Lecture Notes in Computer Science 11188

Commenced Publication in 1973
Founding and Former Series Editors:
Gerhard Goos, Juris Hartmanis, and Jan van Leeuwen

More information about this series at http://www.springer.com/series/7412

Zhaoxiang Zhang · David Suter
Yingli Tian · Alexandra Branzan Albu
Nicolas Sidère · Hugo Jair Escalante (Eds.)

Pattern Recognition and Information Forensics

ICPR 2018 International Workshops, CVAUI, IWCF, and MIPPSNA
Beijing, China, August 20–24, 2018
Revised Selected Papers

 Springer

Editors
Zhaoxiang Zhang
Chinese Academy of Sciences
Beijing, China

David Suter
University of Adelaide
North Terrace, SA, Australia

Yingli Tian
City College of New York
New York, NY, USA

Alexandra Branzan Albu
University of Victoria
Victoria, BC, Canada

Nicolas Sidère
University of La Rochelle
La Rochelle, France

Hugo Jair Escalante
National Institute of Astrophysics, Optics
and Electronics
Puebla, Mexico

ISSN 0302-9743   ISSN 1611-3349   (electronic)
Lecture Notes in Computer Science
ISBN 978-3-030-05791-6   ISBN 978-3-030-05792-3   (eBook)
https://doi.org/10.1007/978-3-030-05792-3

Library of Congress Control Number: 2018964095

LNCS Sublibrary: SL6 – Image Processing, Computer Vision, Pattern Recognition, and Graphics

This Springer imprint is published by the registered company Springer Nature Switzerland AG
The registered company address is: Gewerbestrasse 11, 6330 Cham, Switzerland

Preface

Welcome to the proceedings of the 24th International Conference on Pattern Recognition Workshops held in Beijing, China. ICPR has now become an international forum for discussions on recent advances in the fields of pattern recognition, machine learning, and computer vision, and on applications of these technologies in various fields, with growing popularity and increasing quality. This year, we had 12 workshops of which four were new to ICPR. It is thanks to the workshop organizers and their Program Committees that each workshop had a fascinating program designed to foster new ideas and discussions.

The 24th International Conference on Pattern Recognition Workshops were:

- CVAUI: Computer Vision for Analysis of Underwater Imagery
- IWCF: International Workshop on Computational Forensics
- MIPPSNA: Multimedia Information Processing for Personality and Social Networks Analysis Workshop
- CPPR: Correspondence Problem in Pattern Recognition
- DLPR: Deep Learning for Pattern Recognition
- FFER: Face and Facial Expression Recognition from Real World Video
- PRIFR: Pattern Recognition in Intelligent Financial Analysis and Risk Management
- RRPR: Reproducible Research in Pattern Recognition
- VAIB: Visual Observation and Analysis of Vertebrate And Insect Behavior
- MPRSS: Multimodal Pattern Recognition for Social Signal Processing in Human–Computer Interaction
- DLDAR: Deep Learning for Document Analysis and Recognition

This volume of *Lecture Notes in Computer Science* constitutes the proceedings of the ICPR 2018 International Workshops, CVAUI, IWCF, and MIPPSNA. CVAUI (held since 2014) provided a forum for researchers to share and discuss the new methods and applications for underwater image analysis. IWCF (held since 2007) aimed at addressing the theoretical and practical issues related to this field, i.e., the role of PR techniques for analyzing problems in forensics. MIPPSNA aimed to compile the latest efforts on automatic analysis of unconscious human behavior in the context of social media.

We wish to thank all members of the Organizing Committee, the area chairs, the reviewers, and the authors for making this event possible. We are grateful to all the speakers, authors, and participants for their support. We are also indebted to the publisher, Springer, for their cooperation in publishing the proceedings in the prestigious series of *Lecture Notes in Computer Science*. Finally, we wish to thank in particular our main conference Organizing Committee chairs:

- CVAUI: Alexandra Branzan Albu, Maia Hoeberechts
- IWCF: Jean-Marc Ogier, Chang-Tsun Li, Nicolas Sidere

- MIPPSNA: Hugo Jair Escalante, Bogdan Ionescu, Esaú Villatoro, Gabriela Ramírez, Sergio Escalera, Martha Larson, Henning Müller, Isabelle Guyon

November 2018

Zhaoxiang Zhang
David Suter
Yingli Tian

Organization

These proceedings contain the papers presented at the ICPR 2018 Workshops, consisting of CVAUI 2018 (Computer Vision for Analysis of Underwater Imagery), IWCF 2018 (International Workshop on Computational Forensics), and MIPPSNA 2018 (Multimedia Information Processing for Personality and Social Networks Analysis).

Organizing Committee

Workshop Chairs

Zhaoxiang Zhang	Institute of Automation, Chinese Academy of Sciences, China
David Suter	University of Adelaide, Australia
Yingli Tian	The City College of New York, USA

CVAUI 2018 Chairs

Alexandra Branzan Albu	University of Victoria, BC, Canada
Maia Hoeberechts	Ocean Networks Canada, Victoria, BC, Canada

IWCF 2018 Chairs

Jean-Marc Ogier	University of La Rochelle, France
Chang-Tsun Li	Charles Sturt University, Australia University of Warwick, UK
Nicolas Sidere	University of La Rochelle, France

MIPPSNA 2018 Chairs

Hugo Jair Escalante	National Institute of Astrophysics, Mexico
Bogdan Ionescu	University Politehnica of Bucharest, Romania
Esaú Villatoro	Universidad Autónoma Metropolitana, Cuajimalpa, Mexico
Gabriela Ramírez	Universidad Autónoma Metropolitana, Cuajimalpa, Mexico
Sergio Escalera	Computer Vision Center and University of Barcelona, Spain
Martha Larson	Multimedia Information Retrieval Lab Delft University of Technology, The Netherlands
Henning Müller	University of Applied Sciences Western Switzerland, Switzerland
Isabelle Guyon	UPSud and Inria (Université Paris-Saclay), France

CVAUI 2018 Program Committee

Jacopo Aguzzi	Spanish National Research Council, Spain
Konstantinos Avgerinakis	Centre for Research and Technology Hellas, Greece
Duane Edgington	Monterey Bay Aquarium Research Institute, USA
Bob Fisher	University of Edinburgh, UK
Hervé Glotin	University of Toulon, France
Tim Nattkemper	Bielefeld University, Germany
Timm Schoening	Helmholtz Centre for Ocean Research, Kiel, Germany

IWCF 2018 Program Committee

Yoshinori Akao	National Research Institute of Police Science, Japan
Mickaël Coustaty	University of La Rochelle, France
Ali Dehghantanha	University of Guelph, UK
Katrin Franke	Norwegian University of Science and Technology, Norway
Utpal Garain	Indian Statistical Institute, Kolkata, India
Xufeng Lin	Charles Sturt University, Australia
Cheng-Lin Liu	Institute of Automation of Chinese Academy of Sciences, China
Josep Llados	Universitat Autònoma de Barcelona, Spain
Weiqi Luo	Sun Yat-Sen University, China
Faisal Shafait	National University of Sciences and Technology, Pakistan

CVAUI 2018 Invited Talks

Extracting Ecological Information from Deep-Sea Imagery

S. Kim Juniper[1, 2]

[1] Ocean Networks Canada, Victoria, BC, Canada
[2] School of Earth and Ocean Sciences, University of Victoria, BC, Canada
kjuniper@uvic.ca

Abstract. The development of tools for the acquisition of deep-sea imagery has surpassed the development of tools for extracting biological information from growing video and photo archives. Yet these imagery archives contain a wealth of information on the spatial and temporal distribution of deep-sea species, and their natural dynamics. Ocean Networks Canada has been operating cabled deep-sea observatories in the northeast Pacific since 2006. Traditional manual extraction of biological information from ONC's archived imagery has revealed the potential power of time series biological observations in understanding the response of deep-sea species to short- and long-term environmental variability. However, as imagery accumulates in the archive, it is becoming impossible for researchers to exploit the full potential of the thousands of hours of video from multiple deep-sea cameras connected to the network. Ocean Networks Canada has begun developing other solutions from extracting biological information from underwater imagery. This include working with computer scientists to develop machine vision tools that recognize and enumerate species, and the development of a crowd-sourcing tool that allows members of the public to annotate segments of archived video imagery, with information about species present and habitat properties. This presentation will provide an overview of recent research results that have used Ocean Networks Canada imagery combined with oceanographic sensor data to study seafloor ecosystem dynamics. The presentation will conclude with a review of a recent study that compared crowd sourcing results with expert annotation and computer algorithms to quantify the abundance of sablefish in a submarine canyon habitat.

Bio. Dr. Kim Juniper is Chief Scientist with Ocean Networks Canada, a University of Victoria-based organization that operates cabled ocean observatories in the Pacific and Arctic Oceans. He is also Professor in UVic's School of Earth and Ocean Sciences, and holder of the British Columbia Leadership Chair in Ocean Ecosystems and Global Change. He has authored more than 120 peer-reviewed publications on the microbiology, biogeochemistry and ecology of deep-sea hydrothermal vents and other marine habitats. He pioneered the early use of deep-sea video imagery for the study of the natural dynamics of cold seep and hot vent ecosystems in deep ocean trenches and on underwater volcanic ridges. He has provided occasional scientific expertise to the International Seabed Authority since 2000, in relation to the development of regulations for deep-sea mining, and co-authored the Marine Genetic Resources chapter in the recent UN World Ocean Assessment. He is a participant scientist and member of the Scientific Advisory Committee for the Canadian Healthy Oceans Network, a government-academia partnership that is researching the ecological importance of biodiversity in Canada's three oceans.

Collecting, Cleaning and Analyzing a Large Fish Dataset

Robert B. Fisher

School of Informatics, University of Edinburgh, Scotland, UK
rbf@inf.ed.ac.uk

Abstract. The Fish4Knowledge project captured approximately 1.4 billion images of tropical reef fish from 10 underwater cameras off the coast of Taiwan, over 2010–2013. The project investigated fish detection, tracking and species-level recognition, which ultimately led to the large database. The database was then used for further research, in particular:

(1) Methods for cleaning the many false positive fish detections, and

(2) Exploring the relation between fish swimming speed and water temperature (a big noisy data problem).

The talk will cover aspects of both the initial data collection, and also of the post-collection analysis. For fun, we'll also present work on recognizing individual clownfish.

Bio. Prof. Robert B. Fisher FIAPR, FBMVA received a BS (Mathematics, California Institute of Technology, 1974), MS (Computer Science, Stanford, 1978) and a PhD (Edinburgh, 1987). Since then, Bob has been an academic at Edinburgh University, including a stint as of Dean of Research in the College of Science and Engineering. He has been the Education Committee chair and is currently the Industrial Liaison Committee chair for the Int. Association for Pattern Recognition. His research covers topics in high level computer vision and 3D and 3D video analysis, focussing on reconstructing geometric models from existing examples, which contributed to a spin-off company, Dimensional Imaging. More recently, he has also been researching video sequence understanding, in particular attempting to understand observed animal behaviour. The research has led to 5 authored books and more than 288 peer-reviewed scientific articles or book chapters. He has developed several on-line computer vision resources, with over 1 million hits. Most recently, he is the coordinator of an EU funded project developing a robot hedge-trimmer. He is a Fellow of the Int. Association for Pattern Recognition (2008) and the British Machine Vision Association (2010).

IWCF 2018 Invited Talks

Applications of Multimedia Forensics
in Law Enforcement

Chang-Tsun Li

University of Warwick (UK), Charles Sturt University, Australia
chli@csu.edu.au

Abstract. Similar to people identification through human fingerprint analysis, multimedia forensics through device fingerprint analysis has attracted great attention among scientists, practitioners and law enforcement agencies around the world in the past decade. Device information, such as model and serial number, stored in the EXIF are useful for identifying the devices responsible for the creation of the images in question. However, stored separately from the content, the metadata in the EXIF can be removed and manipulated at ease. Device fingerprints deposited in the content by the device provide a more reliable alternative to aid forensic investigations. The hardware or software of each stage in the digital image acquisition process leaves artifacts in the content that can be used as device fingerprints to identify the source devices. This talk will start with a brief introduction to various types of device fingerprints, their applications and limitations. A more focused presentation on the application of sensor pattern noise, as a form of device fingerprint, to source device identification, source device verification common source inference, content authentication and source-oriented image clustering will then be delivered.

Biography: (including the photo of the speaker) Chang-Tsun Li received the BEng degree in electrical engineering from National Defence University (NDU), Taiwan, in 1987, the MSc degree in computer science from U.S. Naval Postgraduate School, USA, in 1992, and the PhD degree in computer science from the University of Warwick, UK, in 1998. He was an associate professor of the Department of Electrical Engineering at NDU during 1998–2002 and a visiting professor of the Department of Computer Science at U.S. Naval Postgraduate School in the second half of 2001. He was a professor of the Department of Computer Science at the University of Warwick, UK, until Dec 2016. He is currently a professor of the School of Computing and Mathematics, and Director of Data Science Research Unit, Charles Sturt University, Australia. His research interests include multimedia forensics and security, biometrics, data mining, machine learning, data analytics, computer vision, image processing, pattern recognition, bioinformatics, and content-based image retrieval. The outcomes of his multimedia forensics research have been translated into award-winning commercial products protected by a series of international patents and have been used by a number of police forces and courts of law around the world. He is currently Associate Editor of the EURASIP Journal of Image and Video Processing (JIVP) and Associate of Editor of IET Biometrics. He involved in the organisation of many international conferences and workshops and also served as member of the international program committees for several international conferences. He is also actively contributing keynote speeches and talks at various international events.

In the past 6 years, Chang-Tsun Li has been active in facilitating the cross-fertilisation of multimedia forensics and biometrics, and has secured a number of major EU funding to achieve this objective. He was the Coordinator and Principal Investigator of the international project entitled Digital Image and Video Forensics funded by the EU's Seventh Framework Programme (FP7) 2010 to 2014. He was a Working Group Chair of the recently completed EU COST Action IC1106: Integrating Biometrics and Forensics for the Digital Age funded by European Cooperation in Science and Technology (COST) from 2012 to 2016. He is currently the Coordinator and Principal Investigator of the EU Horizon 2020 project, entitled Computer Vision Enabled Multimedia Forensics and People Identification (acronym: IDENTITY). The IDENTITY project has a consortium consisting of 16 institutions from 12 countries and will be running for four years, from January 2016 to December 2019. He is also the representative of CSU as International Partner of the EU COST Action CA16101: Multi-modal Imaging of Forensic Science Evidence – Tools for Forensic Science, 2017 to 2021.

Document Fraud: Reality and Challenge for Companies

Saddok Kebairi

Yooz, France
saddok.kebairi@yooz.fr

Abstract. These last years, process digitalization in companies helped increasing productivity, efficiency and cost reduction. However, it also led to an increase of cyber-attacks and document fraud. In this presentation, we will focus on document fraud. We will first expose the real challenges such fraud represents for companies, the different ways a fraud can happen, its evolution through time, and the different strategies to prevent it, detect it and fight against it. These strategies have three main pillars: internal organization of teams and processes, increasing employees awareness and introducing new technologies to detect fraud at an early stage. Finally, we will expose some fraud detection techniques and solutions.

Biography: Saddok Kebairi is a researcher and project director at ITESOFT Group/YOOZ. He has more than 20 years of experience in implementing industrial document analysis and recognition solutions. He has a very deep knowledge of image processing, writing recognition and project management. He managed several collaborations between European universities and industry and pushed several techniques to production. Currently, his main focus is the fraud detection project at YOOZ.

Apparent Personality Computing
(MIPPSNA 2018 Invited Talk)

Sergio Escalera

University of Barcelona, Barcelona, Spain
sergio.escalera.guerrero@gmail.com

Abstract. Automatic analysis of humans via computer vision and multi-modal approaches requires from large sets of annotated data when working in the supervised scenario. In many situations annotated data is difficult to be collected or the annotation task is influenced by factors such as the acquisition protocol or the subjectivity of the labelers/raters. In the later, we consider the annotated data to contain apparent labels. Apparent labels can be useful for training machines to perceive human attributes and behaviors in a similar way humans do. In this talk, I will present recent research and competitions organized by HuPBA group and ChaLearn Looking at people in the field of Apparent Personality Computing, discussing the bias introduced by different subjective attributes. Collected data, organized competitions, and deep learning approaches in order to deal with the task will be presented.

Biography: Sergio Escalera obtained the P.h.D. degree on Multi-class visual categorization systems at Computer Vision Center, UAB. He obtained the 2008 best Thesis award on Computer Science at Universitat Autònoma de Barcelona. He leads the Human Pose Recovery and Behavior Analysis Group at UB, CVC, and the Barcelona Graduate School of Mathematics. He is an associate professor at the Department of Mathematics and Informatics, Universitat de Barcelona. He is an adjunct professor at Universitat Oberta de Catalunya, Aalborg University, and Dalhousie University. He has been visiting professor at TU Delft and Aalborg Universities. He is a member of the Visual and Computational Learning consolidated research group of Catalonia. He is also a member of the Computer Vision Center at UAB. He is series editor of The Springer Series on Challenges in Machine Learning. He is Editor-in-Chief of American Journal of Intelligent Systems and editorial board member of more than 5 international journals. He is vice-president of ChaLearn Challenges in Machine Learning, leading ChaLearn Looking at People events. He is co-creator of Codalab open source platform for challenges organization. He is co-founder of PhysicalTech and Care Respite companies. He is also member of the AERFAI Spanish Association on Pattern Recognition, ACIA Catalan Association of Artificial Intelligence, INNS, and Chair of IAPR TC-12: Multimedia and visual information systems. He has different patents and registered models. He has published more than 250 research papers and participated in the organization of scientific events, including CCIA04, ICCV11, CCIA14, AMDO16, FG17, NIPS17, NIPS18, FG19, and workshops at ICCV11, ICMI13, ECCV14, CVPR15, ICCV15, CVPR16, ECCV16, ICPR16, NIPS16, CVPR17, ICCV17, NIPS17, ICPR18. He has been guest editor at JMLR, TPAMI, IJCV, TAC, PR, MVA,

JIVP, Expert Systems, and Neural Comp. and App. He has been area chair at WACV16, NIPS16, AVSS17, FG17, ICCV17, WACV18, FG18, BMVC18, NIPS18, FG19 and competition and demo chair at FG17, NIPS17, NIPS18 and FG19. His research interests include, statistical pattern recognition, affective computing, and human pose recovery and behavior understanding, including multi-modal data analysis, with special interest in characterizing people: personality and psychological profile computing.

Contents

**Multimedia Information Processing for Personality and Social
Networks Analysis Workshop (MIPPSNA 2018)**

Computer Vision for Analysis of Underwater Imagery (CVAUI 2018)

Message from the Chairs

The 3rd Workshop on Computer Vision for Analysis of Underwater Imagery (CVAUI 2018), was held in conjunction with the International Conference on Pattern Recognition (ICPR) on 20 August 2018 in Beijing, China. This workshop further consolidated the series that was started in Stockholm (CVAUI 2014), and continued in Cancun (CVAUI 2016).

Monitoring marine and freshwater ecosystems is of critical importance in developing a better understanding of their complexity, including the effects of climate change and other anthropogenic influences. The collection of underwater video and imagery, whether from stationary or moving platforms, provides a non-invasive means of observing submarine ecosystems in situ, including the behaviour of organisms. Oceanographic data acquisition has been greatly facilitated by the establishment of cabled ocean observatories, whose co-located sensors support interdisciplinary studies and real-time observations. Scheduled recordings of underwater video data and static images are gathered with Internet-connected fixed and PTZ cameras, which observe a variety of biological processes. These cabled ocean observatories, such those operated by Ocean Networks Canada (www.oceannetworks.ca), offer a 24/7 presence, resulting in unprecedented volumes of visual data and a "big data" problem for automated analysis. Due to the properties of the environment itself, the analysis of underwater imagery imposes unique challenges which need to be tackled by the computer vision community in collaboration with biologists and ocean scientists.

This workshop provided a forum for researchers to share and discuss new methods and applications for underwater image analysis. We received 10 submissions, out of which 8 were accepted based on a thorough peer review process. Most of the submitted papers were of excellent quality, so the high acceptance rate reflects a self-selection process performed by the authors. We thank the members of Program Committee for lending their time and expertise to ensure the high quality of the accepted workshop contributions.

The technical program covered a variety of topics, including but not limited to underwater image quality enhancement and evaluation, deep learning methods for object classification and image restoration, as well as behaviour tracking. We were also pleased to host two keynote talks given by prominent researchers from marine biology and computer science perspectives. Dr. Kim Juniper, Ocean Networks Canada, talked about *"Extracting Ecological Information from Deep-Sea Imagery,"* highlighting the critical need to bridge the gap between the rapid evolution of tools for acquiring deep-sea imagery and the development of accurate methods for the automatic quantitative analysis of this huge amount of visual data. Dr. Robert B. Fisher, University of Edinburgh, Scotland, UK, offered valuable perspectives about the impact of Big Data on the design and performance of computer vision algorithms in his presentation titled *"Collecting, Cleaning, and Analyzing a Large Fish Dataset."*

We hope that all workshop attendees have been inspired in their research by participating in CVAUI 2018, and that this workshop will foster many fruitful conversations and open new areas for collaborative interdisciplinary research in underwater image analysis.

Alexandra Branzan Albu
Maia Hoeberechts

Deep Active Learning for In Situ Plankton Classification

Erik Bochinski[1]([✉]), Ghassen Bacha[1], Volker Eiselein[1], Tim J. W. Walles[2],
Jens C. Nejstgaard[2], and Thomas Sikora[1]

[1] Communication System Group, Technische Universität Berlin, Berlin, Germany
{bochinski,sikora}@nue.tu-berlin.de
[2] Leibnitz-Institute of Freshwater Ecology and Inland Fisheries, Stechlin, Germany
{walles,nejstgaard}@igb-berlin.de

Abstract. Ecological studies of some of the most numerous organisms on the planet, zooplankton, have been limited by manual analysis for more than 100 years. With the development of high-throughput video systems, we argue that this critical bottle-neck can now be solved if paired with deep neural networks (DNN). To leverage their performance, large amounts of training samples are required that until now have been dependent on manually created labels. To minimize the effort of expensive human experts, we employ recent active learning approaches to select only the most informative samples for labelling. Thus training a CNN using a nearly unlimited amount of images while limiting the human labelling effort becomes possible by means of active learning. We show in several experiments that in practice, only a few thousand labels are required to train a CNN and achieve an accuracy-level comparable to manual routine analysis of zooplankton samples. Once trained, this CNN can be used to analyse any amount of image data, presenting the zooplankton community the opportunity to address key research questions on transformative scales, many orders of magnitude, in both time and space, basically only limited by video through-put and compute capacity.

Keywords: Classification · Zooplankton · Active learning
Automatic identification and sizing · Cost-effective active learning
In situ

1 Introduction

The aquatic planktonic microorganisms are the basis of life in the largest part of our planet, the oceans and lakes, and thus of vital importance also for humanity by providing food, oxygen, as well as many other ecosystems services. However, the increasing pressure of humanity on the same ecosystems has created

T.J.W. Walles was supported by a Leibniz Competition grant ILES "Illuminating Lake Ecosystems", and technical investment was supported by IGB-startup funds to J.C. Nejstgaard.

© Springer Nature Switzerland AG 2019
Z. Zhang et al. (Eds.): ICPR 2018 Workshops, LNCS 11188, pp. 5–15, 2019.
https://doi.org/10.1007/978-3-030-05792-3_1

an urgent need to understand how these systems function and respond to the changing environment [2,21]. To better understand this, it is critical to be able to measure fundamentals such as - who is where when and does what to whom. For plankton this has been an enormous challenge due to a strong mismatch between available time-consuming manual analytic methods, and the need for high numbers of samples to cover the wide range of scales in time and space that the zooplankton operate in [6]. However, here we show that with effectively trained deep learning approaches to lab and in-situ image systems, this has a great promise to ease these key limitations.

In order to yield high quality data at high temporal and spatial scales, adequate tools for data acquisition as well as analysis are required. For the imagery, several camera-based systems have been developed in the recent past [1,8] to gather considerable amounts of data in an automated way [5,15]. Analysing these amounts of data by traditional methods, including manual annotation, are unfeasible. This raises the need for reliable automated labelling tools [14]. Otherwise it would not be possible to effectively explore this new scale of available imagery.

Recent advances in the computer vision domain, accelerated by the rediscovery of convolutional neural networks (CNNs) and deep learning methods in general [11], have greatly improved the possibilities for reliable automated labelling tools. One of the major challenges that prevents the direct application of such tools for successful plankton classification, is the general need for large, manually labelled training data. Since zooplankton appears in very many species, forms and stages, large training sets for each environment and image acquisition system would be needed. Furthermore, it is hard to decide which samples need to be manually annotated for the successful training of a CNN. This becomes even harder as there are commonly great class imbalances in plankton data [4,12,22], while CNN training generally benefits from balanced training data. It seems therefore natural to approach the problems of training data annotation and classification of large datasets in a joint way. This process is known as active learning [18]. It aims at training a classifier on a small initial training set and then selects the most informative samples from a larger unlabelled dataset to query them for labelling to e.g. a human expert for further training. Iteratively performed, this can greatly reduce the number of needed annotations till convergence. Furthermore, samples that were classified with high-confidence can also be included in the training set with a pseudo-label equally to the predicted class. This can further accelerate the training process and therefore reduce the need for manually created annotations.

The additional use of high-confidence samples in the training of CNNs for image classification in an active learning manner was first introduced in [23] as Cost-Effective Active Learning (CEAL). This approach was adapted later for face identification [13], melanoma segmentation [7] and cancerous tissue recognition [20]. The authors of [4] proposed using a CNN to classify microscopic grayscale images of plankton. Several different network architectures were explored and superior results over traditional approaches reported.

A Generative Adversarial Network is used in [22] to generate additional training samples to handle the class imbalance often found in plankton datasets caused by the uneven distribution of plankton presence in nature. The same problem is tackled in [12] using CNNs and transfer learning. [9] analyzes different methods for segmenting the plankton from the background and its impact on the classification accuracy.

The contribution of this paper is manifold: We propose a novel CNN-based classification system that is robust against the background noise in images and therefore does not require any instance segmentation for background removal. To our knowledge, we are the first to report the successful application of Cost-Effective Active Learning to the task of zooplankton classification. Our experiments show that the proposed system is able to solve the classification problem with accuracy levels comparable to manual routine analysis of zooplankton samples, after just a few active learning iterations. We further apply the method to a second dataset captured with a different camera in a different lake environment with the presence of a new prominent phytoplankton distractor class. The previously trained system is able to successfully classify this new data. With just one additional active learning update the same performance level as of the original dataset is reached, showing the validity of the system. As the numbers of organisms counted and sized increases with orders of magnitudes this has several critical advances: (1) numbers of rare organisms, typically larger sized than the numerous smaller organisms, can now be better estimated. (2) the estimate of total biomass and size distributions will now be much more accurate due to much higher and more accurate automatic size estimates, (3) the statistical power will increase due to higher numbers, (4) the high throughput enables sampling and in situ analyses on a much higher spatio-temporal scale, offering completely new options for future (zoo)plankton studies like real-time in situ profiles.

2   Method

2.1   Active Learning

Given a dataset D, the aim of active learning for training a classifier's parameters $\mathcal{W}$ is to minimize the number of required annotated training samples $D^L \subseteq D$ from a larger, initially unlabeled dataset $D^U \subseteq D$ while still obtaining satisfactory training results. This becomes possible due to the assumption that not all samples are equally informative for training and can be exploited by an iterative process of training the classifier using already annotated samples D^L and then classifying all samples of the unlabeled set D^U with it. Samples with the lowest classification confidence are considered the most informative for the future training step. Therefore, the top K least confident predictions are queried to e.g. a human annotator for labeling and moved to D^L. This is repeated until a termination criteria is fulfilled, e.g. the training loss is converged or a certain accuracy of the classifier is reached.

To measure the confidence of a predicted sample, several confidence criteria were proposed in literature. We considered the 3 most common criteria in our approach:

Least confidence [18]:

$$x^*_{LC} = \max_j \left(P(y_i = j | x_i; \mathcal{W}) \right) \tag{1}$$

with $P(y_i = j | x_i; \mathcal{W})$ denoting the probability of x_i belonging to the j-th class which translates to the most probable softmax classification score for the j-th category. The lower this value the higher the uncertainty.

Margin sampling [17]:

$$x^*_{MS} = P(y_i = j_1 | x_i; \mathcal{W}) - P(y_i = j_2 | x_i; \mathcal{W}) \tag{2}$$

The margin between the best $(P(y_i = j_1 | x_i; \mathcal{W}))$ and second best $(P(y_i = j_2 | x_i; \mathcal{W}))$ classification score is used as confidence value. Lower values represent a higher grade of uncertainty.

Entropy [19]:

$$x^*_{EN} = - \sum_i P(y_i = j | x_i; \mathcal{W}) \log P(y_i = j | x_i; \mathcal{W}) \tag{3}$$

The entropy criterion inspired by information theory takes all predicted class labels into account and is accordingly defined by the entropy of the set of all classification scores $P(y_i = j | x_i; \mathcal{W})$. Higher values denote higher uncertainties.

2.2   Cost-Effective Active Learning

The plain active learning approach only takes advantage of the most informative samples and their retrieved labels. For cost-effective active learning [23], the class predictions of the high-confidence samples are used as pseudo-labels and added temporarily to D^L for the next training step of the classifier as they can still contribute to the training process. In [23] it was proposed to use the entropy criteria for the selection of the high-confidence samples. We consider all three as possible criteria in our experiments for pseudo-labeling:

$$j^* = \operatorname*{argmax}_j \left(P(y_i = j | x_i; \mathcal{W}) \right) \tag{4}$$

$$y_i = \begin{cases} j^*, & x^*_{LC,MS} > \delta \text{ or } x^*_{EN} < \delta \\ 0, & \text{otherwise} \end{cases} \tag{5}$$

with:

$$\delta = \begin{cases} \delta_0, & t = 0 \\ \delta + dr \cdot t, & t > 0 \end{cases} \tag{6}$$

as a threshold for the selection of the high-confidence samples with δ_0 as the start value and dr as the decay rate. The decaying threshold allows for the selection of more high-confidence samples at the beginning and enforces a higher confidence of the samples towards the end of the active learning process.

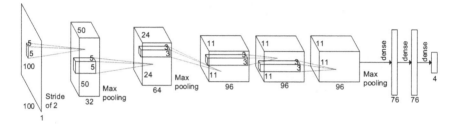

Fig. 1. Employed CNN architecture

2.3 Classifier

As classifier, a Convolutional Neural Network (CNN) as shown in Fig. 1 is employed. The architecture is based on the popular AlexNet [11] and was carefully adapted to fit the requirements of the used plankton image data. ReLU activation is performed after each layer except for the last one which consists of C softmax activated outputs where C denotes the number of possible classes. A dropout of 50% was used while training the dense layers to prevent overfitting. As loss function the cross-entropy is employed:

$$\mathcal{L}(\mathbf{x}, y, \mathcal{W}) = - \sum_{c=1}^{C} \mathbb{1}_{y=c} \log P(y = j | \mathbf{x}; \mathcal{W}) \tag{7}$$

where $\mathbb{1}_{y=c}$ is 1 if y equals c or otherwise 0 and $P(y = j | \mathbf{x}; \mathcal{W})$ the softmax output of the CNN for the jth class. The task is then to find a parameter set $\mathcal{W}$ of the CNN satisfying the following minimization problem in each active learning iteration T:

$$\min_{\{\mathcal{W}, n=|D|\}} = \frac{1}{n} \sum_{i=1}^{n} \mathcal{L}(\mathbf{x}_i, y_i, \mathcal{W}) \tag{8}$$

The non-optimal optimization can then be performed using ordinary gradient descent methods.

3 Experiments

Several experiments were conducted in order to assess the effectiveness of cost-effective active learning for training a CNN for zooplankton classification. Two datasets from different biological environments were captured and analysed. The first dataset is used to analyse the achievable accuracy of the CNN and how the cost-effective active learning can be used to minimize the number of required annotations. The second dataset is used to examine the generalization ability of the CNN and if the CEAL method can be used to fine-tune the system to adapt to the characteristics of this new data.

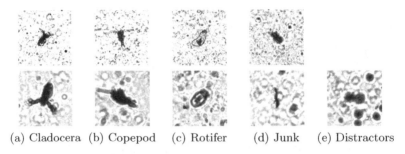

(a) Cladocera (b) Copepod   (c) Rotifer   (d) Junk   (e) Distractors

Fig. 2. Example images of the ILES (top row) and CZECH (bottom row) datasets. Different scales, rotations and background clutter pose challenges for the classification system.

3.1 Datasets

All images used in the experiments were captured using the in-situ imager described in [3]. The first dataset ILES contains about 840K images. They were divided into 4 classes: *cladocera, copepod, rotifer* and *junk* whereas the latter one comprises everything which can not be certainly assigned to one of the other classes. The dataset is further split into two subsets A and B. Subset A comprises about 60K fully annotated images in order to evaluate the cost-effective active learning framework with 80% of the data as training and the remaining 20% as testing data. Subset B contains the other 780K images and was used to validate the approach and further investigation concerning suitability of the results for analyses from the biological perspective. The second dataset CZECH contains about 167K all unlabelled images. It was collected by the same imager but equipped with a different camera and is used to further validate the approach using data captured in a different environment. The major challenge is the prominent presence of a new phytoplankton distractor class shown in Fig. 2e. A total of $10K/5K$ randomly selected images of ILES B/CZECH were labelled for performance analysis.

3.2 Preprocessing

Only a two dimensional projection of the three dimensional object with an unknown spacial orientation serves as input image for classifying the object. This greatly differs to most of the well-researched computer vision applications as they are focused to non-microscopic and non-aquatic images. To support the CNN to deal with the induced rotation invariance, we use a pre-processing pipeline as sketched in Fig. 3. First, the approximate shape of the object is determined by otsu thresholding [16]. The main axis is then calculated using principal component analysis. The image is rotated in a way that the rotation of this axis is strictly vertical. Finally, the center crop of the resulting image is used. Note that the segmentation using otsu thresholding is only used for rotation but not for cropping or removal of the background (as eg. in [9]) as we find that no current segmentation approach is able to perform this task reliably enough to not remove fine-grained details belonging to the planktonic object. Instead we rely on the CNN to learn the differentiation between background and foreground features during training. The ILES A training set consists of about $20\,K$ samples for each of the *cladocera* and *junk* classes, about $5\,K$ samples for *copepod* and only $1.3K$ samples belonging to the *rotifer* class. To handle this imbalance during training, the *copepod* images were mirrored horizontally and vertically, quadrupling the amount of training samples to a total of $20K$. Also $20K$ samples for *rotifer* were created by mirroring and rotating to produce 15 samples per image including the original. The rotations render the normalization regarding the orientation useless, however there is no practical impact to the training since the *rotifer* individuals have a distinct round shape (see Fig. 2c) which still causes that class to be the most reliable during classification.

Fig. 3. Preprocessing pipeline for the images.

3.3 Training Procedure

The first training evaluation was performed using the ILES A dataset. Since this dataset is fully annotated, the active learning strategies can be simulated.

As initial labelled training set D^L, 10% of the augmented training data was used. Training is performed for 11 active learning iterations T with $K = 2200$. An initial threshold $\delta_0 = 0.995$ and a decay rate of $dr = 0.33 \cdot 10^{-5}$ was chosen for least confidence (LS) and margin sampling (MS) and $\delta_0 = 0.4 \cdot 10^{-4}$, $dr = -0.2 \cdot 10^{-5}$ for entropy-based (EN) high-confidence sample selection. In each iteration, the CNN was trained for 10 epochs with a batch size of 32 on D^L including the temporarily added high-confidence samples. Training was performed using the adam algorithm [10] with a learning rate of 10^{-4}. The remaining parameters are set to the default values of $\beta_1 = 0.9, \beta_2 = 0.999, \epsilon = 10^{-8}$ in all experiments.

3.4 Results

First, the maximum achievable CNN accuracy was determined by training on dataset ILES A without employing any active learning strategy. Otherwise, the training procedure previously described in Sect. 3.3 was followed. An accuracy of 83.84% was achieved and serves as baseline for the subsequent experiments using the active learning approaches. Figure 4a shows the development of the CNN accuracy depending on the percentage of labelled training samples for the EN, LC and MS cost-effective active learning strategies. It can be seen that there is no significant difference in the performance of the different confidence metrics. Margin sampling however was slightly better than the other two strategies and was therefore selected for the subsequent experiments. In Fig. 4b, a comparison between CEAL with margin sampling (MS), plain active learning (AL) and a random selection of samples queried for labelling is shown. In addition, ALL denotes the baseline accuracy without any active learning. It can be observed that CEAL performs favourably and is the only method reliably reaching the peak accuracy of 83.84%. This is achieved while only requiring labels for one third of the available training samples which translates to about $16K$ required labels in total.

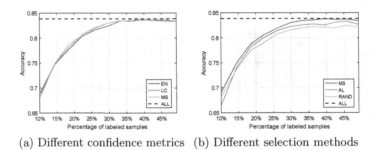

(a) Different confidence metrics   (b) Different selection methods

Fig. 4. Comparison of different sample selection methods and confidence metrics.

3.5   Generalization

In addition to the experiments on the fully labelled dataset, experiments under real conditions were conducted. The final model from the previous experiments trained on the dataset ILES A is evaluated on the ILES B and CZECH datasets. Initially, a drop in the accuracy for the ILES B dataset is noticed. For the CZECH dataset, a high accuracy of about 91% is achieved. The reason is the prominent presence of a new phytoplankton class which is mostly classified correctly as *junk*, which makes up about 88% of the whole test set. Following [15], the predictions were also evaluated using the unweighted F1 score to get more meaningful results. This reveals that the performance on the CZECH dataset is with an F1 score of 0.55 indeed considerably worse than on the ILES A set with 0.85.

To adopt the CNN classifier to the two new unlabelled datasets, a final cost-effective active learning iteration was performed. In order to do so, 5.35% of the ILES B and 3.37% of the CZECH dataset were labelled by a human expert. The samples with the least margin sampling confidence were selected. Additionally, the high-confidence samples using the same confidence metric were pseudo-labelled as in the previous experiment. With these new samples, the CNN was fine-tuned. The results are presented in Table 1.

Table 1. Comparison of the classification performance for all datasets.

Dataset	Accuracy	F1
ILES A	83.84%	0.85
ILES B (no fine-tuning)	72.78%	0.75
ILES B (with fine-tuning)	86.23%	0.86
Czech (no fine-tuning)	90.87%	0.55
Czech (with fine-tuning)	96.08%	0.80

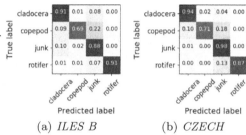

(a) *ILES B*   (b) *CZECH*

Fig. 5. Confusion matrices for both validation datasets.

The accuracy as well as the F1 score improved. In the case of the ILES B, the performance compared to the initial ILES A was even slightly increased. For the more challenging CZECH dataset, the accuracy was raised to 96% and the F1 score is with 0.80 only slightly behind the ILES datasets. Still, this result shows that the approach is able to adapt not only to the different lake environment of the CZECH dataset, but to a different camera setup with different visual properties (see Fig. 2) as well. In Fig. 5, confusion matrices for both datasets are presented. It shows that the *cladocera* and *rotifer* classes are predicted most robustly while the performance for *rotifer* is slightly decreased for the CZECH dataset. Most likely this is due to the visual similarity to the new phytoplankton distractor only present in this dataset. Otherwise, the *copepod* and *junk* classes are confused sometimes. The most probable reason for this is that there are many *copepod* samples which are not focused properly, rendering the antennas as most distinguishing visual feature invisible.

4 Conclusion

In this paper, we investigated the adaptability of the cost-effective active learning (CEAL) approach to train a Convolutional Neural Network (CNN) for the task of zooplankton classification. Various experiments showed that CNNs are indeed suitable for this task. With CEAL, just a fraction of the samples need to be annotated by a human expert to reach the maximum possible accuracy of the CNN. It was shown that the system is further capable of adapting to different camera setups, lake environments and is even robust to a new, unseen distractor class. Hence, the proposed approach contributes to close the gap between automated, large-scale image data acquisition systems and the actual interpretation of the data from the biological application side by efficiently inferring the required annotations automatically. This contribution reduces the effort of training and using such systems significantly. When adapted in the ecological research community together with the necessary optical equipment this will yield possibilities to acquire key zooplankton data at an unprecedented magnitude in both temporal and spatial scales, in its turn expected to create transformative changes in plankton ecology in the near future.

References

1. Benfield, M.C., et al.: RAPID: research on automated plankton identification. Oceanography **20**, 172–187 (2007)
2. Connor, R.: The United Nations World Water Development Report 2015: Water for a Sustainable World. UNESCO Publishing, Paris (2015)
3. Cowen, R.K., Guigand, C.M.: In situ ichthyoplankton imaging system (ISIIS): system design and preliminary results. Limnol. Oceanogr. Methods **6**, 126–132 (2008)
4. Dai, J., Wang, R., Zheng, H., Ji, G., Qiao, X.: ZooplanktoNet: deep convolutional network for zooplankton classification. In: OCEANS (2016)
5. Douglas, K., Juniper, S., Jenkyns, R., Hoeberechts, M., Macoun, P., Hillier, J.: Developing spatial management tools for offshore marine protected areas. In: OCEANS-Anchorage (2017)
6. Hofmann, E.E., Klinck, J.M.: Future marine zooplankton research - a perspective. Marine Ecol. Progress Ser. **222**, 297–308 (2001)
7. Gorriz, M., Carlier, A., Faure, E., Giro-i Nieto, X.: Cost-effective active learning for melanoma segmentation. arXiv preprint arXiv:1711.09168 (2017)
8. Gorsky, G., et al.: Digital zooplankton image analysis using the zooscan integrated system. J. Plankton Res. **32**, 285–303 (2010)
9. Hirata, N.S., Fernandez, M.A., Lopes, R.M.: Plankton image classification based on multiple segmentations. In: ICPR CVAUI Workshop (2016)
10. Kingma, D., Ba, J.: Adam: a method for stochastic optimization. In: International Conference for Learning Representations (2015)
11. Krizhevsky, A., Sutskever, I., Hinton, G.E.: ImageNet classification with deep convolutional neural networks. In: NIPS (2012)
12. Lee, H., Park, M., Kim, J.: Plankton classification on imbalanced large scale database via convolutional neural networks with transfer learning. In: IEEE International Conference on Image Processing (2016)
13. Lin, L., Wang, K., Meng, D., Zuo, W., Zhang, L.: Active self-paced learning for cost-effective and progressive face identification. IEEE Trans. Pattern Anal. Mach. Intell. **40**, 7–19 (2018)
14. MacLeod, N., Benfield, M., Culverhouse, P.: Time to automate identification. Nature **467**, 154 (2010)
15. Orenstein, E.C., Beijbom, O., Peacock, E.E., Sosik, H.M.: WHOI-plankton-a large scale fine grained visual recognition benchmark dataset for plankton classification. arXiv preprint arXiv:1510.00745 (2015)
16. Otsu, N.: A threshold selection method from gray-level histograms. IEEE Trans. Syst. Man Cybern. **9**, 62–66 (1979)
17. Scheffer, T., Decomain, C., Wrobel, S.: Active hidden Markov models for information extraction. In: International Symposium on Intelligent Data Analysis (2001)
18. Settles, B.: Active learning literature survey. Computer Sciences Technical report 1648 (2010)
19. Shannon, C.E.: A mathematical theory of communication. ACM SIGMOBILE Mob. Comput. Commun. Rev. **5**, 3–55 (2001)
20. Stanitsas, P., Cherian, A., Truskinovsky, A., Morellas, V., Papanikolopoulos, N.: Active convolutional neural networks for cancerous tissue recognition. In: IEEE International Conference on Image Processing (2017)
21. Vörösmarty, C.J., et al.: Global threats to human water security and river biodiversity. Nature **467**, 555 (2010)

22. Wang, C., Yu, Z., Zheng, H., Wang, N., Zheng, B.: CGAN-plankton: towards large-scale imbalanced class generation and fine-grained classification. In: IEEE International Conference on Image Processing (2017)
23. Wang, K., Zhang, D., Li, Y., Zhang, R., Lin, L.: Cost-effective active learning for deep image classification. IEEE TCSVT **27**, 2591–2600 (2017)

Marine Snow Removal Using a Fully Convolutional 3D Neural Network Combined with an Adaptive Median Filter

Michał Koziarski and Bogusław Cyganek[✉]

Department of Electronics, AGH University of Science and Technology,
Al. Mickiewicza 30, 30-059 Kraków, Poland
{michal.koziarski,cyganek}@agh.edu.pl

Abstract. Marine snow is a type of noise that affects underwater images. It is caused by various biological and mineral particles which stick together and cause backscattering of the incident light. In this paper a method of marine snow removal is proposed. For particle detection a fully convolutional 3D neural network is trained with a manually annotated images. Then, marine snow is removed with an adaptive median filter, guided by the output of the neural network. Experimental results show that the proposed solution is capable of an accurate removal of marine snow without negatively affecting the image quality.

Keywords: Marine snow removal · Underwater image processing Deep neural networks · Median filtering

1 Introduction

Images acquired in underwater conditions are exposed to different physical and environmental conditions compared to the atmospheric surroundings. Thus, underwater images suffer from blur, vanishing colors, as well as various types of noise [8,11]. To remedy these, artificial lighting is employed, which assures proper illumination level and helps in retaining colors. However, in marine conditions there are frequently billions of biological and mineral particles which join together and move in different directions. They cause light back scattering which manifest in images as white blobs of various size and shape, as shown in Fig. 1. This effect was observed by the biologist and deep exploration pioneer William Beebe and called marine snow, since the clusters of particles resemble falling snowflakes [2,7]. Their structure and biological origin were analyzed by researchers [16,18]. An overview is presented in a paper by Silver [19].

Marine snow can severely obfuscate image what can for example distract processing algorithms of underwater ROVs since the particles are large and resemble nearby falling objects. However, structure and statistical properties of this noise are significantly different than the ones encountered in the airy conditions.

© Springer Nature Switzerland AG 2019
Z. Zhang et al. (Eds.): ICPR 2018 Workshops, LNCS 11188, pp. 16–25, 2019.
https://doi.org/10.1007/978-3-030-05792-3_2

Fig. 1. Examples of marine snow in underwater images: maneuvering inside a wreck in the Indian Ocean (left), inspecting underwater constructions in the artificial lake Jaworzno (right). Marine snow shows near light source, due to the back scattering effect, as moving white particles of various size and shape.

Hence, only the smallest particles can be treated as e.g. salt-and-pepper noise and be removed with the median filter. Thus, to filter other types of particles some modifications of the median filter were recently proposed. One of the first is the work by Banerjee et al. [1]. This method is a modification of the median filter weighted by the probability of marine snow existence. The latter is computed based on the proposed marine snow model of observing sparse number of high intensity pixels in two patches of various size. However, this method can cope only with relatively small particles and will not remove the ones presented in Fig. 1. A modification was proposed by Farhadifard et al. [4]. Their method assumes median filtering with a supervised noise detection by a multi scale patch search. However, all these methods operate on a single video frame at a time and can only remove relatively small particles. In this paper, marine snow detection is proposed to be done with the properly designed and trained 3D convolutional neural network (3D-CNN). Application of 3D convolutions allows for direct computation of spatial and temporal properties of the particles. More specifically, only a 3D convolution allows for proper detection of a relatively large and light particle which moves so fast, it is only visible on a single video frame. However, to train a network a number of underwater sequences with marine snow particles had to be manually annotated, as shown in Fig. 7. Thanks to this it was possible to train the 3D-CNN, as will be discussed. The trained network can reliably detect marine snow particles in real underwater sequences. These, in turn, can be filtered out thanks to the proposed 3D median filter. Experimental results are evaluated on images acquired in various underwater conditions. These show high detection accuracy, as well as fast operation of the proposed method. Therefore it can be used as a pre-filtering module of the ROVs vision front-end, etc.

2   Method Description

Marine snow differs significantly from standard noise models, such as the Gaussian or salt-and-pepper noise. Because of that, most existing filtering techniques are ill-suited for the task of the marine snow removal. To accommodate for the unique characteristics of the marine snow we propose a novel pipeline, in which the strength of the filtering is locally adjusted based on the output of the marine

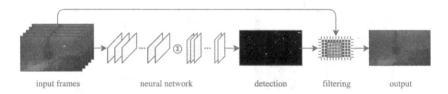

input frames   neural network   detection   filtering   output

Fig. 2. The proposed marine snow filtering pipeline. Firstly, a stack of frames is passed through a convolutional neural network that detects marine snow particles. Secondly, a filtering procedure, guided by the produced detection mask, is conducted on the central frame.

snow detection module. A graphical overview of the proposed pipeline was presented in Fig. 2.

The proposed pipeline is based on two novel ideas. First of all, that using the consecutive video frames, rather than a single one, can aid the process of marine snow detection. Since marine snow particles are not stationary and often move at a high velocity, using the temporal information can be beneficial for detecting their positions. Secondly, it is proposed to use the detected positions of the particles to control the filtering strength. We propose taking advantage of the first idea by introducing a novel, fully convolutional architecture of a neural network. This architecture relies on the 3D convolutions to learn a spatiotemporal features, and is used in the marine snow detection task. Afterwards, to take advantage of the second idea we propose an adaptive median filtering algorithm that uses the detected marine snow positions to locally alter the filtering strength. In the remainder of the section we give a detailed description of both building blocks constituting the proposed marine snow removal pipeline.

2.1 Fully Convolutional 3D Neural Network

In the recent years convolutional neural networks achieved a state-of-the-art performance in various computer vision problems. Most notable example of that trend is the image recognition task [6,13,20]. They were also successfully used in other areas, such as the inverse problems: image super-resolution [14], denoising [12] and inpainting [22], as well as the image segmentation [15,17]. One of the main reasons behind the recent resurgence of neural networks is the increasing availability of a large quantities of training data, as well as computational power of computers. However, when the ground truth data is limited, for instance when the labeling process is time-consuming, as is the case of the manual marine snow annotation, training becomes more difficult and the number of networks parameters has to be limited to avoid overfitting. Using convolutional layers in favor of a fully connected layers can help mitigate this issue. This has been demonstrated in several recent papers, such as [15] and [9], in which neural networks consisting solely of the convolutional layers were successfully used.

In this paper we propose extending the idea of a fully convolutional network by using the 3D convolutional layers instead of the traditional 2D convolutions.

3D convolutional layers were recently used by Tran et al. [21] for video classification with an architecture combining convolutional and fully connected layers. Compared to the 2D convolutional layers, which process 3-dimensional inputs, such as RGB images, with the 2D convolutions, 3D convolutional layers can be used to process a 4-dimensional inputs, such as videos, with a 3D convolution operation. Networks consisting of 3D convolutional layers learn features in both spatial and temporal dimensions and, as a result, are able to detect movement, such as that of the marine snow particles.

For the marine snow detection task, we propose an architecture of a fully convolutional neural network presented in Fig. 3. It consists of m 3D convolutional layers with a filter of size $3 \times 3 \times 3$, following the practice of using small filter size as e.g. in Tran et al. [21]. Each of the layers consists of 64 filters and is followed by the ReLU activation function. After the last 3D convolutional layer we apply a summation over the original temporal dimension and use n 2D convolutional layers, each with a 64 filters of size 3×3. Each 2D convolutional layer except the last one is also followed by the ReLU function. The last layer is followed by the ReLU1, defined as $f(x) = min(max(x, 0), 1)$, to constrain the networks outputs in range from 0 to 1. We introduce the temporal summation operation and move from 3D to 2D convolutional layers because we intend to use a small number of frames, or in other words temporal size, and suspect that using a small number of 3D convolutions will be sufficient.

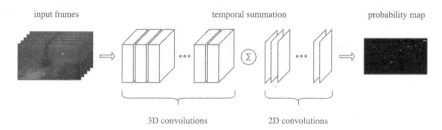

Fig. 3. The proposed fully convolutional 3D neural network. It consists of a stack of 3D convolutional layers, followed by a summation across the original temporal dimension and an optional stack of 2D convolutional layers.

2.2   Adaptive Median Filtering

As alluded to previously, the process of marine snow removal is twofold. First, a potential marine snow affected regions in images are detected with the 3D convolutional neural network, trained with relatively large, hand annotated marine snow examples, as described in the previous section. However, due to high generalizing properties of this network, in operation time it is able to detect marine snow regions of various shape and size. The second step is to substitute these regions in images with neighboring signals which are not affected by the marine snow. In the proposed method this is done with the new adaptive version of the median filter. The idea of this algorithm is to start processing at a given pixel, which was detected as a marine snow, and traverse its neighboring pixels looking for the ones which are not marine snow affected ("healthy" ones). The traversed neighborhood is gradually enlarged to encompass regions up to a certain maximal size. This process is stopped after collecting a sufficient number of "healthy" pixels (based on our experiments, in most cases at least 3–5), from which a median value is computed and used as a substitute for a marine snow affected pixel. Operation of this algorithm is explained in the diagrams in Fig. 4. The adaptive filtering is then repeated in every pixel position marked by the neural network as a marine snow. The idea behind the proposed procedure is to limit filtering to the minimum so that the image quality is not affected, and at the same time to adapt the size of the filter to a given marine snow particle. The latter is necessary since the marine snow particle can vary in size significantly.

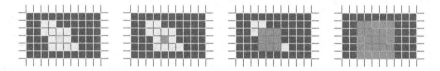

Fig. 4. The proposed adaptive median filter. From the left: (1) sample detection mask, white pixels representing detected marine snow, blue representing filtering positions, (2–3) consecutively increasing kernel size, with red indicating detected marine snow, (4) further increased kernel up to the point of finding pixels that are not marine snow, indicated in green, from which median is computed. (Color figure online)

3   Experimental Study

To assess the practical usefulness of the proposed filtering pipeline we performed an experimental study consisting of two stages. In the first one we evaluated the detection capabilities of the proposed fully convolutional 3D neural network. In the second stage we combined the obtained detection model with the proposed adaptive median filter and compared the performance of the whole pipeline in the marine snow removal task with the available baseline methods.

For experiments two underwater video sequences were used. The first one was acquired during a SCUBA diving in the sea waters of Antarctica, near Port Lockroy (64°49'31"S 63°29'40"W). The second one was filmed in the lake in the quarry Zakrzowek, Poland (50°02'11"N 19°54'38"E). These are color videos with frames of 1920 × 1080 pixels for the Antarctica, and 1280 × 720 pixels for Zakrzowek sequence, 24 frames per second, and duration 45 and 50 min, respectively. From these, three separate scenes were extracted: one from the Antarctica sequence, consisting of 30 consecutive frames, and two from the Zakrzowek sequence, referred to as Zakrzowek-A and Zakrzowek-B, consisting of 22 and

24 frames, respectively. Marine snow particles were manually annotated by a human examiner in every frame in a form of binary mask. For the experiments, partitions Antarctica and Zakrzowek-A were used as a training data, whereas Zakrzowek-B was used for the evaluation of the model. The experiments were conducted on a computational cluster. Each run used a single core of the Intel Xeon E5-2680 v3 processor combined with the Nvidia Tesla K40 XL GPU.

3.1   Results of Marine Snow Detection

In the first part of the experimental study, the proposed neural network was evaluated in the marine snow detection task. The goal of this part of the evaluation was not only measuring the performance of the proposed model, but also evaluating if, and under what conditions, introduction of 3D convolutions is beneficial to the networks performance. To this end two separate experiments were conducted. In the first one we varied the number of consecutive frames used by the network to produce a single detection mask. We considered the number of input frames in $\{1, 3, 5, 7\}$, where using a single frame is equivalent to a single image marine snow detection. In this experiment the architecture of the neural network was fixed. Based on the results of Kim et al. [9], we used a model consisting of 20 convolutional layers, in our case using 3D convolutions. In the second experiment we evaluated the impact of the number of 3D layers on the models performance. We kept the total number of layers fixed at 20, but varied the number of 3D layers, using values in $m \in \{1, 5, 10, 15, 20\}$. After the last 3D layer the networks output was flattened, and 2D convolutions were used until the network reached the depth of 20 layers. In this experiment the number of input frames was fixed at 3.

In both experiments, the networks were trained using Adam optimizer [10] with learning rate equal to $1e-5$, β_1 equal to 0.9, β_2 equal to 0.999, ϵ equal to $1e-8$ and the loss function being the mean squared error between networks outputs and ground truth annotations. The weights of the network were initialized using the procedure described by Glorot and Bengio [5]. The training was conducted in a batch mode, with batch size of 32, using patches of size 40×40, extracted from the original frames with a stride of 20. The training lasted for 2 epochs. This value was chosen based on the performance on the validation set in the initial runs, in which half of the training data was set aside as a validation partition. For every network variant training procedure was repeated 10 times with a random initialization.

Due to high data imbalance, to numerically assess the performance of the networks we considered four metrics: accuracy, precision, recall and F-measure [3]. Each metric was computed on the pixel level for the whole dataset. In the Fig. 5 we present the values of F-measure, averaged over the random network initializations, as a functions of the number of input frames and the number of 3D convolutional layers. As can be seen, when using only a single frame, the observed performance is significantly lower than in the case in which additional frames are used. Similarly, using a higher number of 3D layers than 1 is beneficial to the networks performance. However, increasing the number of frames beyond

3 and the number of 3D layers beyond 5 did not lead to a significant increase in performance. Since both the training and the evaluation time increase approximately linearly with the number of input frames and the number of 3D layers, as can be seen in Fig. 6, the architecture using 3 input frames and 5 3D layers was chosen to be used in the further experiments. The numerical values of all of the considered performance metrics for the chosen architecture were presented in Table 1. As can be seen, proposed network performs well in the imbalanced data setting. It should be noted the measured performance was lowered due to the inaccuracies in the hand annotated ground truth data. In particular, very small particles very usually not labeled by the annotator, but were still, usually correctly, detected by the network. Finally, the detection mask produced by the network on a sample image were presented in Fig. 7. As can be seen, the network is able to detect most of the annotated marine snow particles. Furthermore, it is able to generalize to smaller particles, which were left out in the annotating process due to a high cost of manual labeling.

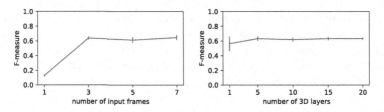

Fig. 5. Average and standard deviation of the networks F-measure in the marine snow detection task as a function of the number of input frames (left) and the number of 3D convolutional layers (right).

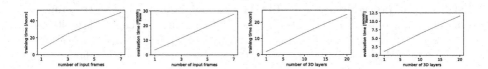

Fig. 6. From the left: observed training and evaluation time as a function of the number of input frames and the number of 3D convolutional layers.

3.2 Results of Marine Snow Removal

In the second part of the experimental study we combined previously described fully convolutional 3D neural network with the proposed adaptive filtering algorithm. Since the evaluation was conducted on a real data, the ground truth

Table 1. Average and standard deviation of various performance metrics for the proposed model in the marine snow detection task.

Accuracy	Precision	Recall	F-measure
99.405 ± 0.129	0.620 ± 0.109	0.668 ± 0.061	0.632 ± 0.030

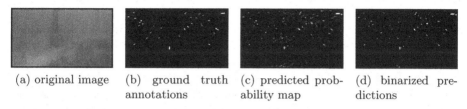

(a) original image   (b) ground truth annotations   (c) predicted probability map   (d) binarized predictions

Fig. 7. A sample image, associated ground truth annotations and the predictions made by the neural network in the detection task.

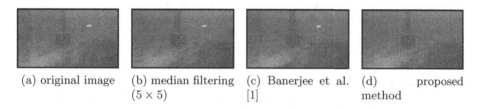

(a) original image   (b) median filtering (5×5) (c) Banerjee et al. [1]   (d) proposed method

Fig. 8. A comparison of the proposed filtering pipeline with the reference methods. Proposed approach deals with all sizes of the marine snow particles, at the same time preserving the quality of the original image in the areas unaffected by the marine snow.

images with no marine snow were not available. Because of that the examination was limited to a visual assessment of the produced filtered images. For the comparison we examined two baseline methods: a standard median filtering with a window size equal to 5×5, as well as the probabilistic approach proposed by Banerjee et al. [1].

A sample filtered image was presented in Fig. 8. The remaining test images, filtered by all of the methods, are available as a supplement[1]. As can be seen, standard median filtering is unsuitable for the marine snow removal task at the tested window size. Further increase of the window size not only negatively affects the quality of the image, but also fails to significantly improve the performance. The approach proposed by Banerjee et al. [1] also fails to filter all of the marine snow particles, especially the larger ones. The method proposed in this paper reliably filters marine snow particles of all sizes, at the same time minimally affecting the image quality, since only the positions at which marine snow was detected are altered.

---

[1] http://home.agh.edu.pl/~cyganek/MS_ICPR2018.zip.

4 Conclusions

In the paper a novel and efficient method of marine snow noise removal from underwater videos is proposed. This type of noise, caused by clustered biological and mineral particles, hinders scene analysis in underwater operations and should be removed. However, the problem is difficult since its statistical properties are significantly different from other types of noise. It was observed that marine snow particles tend to have high luminance and low color saturation. Also, the particles usually move fast from frame to frame. The novelty of the proposed method is that it takes full advantage of these spatial and temporal properties. First stage of operation is marine snow detection with the especially designed fully convolutional 3D neural network. It is trained with real underwater images with hand annotated places of marine snow occurrence. Thanks to high generalization abilities of this type of network, noise is well detected in underwater videos of various category. In the next step, all places which were detected as marine snow are removed with the novel version of the adaptive median filter. Experimental results show high accuracy in marine snow detection. This way filtered underwater images have majority of marine snow removed whereas details of other small objects are retained.

Acknowledgments. This work was supported by the National Science Center NCN, Poland, under the grant no. 2016/21/B/ST6/01461. The support of the PLGrid infrastructure is also greatly appreciated.

References

1. Banerjee, S., Sanyal, G., Ghosh, S., Ray, R., Shome, S.N.: Elimination of marine snow effect from underwater image - an adaptive probabilistic approach. In: 2014 IEEE Students' Conference on Electrical, Electronics and Computer Science (SCEECS), pp. 1–4. IEEE (2014)
2. Carson, R.: The Sea Around Us. Oxford University Press, Cary (1951)
3. Cyganek, B.: Object Detection and Recognition in Digital Images: Theory and Practice. Wiley, Hoboken (2013)
4. Farhadifard, F., Radolko, M., von Lukas, U.F.: Single image marine snow removal based on a supervised median filtering scheme. In: VISIGRAPP (4: VISAPP), pp. 280–287 (2017)
5. Glorot, X., Bengio, Y.: Understanding the difficulty of training deep feedforward neural networks. In: Proceedings of the Thirteenth International Conference on Artificial Intelligence and Statistics, pp. 249–256 (2010)
6. He, K., Zhang, X., Ren, S., Sun, J.: Deep residual learning for image recognition. In: Proceedings of the IEEE Conference on Computer Vision and Pattern Recognition, pp. 770–778 (2016)
7. Hines, C.L.: The official William Beebe web site. https://sites.google.com/site/cwilliambeebe/Home/bathysphere. Accessed 14 Mar 2018
8. Jaffe, J.: Underwater optical imaging: the past, the present, and the prospects. In: IEEE Journal of Oceanic Engineering, pp. 683–700. IEEE (2015)

9. Kim, J., Kwon Lee, J., Mu Lee, K.: Accurate image super-resolution using very deep convolutional networks. In: Proceedings of the IEEE Conference on Computer Vision and Pattern Recognition, pp. 1646–1654 (2016)

10. Kingma, D.P., Ba, J.: Adam: a method for stochastic optimization. arXiv preprint arXiv:1412.6980 (2014)

11. Kocak, D.M., Dalgleish, F.R., Caimi, F.M., Schechner, Y.Y.: A focus on recent developments and trends in underwater imaging. Mar. Technol. Soc. J. **42**(1), 52–67 (2008)

12. Koziarski, M., Cyganek, B.: Image recognition with deep neural networks in presence of noise-dealing with and taking advantage of distortions. Integr. Comput.-Aided Eng. **24**(4), 337–349 (2017)

13. Krizhevsky, A., Sutskever, I., Hinton, G.E.: ImageNet classification with deep convolutional neural networks. In: Advances in Neural Information Processing Systems, pp. 1097–1105 (2012)

14. Lim, B., Son, S., Kim, H., Nah, S., Lee, K.M.: Enhanced deep residual networks for single image super-resolution. In: The IEEE Conference on Computer Vision and Pattern Recognition (CVPR) Workshops, vol. 1, p. 3 (2017)

15. Long, J., Shelhamer, E., Darrell, T.: Fully convolutional networks for semantic segmentation. In: Proceedings of the IEEE Conference on Computer Vision and Pattern Recognition, pp. 3431–3440 (2015)

16. Orzech, J.K.; Nealson, K.: Bioluminescence of marine snow: its effect on the optical properties of the sea. In: Proceedings of SPIE 0489, Ocean Optics VII. SPIE (1984)

17. Paszke, A., Chaurasia, A., Kim, S., Culurciello, E.: ENet: a deep neural network architecture for real-time semantic segmentation. arXiv preprint arXiv:1606.02147 (2016)

18. Riley, G.: Organic aggregates in seawater and the dynamics of their formation and utilization. Limnol. Oceanogr. **8**, 372–381 (1963)

19. Silver, M.: Marine snow: a brief historical sketch. Limnol. Oceanogr. Bull. **24**, 5–10 (2015)

20. Simonyan, K., Zisserman, A.: Very deep convolutional networks for large-scale image recognition. arXiv preprint arXiv:1409.1556 (2014)

21. Tran, D., Bourdev, L., Fergus, R., Torresani, L., Paluri, M.: Learning spatiotemporal features with 3D convolutional networks. In: 2015 IEEE International Conference on Computer Vision (ICCV), pp. 4489–4497. IEEE (2015)

22. Xie, J., Xu, L., Chen, E.: Image denoising and inpainting with deep neural networks. In: Advances in Neural Information Processing Systems, pp. 341–349 (2012)

Strategies for Tackling the Class Imbalance Problem in Marine Image Classification

Daniel Langenkämper[(⊠)], Robin van Kevelaer, and Tim W. Nattkemper

Biodata Mining Group, Faculty of Technology, Bielefeld University,
33615 Bielefeld, Germany
dlangenk@cebitec.uni-bielefeld.de
https://www.cebitec.uni-bielefeld.de/biodatamining/

Abstract. Research of deep learning algorithms, especially in the field of convolutional neural networks (CNN), has shown significant progress. The application of CNNs in image analysis and pattern recognition has earned a lot of attention in this regard and few applications to classify a small number of common taxa in marine image collections have been reported yet.

In this paper, we address the problem of class imbalance in marine image data, i.e. the common observation that 80%–90% of the data belong to a small subset of L' classes among the total number of L observed classes, with $L' \ll L$. A small number of methods to compensate for the class imbalance problem in the training step have been proposed for the common computer vision benchmark datasets. But marine image collections (showing for instance megafauna as considered in this study) pose a greater challenge as the observed imbalance is more extreme as habitats can feature a high biodiversity but a low species density.

In this paper, we investigate the potential of various over-/ undersampling methods to compensate for the class imbalance problem in marine imaging. In addition, five different balancing rules are proposed and analyzed to examine the extent to which sampling should be used, i.e. how many samples should be created or removed to gain the most out of the sampling algorithms. We evaluate these methods with AlexNet trained for classifying benthic image data recorded at the Porcupine Abyssal Plain (PAP) and use a Support Vector Machine as baseline classifier. We can report that the best of our proposed strategies in combination with data augmentation applied to AlexNet results in an increase of thirteen basis points compared to AlexNet without sampling. Furthermore, examples are presented, which show that the combination of oversampling and augmentation leads to a better generalization than pure augmentation.

Keywords: Class imbalance · CNN · Marine imaging
Deep learning · Taxonomic classification

© Springer Nature Switzerland AG 2019
Z. Zhang et al. (Eds.): ICPR 2018 Workshops, LNCS 11188, pp. 26–36, 2019.
https://doi.org/10.1007/978-3-030-05792-3_3

1   Introduction

1.1   Motivation

The classification of objects is of central importance for a multitude of areas, e.g. autonomous driving, biodiversity studies, public surveillance, etc. With the emergence of deep neural networks, especially convolutional neural networks (CNNs), computer science has made a great leap forward in solving this problem. In recent years, the performance on benchmark datasets has even surpassed human performance for the first time [9].

However, in contrast to natural images, i.e. images showing everyday objects, or even customized benchmark data such as ImageNet [4], biological data have some unique characteristics in contrast to those mentioned above. The main differences are (a) data quality issues, (b) lack of training data and (c) class imbalance. The quality issues are mainly caused by the heterogeneity in capture setups, i.e. different light sources, occlusion, cast shadows, different camera angles, different camera equipment, development of the images (white balancing, etc.) and others. The lack of training data is inherent in that the captured objects are not everyday objects. It is, therefore, more difficult to encounter these objects and harder to annotate these. For everyday objects, citizen science solutions are a quick way to acquire a lot of valid annotations. Otherwise, trained experts are needed to acquire a limited number of error-prone annotations. The class imbalance, i.e. the common observation that 80%-90% of the training data belong to a small subset of L' classes among the total number of L observed classes, with $L' \ll L$, is usually present to varying degrees in biological data, e.g. established by prey and predator relationships, where the prey is more abundant than the predators.

Marine images are also a special type of this biological data. Data is scarce due to the high investment in equipment and difficult setup of the imaging system needed to acquire underwater imagery. The annotation problem is exacerbated by the high diversity - low abundance phenomena observed in the deep sea. Trained experts' time is limited, and citizen science projects are difficult to establish, although public interest is generally high. This annotation problem further skews the class imbalance, since easy to spot/annotate objects will be annotated much more frequently.

1.2   Prior Work

Different methods for compensating class imbalances exist. These are over- and undersampling of data [3,8,18], class weights/class aware loss functions/cost sensitive learning [5,11] and postprocessing the output class probabilities also known as thresholding, which could be regarded as a special case of cost-sensitive learning [12,16]. While class weights are dependent on the algorithm used, e.g. applicable for the SVM, over-/undersampling are applied before the classification is run and are therefore independent of the algorithm used. Class aware loss functions were proposed for example for some CNN types. They are a powerful instrument but are algorithm dependent and not easy to tune.

Prior work has been published to investigate the influence of class imbalance on machine learning algorithms, e.g. [2], but no investigation concerning the case of marine imaging is known to the authors. For a review have a look at [7].

2   Dataset

The images used in this study were recorded using an autonomous underwater vehicle (AUV) at the Porcupine Abyssal Plain (PAP) [13], located southwest of the UK in international waters. The image set is composed of 12116 images $\mathcal{I}_{i=0...12115}$. 30149 circular annotations $\mathcal{A}_j = (x, y, r, i, l)$ (with x, y being the center of the circle with radius r on image $\mathcal{I}_i$) divided into 19 classes, i.e. morphtoypes/taxa l (see Fig. 1) were done by experts. These were used to extract rectangular image patches $\mathcal{P}_{j=0...30148}$ containing the annotated object. As can be seen in Fig. 1 the distribution of the classes l is skewed, and a class imbalance problem is present.

For the SVM, features are generated by flattening the RGB patches from $\mathcal{P}_j \in \mathbb{N}^{30149 \times \text{width} \times \text{height} \times 3}$ to $\mathcal{P}'_j \in \mathbb{N}^{30149 \times (\text{width} * \text{height} * 3)}$. Then dimensionality reduction using a PCA on the patches $\mathcal{P}'_j$ is applied to get the dataset $\Gamma_{\text{SVM}} = \{PCA(\mathcal{P}'_j)\} \in \mathbb{R}^{30149 \times 64}$.

For the CNN the image patches $\mathcal{P}_j$ were resized to patches P''_j of size $64 \times 64 \times 3$. These form the dataset $\Gamma_{\text{CNN}} = \{\mathcal{P}''_|\} \in \mathbb{N}^{30149 \times 64 \times 64 \times 3}$.

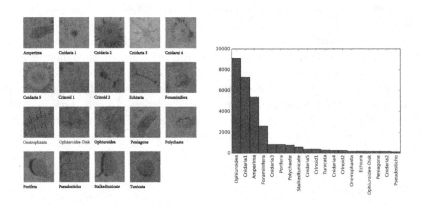

Fig. 1. Example image patches of all classes l and histogram of the classes

3   Methods

3.1   Over/Undersampling Methods

Random Oversampling. Random oversampling (ROS) [1] is a simple method designed to balance a dataset. With this method, $\mathcal{P}_j$ belonging to the classes that are to be oversampled are drawn with replacement and added to the data set until the desired class sizes are reached. This results in a larger data set that contains some of the $\mathcal{P}_j$ multiple times.

SMOTE. Synthetic Minority Over-sampling Technique (SMOTE) [3] is an algorithm that generates synthetic samples from the existing ones of a dataset. It was originally formulated for two-class classification problems. If $s'(l)$ new samples are to be created for a class l, $s'(l)$ image patches $\{\mathcal{P}_j\}_{j=1,\ldots,s'(l)} \subset \Gamma$ of this class are randomly selected. For each of these $\mathcal{P}_j$, the K nearest neighbors in Γ are estimated forming $P_{k=1,\ldots,K}$, while K is a hyper-parameter and must be determined. One of these K nearest neighbors P_k is selected randomly. The new sample is determined to be:

$$\hat{P} = P_j + \lambda * (P_k - P_j) \tag{1}$$

with λ [0, 1] being a random number.

ADASYN. Adaptive Synthetic Sampling (ADASYN) [8] is an oversampling method that generates synthetic samples similar to the SMOTE algorithm and was originally formulated for a two-class classification problem. Unlike SMOTE, it does not select the sample pairs from which a new sample is generated only randomly, but according to the distribution of the data. The K nearest neighbors for every data point are computed. For each sample P_j of the minority class, the ratio $r_j = \frac{\delta_j}{k}$ with $\delta_j = |\{P_k : l(P_k) == P_{maj}\}|$ being the number of samples labeled with l_{maj} in the k neighborhood is determined.

All r_j are normalized $\hat{r}_j = r_j / \sum_j r_j$ so that the result is a probability distribution $\hat{r} = \sum_j \hat{r}_j = 1$. The number of synthetic samples s'_j that are generated for each P_j is computed as $s'_j = \hat{r}_j * s'(l)$. A new sample $\hat{P}$ is computed as follows:

$$\hat{P} = P_j + \lambda(P_k - P_j) \tag{2}$$

This algorithm results in more samples being created for a sample that has many neighbors from the majority class than for samples that have fewer such neighbors. If a sample has no neighbors from the majority class, no samples are created for it.

Data Augmentation. The term *data augmentation* describes the application of different transformations to the training images. This can be e.g. the extraction of sections from images or flipping, rotations, or Gaussian blurring [10,14,15]. It can be used by temporarily creating randomly transformed copies of the training data during training and can therefore also be used additionally if the training set was previously oversampled. It has proven to be helpful to prevent overfitting and to improve classifier performance [10,14].

Transformation Oversampling. The image transformations used for data augmentation can also be applied as part of an oversampling method that can be employed to balance an imbalanced training dataset as proposed by Wang and Perez [15].

To balance the dataset the transformations are applied to image patches P_j from minority classes that are to be oversampled. Hereby, it is paid attention that if possible no transformations are multiply applied to the same P_j, i.e. the same transformation is only applied multiple times to the same P_j if all the other transformations have already been used on it.

The transformations used here are a 90-degree rotation, Gaussian blur with $\sigma = 1$ and flipping using one of both image axes. In the following, this oversampling method is referred to as *Transformation Oversampling* (TROS).

Random Undersampling. Undersampling means that image patches P_j are removed from the data. The method can be applied to the larger classes in an unbalanced dataset to reduce the imbalance. Random undersampling (RUS) [1] is a simple undersampling method that randomly removes P_j from all classes that are to be subsampled until the desired sample size $s(l)$ is reached.

3.2   Balancing Rules

All the used sampling methods introduced above require a desired sample size $s(l)$ for each class l. The sample size is usually expressed as a percentage of the sample size $s(l)$ of the majority class l_{maj}, i.e. the class which is the most common.

The term *balancing rule* will be used to describe the rule that defines which sample size $s(l)$ a class should be sampled to in relation to $s(l_{\text{maj}})$.

Three different rules for oversampling are introduced in this section $\{r_{100}, r_{50}, r_{50,75,100}\}$.

r_{100} is the most intuitive one setting the sample size $s(l)$ to the sample size of the majority class $s(l_{\text{maj}})$.

$$r_{100} : s(l) = s(l_{\text{maj}}) \tag{3}$$

When resampling imbalanced datasets, the synthetically generated samples are derived from only a small number of samples. Thus it may be the case that at some point generating more samples does not significantly increase the accuracy of the classifier trained on the dataset anymore. Additionally, there may be a loss of classification performance on the majority classes if all classes are sampled to the same size.

A solution for this may be oversampling rare classes to a size of $\frac{1}{2}s(l_{\mathrm{maj}})$ and keep the larger classes at their original size.

$$r_{50} : s(l) = \begin{cases} \frac{s(l_{\mathrm{maj}})}{2} & \text{if } s(l) < \frac{s(l_{\mathrm{maj}})}{2} \\ s(l) & \text{else} \end{cases} \tag{4}$$

This rule may increase the classification accuracy of the rare classes keeping that of the common classes reasonably high, thus preventing a high loss of average precision per class caused by misclassification of common classes.

Using the third rule $r_{50,75,100}$ the sample sizes $s(l)$ are divided up into three ranges.

$$r_{50,75,100} : s(l) = \begin{cases} \frac{1}{2}s(l_{\mathrm{maj}}) & \text{if } s(l) \leq \frac{1}{4}s(l_{\mathrm{maj}}) \\ \frac{3}{4}s(l_{\mathrm{maj}}) & \text{if } \frac{1}{4}s(l_{\mathrm{maj}}) < M_k \leq \frac{1}{2}s(l_{\mathrm{maj}}) \\ s(l_{\mathrm{maj}}) & \text{else} \end{cases} \tag{5}$$

In addition two rules $\{\hat{r}_{75}, \hat{r}_{50,100}\}$ combining oversampling with undersampling are evaluated. The first rule r_{75} completely balances the dataset, but decreases the variety of the largest classes by removing a certain share of their training samples randomly. Many of the synthetic minority class samples are generated from a small number of image patches $\mathcal{P}_j$. Because of this, the variance of these classes may be smaller than the variance of the majority classes even after oversampling. Applying this rule may reduce this difference.

$$\hat{r}_{75} : s(l) = \frac{3}{4}s(l_{\mathrm{maj}}). \tag{6}$$

The other rule introduced here is adapted from a combined undersampling and oversampling approach introduced in [3]. The method mentioned there includes undersampling the majority class to half the size and oversampling the minority class to $s(l_{\mathrm{maj}})$ in a two-class classification problem. This is extended to the multiclass classification problem at hand. The desired sample sizes $s(l)$ are computed as follows:

$$\hat{r}_{50,100} : s(l) = \begin{cases} \frac{s(l_{\mathrm{maj}})}{2} & \text{if } s(l) \geq \frac{s(l_{\mathrm{maj}})}{2} \\ s(l_{\mathrm{maj}}) & \text{else } \cdot \end{cases} \tag{7}$$

3.3   Evaluation Metrics

The classification results are evaluated using the macro-averaged recall, precision [17] and the mean f1-score [6]. Macro-averaging means that the measure is first computed for each class separately, then the arithmetic mean of the per-class measures is computed to obtain a performance measure that is suitable for equally weighting all classes regardless of their sample sizes. If the average of the class-wise measures were weighted by class size, as usual, low scores for small classes would lower the average much less, while for common classes the loss would be much stronger. This is important to assess whether a classifier can classify rare classes as well as common classes.

The macro-averaged recall R_{macro} is defined as $R_{\mathrm{macro}} = \frac{1}{L} \sum_l R(l)$ where $R(l)$ denotes the recall of class l.

The macro-averaged precision P_{macro} is defined as $P_{\mathrm{macro}} = \frac{1}{L} \sum_l P(l)$ where $P(l)$ denotes the precision of class l.

To evaluate the overall classification performance, the macro-averaged f1-score $F_{1,\mathrm{macro}}$, which is defined as $F_{1,\mathrm{macro}} = \frac{1}{L} \sum_l F_1(l)$ with $F_1(l) = \frac{2R(l)P(l)}{R(l)+P(l)}$ where $F_1(l)$ is the class-wise f1-score, which is the harmonic mean of $P(l)$ and $R(l)$, with both values weighted equally.

Table 1. CNN results: best results are shown in boldface.

$F_{1,\mathrm{macro}}$	SMOTE	ADASYN	ROS	TROS
baseline	0.6868			
r_{50}	0.7571	0.7404	0.7416	0.7651
$r_{50,75,100}$	0.7525	0.7432	**0.7445**	**0.7766**
r_{100}	0.7581	**0.7434**	0.7433	0.7621
$\hat{r}_{75}$	**0.7653**			0.7607
$\hat{r}_{50,100}$	0.7652			0.7578

(a)

R_{macro}	SMOTE	ADASYN	ROS	TROS
baseline	0.6585			
r_{50}	0.7225	**0.7082**	0.7266	0.7892
$r_{50,75,100}$	0.7332	0.7070	0.7249	0.7900
r_{100}	0.7250	0.7067	**0.7280**	0.7767
$\hat{r}_{75}$	0.7317			0.7888
$\hat{r}_{50,100}$	**0.7400**			**0.7961**

(b)

P_{macro}	SMOTE	ADASYN	ROS	TROS
baseline	0.7345			
r_{50}	**0.8159**	0.7915	0.7688	0.7495
$r_{50,75,100}$	0.7907	0.7985	**0.7739**	**0.7691**
r_{100}	0.8087	**0.8016**	0.7689	0.7563
$\hat{r}_{75}$	0.8153			0.7425
$\hat{r}_{50,100}$	0.8065			0.7334

(c)

	$F_{1,\mathrm{macro}}$	R_{macro}	P_{macro}
baseline	0.6868	0.6586	0.7345
Only DA	0.7213	0.6989	0.7751
DA, SMOTE, r_{50}	0.8000	0.7903	0.8206
DA, TROS, $r_{50,75,100}$	0.7919	0.7847	0.8030
DA, SMOTE, $\hat{r}_{75}$	**0.8145**	0.8110	**0.8248**
DA, SMOTE, $\hat{r}_{50,100}$	0.8120	**0.8136**	0.8157

(d)

4 Results

In Table 1(a) the results of the AlexNet classification using the different balancing rules compared to the classification results without any sampling (baseline) are shown. It is evident that sampling helps in increasing the classification performance significantly. The best results are achieved using TROS with the $r_{50,75,100}$ rule, which results in an increase of roughly 9 basis points for the $F_{1,\mathrm{macro}}$ score. SMOTE oversampling combined with random undersmapling is almost as good comparing the $F_{1,\mathrm{macro}}$ score (-1 basis point) but achieves a much higher macro precision than the aforementioned method (81.5% vs. 76.9%) at the cost of a much lower macro recall value (74% vs. 79,6%). ADASYN and ROS are underperforming therefore the undersampling experiments were not executed.

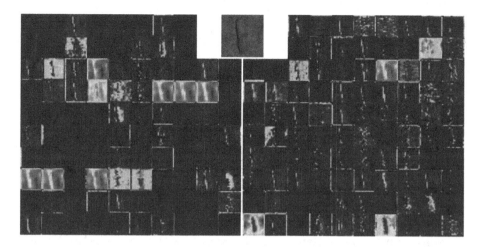

Fig. 2. Example plots of the activations of the first layer of AlexNet. The left image shows the activations for pure data augmentation and the right image of data augmentation combined with the best sampling approach (cmp. Table 1d).

The results of combining the sampling methods with data-augmentation are shown in Table 1(d) and Table 2. Here the runner-up from above – SMOTE combined with the $\hat{r}_{75}$ balancing rule is the best, which gains an additional 5 basis points using data-augmentation. Interestingly, data-augmentation without sampling only gains 3.5 basis points compared to the baseline.

Besides, as can be seen in Fig. 2 according to the activations the AlexNet classifier tends to gain generalization performance, using oversampling in combination with data-augmentation compared to using pure data-augmentation. In this figure we can see that more, and also more unique filters are active and that the filters generated by the convolutional neural network are detecting

Table 2. Single Class F_1 scores including total macro and weighted F_1 score

Class	Baseline F_1	DA, SMOTE, $\hat{r}_{75}$ F_1	Class	Baseline F_1	DA, SMOTE, $\hat{r}_{75}$ F_1
Amperima	0.9378	0.9662	Oneirophanta	0.812	0.9098
Cnidaria 1	0.9683	0.9784	Ophiuroidea	0.932	0.963
Cnidaria 2	0.731	0.7299	Ophiuroidea-Disk	0.3916	0.6063
Cnidaria 3	0.8043	0.9437	Peniagone	0.4663	0.6766
Cnidaria 4	0.78	0.8179	Polychaete	0.7276	0.8956
Cnidaria 5	0.8968	0.9013	Porifera	0.5811	0.7051
Crinoid 1	0.5423	0.8179	Pseudosticho	0.3807	0.7852
Crinoid 2	0.6063	0.7493	Stalkedtunicate	0.684	0.7913
Echiura	0.5178	0.7095	Tunicata	0.4244	0.5829
Foraminifera	0.864	0.9459			
			$F_{1,\text{macro}}$	0.6868	0.8145
			F_1	0.8841	0.935

more edges, or small details like the tentacles of the holothurian, rather than memorizing the whole holothurian.

Table 3. SVM results: best results are shown in boldface.

	SMOTE			ADASYN		
	R_{macro}	P_{macro}	$F_{1,macro}$	R_{macro}	P_{macro}	$F_{1,macro}$
Baseline	**0.5571**	**0.6223**	**0.5796**	**0.5571**	**0.6223**	0.5796
r_{50}	0.5541	0.6095	0.5729	0.5525	0.6074	0.5711
$r_{50,75,100}$	0.5528	0.6123	0.5735	0.5494	0.6045	0.5684
r_{100}	0.5503	0.6036	0.5680	0.5475	0.5986	0.5643

Additionally, we investigated the influence of SMOTE and ADASYN over-sampling on the SVM classifier. The SVM results are listed in Table 3. It can be seen that oversampling is hurting the performance. This is unfortunately inherent with the way the SVM classifies and in that SMOTE and ADASYN are generating data. The SVM tries to find a separating hyperplane between data points of different classes. SMOTE and ADASYN are introducing new data points in between data points of differently labeled data (cmp. Eqs. 1 and 2). Therefore the data is placed near the separating hyperplane, thus increasing the number of support vectors (cmp. Fig. 3) needed to establish a hyperplane still separating the differently labeled data, while still not gaining any better scores. This results in overfitting of the classifier.

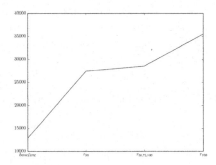

Fig. 3. Number of support vectors compared to the balancing rule applied.

5   Conclusion

To sum up the results of this thesis, it can be said that over-/undersampling is a method that is helpful to improve a classifier's result achieved on imbalanced marine image data. In contrast to other data domains combined over-/undersampling was only stronger than pure oversampling when combined with data augmentation. It was shown that over-/unddersampling is a well-suited method to improve the performance of a convolutional neural network, especially if it is combined with data augmentation. The balancing rules introduced and compared in this paper show a big improvement over the intuitive approach of oversampling every class to the maximum sampling size.

Which sampling algorithm and balancing rule to choose is a question of the desired result. Applying SMOTE alone, for example, yields a good precision while using TROS increases the recall more. If data augmentation is applied additionally to oversampling, the results are more balanced increasing the performance of rare classes. This leads to the best overall classification performance and increased generalization, which makes it recommendable to combine sampling with data augmentation.

Acknowledgment. We thank the National Oceanography Centre for providing the data and consultation and NVIDIA Corporation for donating the GPU used in this project. This project has received funding by Projektträger Jülich (grant no 03F0707C) under the framework of JPI Oceans.

References

1. Batista, G., Prati, R., Monard, M.: A study of the behavior of several methods for balancing machine learning training data. SIGKDD Explor. Newsl. **6**(1), 20–29 (2004)
2. Buda, M., Maki, A., Mazurowski, M.A.: A systematic study of the class imbalance problem in convolutional neural networks. arXiv preprint arXiv:1710.05381 (2017)
3. Chawla, N., Bowyer, K., Hall, L., Kegelmeyer, W.: SMOTE: synthetic minority over-sampling technique. J. Artif. Intell. Res. **16**, 321–357 (2002)
4. Deng, J., Dong, W., Socher, R., Li, L.J., Li, K., Fei-Fei, L.: ImageNet: a large-scale hierarchical image database. In: CVPR 2009, pp. 248–255. IEEE (2009)
5. Elkan, C.: The foundations of cost-sensitive learning. In: IJCAI, vol. 17, pp. 973–978. Lawrence Erlbaum Associates Ltd. (2001)
6. Ferri, C., Hernndez-Orallo, J., Modroiu, R.: An experimental comparison of performance measures for classification. Pattern Recogn. Lett. **30**(1), 27–38 (2009)
7. Haixiang, G., Yijing, L., Shang, J., Mingyun, G., Yuanyue, H., Bing, G.: Learning from class-imbalanced data: review of methods and applications. Expert Syst. Appl. **73**, 220–239 (2017)
8. He, H., Bai, Y., Garcia, E.A., Li, S.: ADASYN: adaptive synthetic sampling approach for imbalanced learning. In: IJCNN 2008, pp. 1322–1328. IEEE (2008)
9. He, K., Zhang, X., Ren, S., Sun, J.: Delving deep into rectifiers: surpassing human-level performance on imagenet classification. In: ICCV, pp. 1026–1034 (2015)
10. Krizhevsky, A., Sutskever, I., Hinton, G.E.: ImageNet classification with deep convolutional neural networks. In: Advances in Neural Information Processing Systems 25, pp. 1097–1105. Curran Associates, Inc. (2012)
11. Kukar, M., Kononenko, I., et al.: Cost-sensitive learning with neural networks. In: ECAI, pp. 445–449 (1998)
12. Lawrence, S., Burns, I., Back, A., Tsoi, A.C., Giles, C.L.: Neural network classification and prior class probabilities. In: Orr, G.B., Müller, K.-R. (eds.) Neural Networks: Tricks of the Trade. LNCS, vol. 1524, pp. 299–313. Springer, Heidelberg (1998). https://doi.org/10.1007/3-540-49430-8_15

13. Morris, K.J., Bett, B.J., Durden, J.M., et al.: A new method for ecological surveyingof the abyss using autonomous underwater vehicle photography. Limnol: Oceanogr. Methods **12**, 795–809 (2014)

14. Pawara, P., Okafor, E., Schomaker, L., Wiering, M.: Data augmentation for plant classification. In: Blanc-Talon, J., Penne, R., Philips, W., Popescu, D., Scheunders, P. (eds.) ACIVS 2017. LNCS, vol. 10617, pp. 615–626. Springer, Cham (2017). https://doi.org/10.1007/978-3-319-70353-4_52

15. Perez, L., Wang, J.: The effectiveness of data augmentation in image classification using deep learning. CoRR abs/1712.04621 (2017). http://arxiv.org/abs/1712.04621

16. Richard, M.D., Lippmann, R.P.: Neural network classifiers estimate Bayesian a posteriori probabilities. Neural Comput. **3**(4), 461–483 (1991)

17. Sokolova, M., Lapalme, G.: A systematic analysis of performance measures for classification tasks. Inf. Process. Manag. **45**(4), 427–437 (2009)

18. Wilson, D.L.: Asymptotic properties of nearest neighbor rules using edited data. IEEE Trans. Syst. Man Cybern. **3**, 408–421 (1972)

An Online Platform for Underwater Image Quality Evaluation

Chau Yi Li[(✉)], Riccardo Mazzon, and Andrea Cavallaro

Centre for Intelligent Sensing, Queen Mary University of London, London, UK
{chau.li,r.mazzon,a.cavallaro}@qmul.ac.uk

Abstract. With the miniaturisation of underwater cameras, the volume of available underwater images has been considerably increasing. However, underwater images are degraded by the absorption and scattering of light in water. Image processing methods exist that aim to compensate for these degradations, but there are no standard quality evaluation measures or testing datasets for a systematic empirical comparison. For this reason, we propose PUIQE, an online platform for underwater image quality evaluation, which is inspired by other computer vision areas whose progress has been accelerated by evaluation platforms. PUIQE supports the comparison of methods through standard datasets and objective evaluation measures: quality scores for images uploaded on the platform are automatically computed and published in a leaderboard, which enables the ranking of methods. We hope that PUIQE will stimulate and facilitate the development of underwater image processing algorithms to improve underwater images.

Keywords: Underwater image processing · Evaluation platform
Benchmark datasets · Underwater image enhancement

1 Introduction

Underwater image analysis is attracting an increasing level of attention [1] and supports applications such as underwater exploration, habitat monitoring and species identification [2]. However, the appearance of underwater scenes is degraded by scattering, which blurs the resulting image, and by wavelength-dependent absorption, which reduces the energy of the light reaching the camera.

Image processing may be used to improve underwater image quality through restoration or enhancement methods. Restoration methods compensate for image distortions using prior information, such as the Dark Channel [3,4] or the Red Channel [5] prior. These methods may assume a uniform [3–6] or a more realistic non-uniform [7] background-light. Enhancement methods remove the colour cast [8–10] using for example global white balancing [8,9].

Figure 1 shows an underwater image processed by three different methods: an important issue is how to objectively assess the processed images as there are currently no benchmark datasets or standard image quality evaluation measures.

© Springer Nature Switzerland AG 2019
Z. Zhang et al. (Eds.): ICPR 2018 Workshops, LNCS 11188, pp. 37–44, 2019.
https://doi.org/10.1007/978-3-030-05792-3_4

(a)   (b)   (c)   (d)

Fig. 1. Image processing results on a sample underwater image. (a) Original image; (b) enhancement by global white balancing [9]; (c) enhancement by [10]; (d) restoration by [7]. Note the colour distortion in (b) and the overexposed areas (e.g. fishes) in (c). (Colour figure online)

In fact, while the evaluation of several computer vision tasks is supported by online benchmarking platforms, such as the Middlebury platform for optical flow [11] and the Multiple Object Tracking (MOT) Challenge for multi-target tracking [12], no platform exists yet for underwater image processing evaluation.

In this paper, we present an online Platform for Underwater Image Quality Evaluation (PUIQE) that supports the development of underwater image processing algorithms by distributing commonly used test images and by calculating underwater image quality scores. The main contribution is having established a common protocol to compare processing results: researchers run their algorithms on the datasets downloaded from the platform and then submit the results, whose evaluation scores are then published on a leaderboard. PUIQE ensures a fair comparison by restricting submissions to contain the complete dataset with the correct image resolution and format. Moreover, unlike the Middlebury and the MOT platforms that enforce the automatic evaluation on complete datasets, PUIQE also allows users to use the platform for private development by testing single images in restricted sessions (see Fig. 2). PUIQE is available at http://puiqe.eecs.qmul.ac.uk/.

2   Evaluation Measures

Most underwater image processing results are assessed subjectively by visual inspection [5,10] or by using no-reference image quality measures [6,8]. Artificial references can be created by taking stereo images with dual cameras to obtain the true scene-to-camera distance [9] or by using a colour chart as reference [9]. However, this additional information is not available outside controlled settings.

The current version of PUIQE includes two quality measures for underwater images, namely Underwater Color Image Quality Evaluation (*UCIQE*) [13] and Human-Visual-System-Inspired Underwater Image Quality Measures (*UIQM*) [14]. These measures quantify the colour degradation due to absorption of light in water and the blurring effect due to scattering. *UCIQE* and *UIQM* combine linearly measures of colour and sharpness, with coefficients obtained from subjective evaluation data. *UCIQE* evaluates the quality of an image only

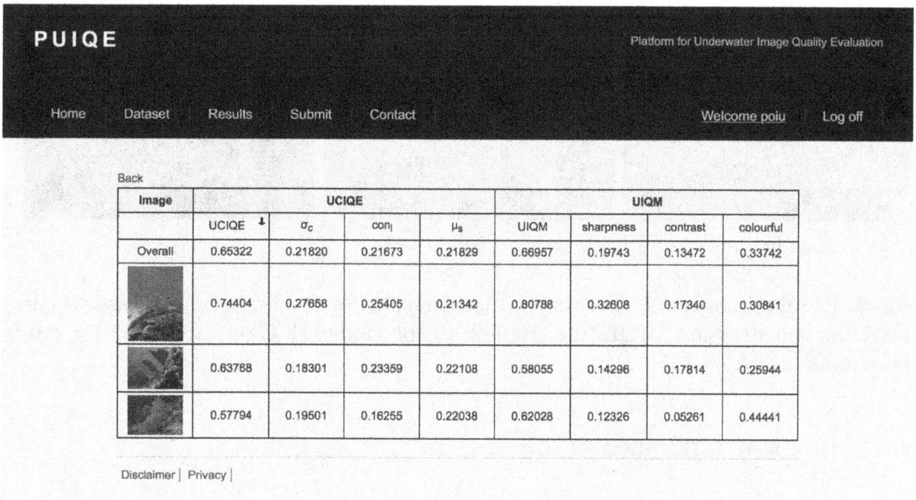

Fig. 2. Example of private session in PUIQE. Individual images are evaluated with *UCIQE* and *UIQM* (Sect. 2).

based on the colour distortion caused by light attenuation, whereas *UIQM* is modelled on the human vision system and also considers the loss of contrast.

Let $I_p = [L_p, a_p, b_p]$ be the value of pixel p in the CIELab space, and L_p, a_p and b_p be the intensity values in the L, a and b channels, respectively. *UCIQE* is a linear combination with weights obtained from a subjective evaluation of 12 subjects on 44 images [13]:

$$UCIQE = 0.4680 \times \sigma_c + 0.2745 \times con_l + 0.2576 \times \mu_s, \qquad (1)$$

where con_l is the contrast of luminance, i.e. the difference between the top 1% and the bottom 1% of the values in $\{L_p | p = 1...N\}$, where N is the number of pixels in the image; σ_c is the standard deviation of chroma:

$$\sigma_c = \frac{1}{N} \sum_{p=1}^{N} \left(C_p^2 - \mu_c^2 \right), \qquad (2)$$

with chroma, C_p, defined as [15]:

$$C_p = \sqrt{a_p^2 + b_p^2}; \qquad (3)$$

and μ_s is the average of saturation:

$$\mu_s = \frac{1}{N} \sum_{p=1}^{N} S_p, \qquad (4)$$

| (a) | (b) | (c) |

Fig. 3. Sample images for illustrating the behaviour of the evaluation measures currently implemented in PUIQE: (a) original; (b) blurred with Gaussian filter ($\sigma = 2.0$); (c) gamma corrected ($\gamma = 2.2$).

with saturation, S_p, defined as [15]:

$$S_p = \frac{C_p}{L_p}. \tag{5}$$

$UIQM$ combines linearly colourfulness, $UICM$, sharpness, $UISM$, and contrast, $UIConM$:

$$UIQM = 0.0282 \times UICM + 0.2953 \times UISM + 3.3753 \times UIConM, \tag{6}$$

with weights obtained from a subjective evaluation of 10 subjects on 14 images. $UICM$, which quantifies the degradation caused by light absorption, is defined by the statistics of the differences between red-green and yellow-blue planes. $UISM$ and $UIConM$ account for the degradation due to scattering: $UISM$ depends on the strength of Sobel edges computed on each colour channel independently; whereas $UIConM$ is obtained using the logAMEE operation [16], which is considered consistent with human visual perception in low light conditions.

In Fig. 3, we mimic the effect of scattering and absorption by artificially distorting an underwater image with Gaussian blur and gamma correction, respectively. The corresponding $UCIQE$ and $UIQM$ values are shown in Table 1. For the Gaussian-blurred image, $UISM$ calculated by $UIQM$ decreases, as expected; for the gamma-corrected image, both the values of colourfulness σ_c of $UCIQE$ and $UICM$ of $UIQM$ decrease, as expected.

Table 1. Effect of blurring and reduced colour intensity on the $UCIQE$ (Eq. 1) and $UIQM$ (Eq. 6) measures, and their components. Numerical values and trends. Key (comparison with respect to the original image): ↓: value decreased; ↑: value increased.

Image	$UCIQE$	σ_c	con_l	μ_s	$UIQM$	$UISM$	$UIConM$	$UICM$
Fig. 3(a)	.6392	.2049	.2218	.2129	.6855	.2073	.1069	.3712
Fig. 3(b)	.6327 ↓	.2048 ↓	.2153 ↓	.2126 ↓	.6579 ↓	.2069 ↓	.0399 ↓	.4111 ↑
Fig. 3(c)	.6326 ↓	.2072 ↑	.1830 ↓	.2424 ↑	.6617 ↓	.1831 ↓	.1452 ↑	.3334 ↓

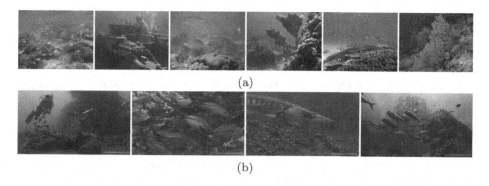

Fig. 4. Datasets currently available in PUIQE: (a) ReefnFish; (b) Bali.

3 Datasets

As no established image dataset for underwater image processing is currently available, researchers use different images for testing, and, even when images of the same scene are used, they might have different resolutions. For example, there is no overlap between the test images used by Berman et al. [9] and Galdran et al. [5], whereas Chiang and Chen [10] used images with lower resolution than the original video [17]. Therefore valid comparisons are in general not possible from published results.

To allow an easy access to frequently used images as first step towards the establishment of standard testing datasets, we gathered two sets of images used in various publications, namely *ReefnFish* and *Bali* (Fig. 4). The Reefn-Fish dataset consists of 6 images that include man-made and natural objects, such as shipwreck, fish and coral, and scenes under low light conditions. These images were used in [5,6,8]. The Bali dataset consists of 4 images used in [6,10] and extracted from a video with scenes with changing background light, scuba divers and varying scene depth. Note that while these images were employed in multiple publications [5,8,10], there is no guarantee that they had the same image resolution and format when used in the experiments. For instance, using the same image but saved with different JPEG compression distortions [18] does not allow a fair comparison of algorithms.

By sharing datasets online, researchers can easily access them along with a standard procedure for comparison. The consistency of testing will be ensured by constraining the entries to the leaderboard only to those algorithms tested on the full datasets, and on images of the same resolution and format as the originals.

4 Leaderboard

Evaluation tables facilitate the comparison of methods, and the identification of their strengths and limitations. PUIQE lists on a leaderboard the details of the methods being tested and their performance scores, as discussed in Sect. 2. To be included in the leaderboard, methods have to process all the images in the ReefnFish or Bali datasets. Submission results can be either associated with the authors and the related publication or remain anonymous at the authors' wish. The online system checks whether the image format is the same as the original datasets and rejects the submission otherwise.

The processed images of the datasets, and the *UCIQE* and *UIQM* measures along with their contributing terms (see Eqs. 1 and 6), are presented in the form of a table summarising the results. Users can select to view a compact table where the details of the methods are hidden, and sort the methods by measure or by their contributing components.

Dataset: ReefnFish (click to see results for individual images)

Team	UCIQE				UIQM			
	UCIQE ↓	σ_c	con_l	μ_s	UIQM	sharpness	contrast	colourful
UWHL	0.673	0.217	0.238	0.218	0.691	0.241	0.152	0.298
Dana Berman, Tali Treibitz, Shai Avidan (result generated by code available in Author's GitHub) Diving into Haze-Lines: Color Restoration of Underwater Images								
DCP	0.669	0.222	0.230	0.217	0.658	0.200	0.151	0.308
He Kaiming (result generated with implementation by MATLAB) Single Image Haze Removal Using Dark Channel Prior								
bglight_icip	0.613	0.200	0.201	0.212	0.625	0.156	0.098	0.371
Chau Yi Li, Andrea Cavallaro Background Light Estimation for Depth-dependent Underwater Image Restoration								
Anonymous	0.606	0.195	0.196	0.215	0.627	0.140	0.098	0.389
Anonymous entry								

[Top]

(a)

Image: fish.png

		UCIQE				UIQM			
	Team	UCIQE ↓	σ_c	con_l	μ_s	UIQM	sharpness	contrast	colourful
	UWHL	0.681	0.247	0.235	0.199	0.810	0.338	0.104	0.368
	DCP	0.662	0.241	0.216	0.205	0.615	0.162	0.132	0.321
	bglight_icip	0.639	0.240	0.194	0.205	0.669	0.190	0.063	0.416
	Anonymous	0.629	0.230	0.192	0.208	0.684	0.152	0.064	0.468

[Top]

(b)

Fig. 5. (a) Snapshot of the leaderboard for the dataset ReefnFish. Three methods are associated to their authors and publications [7,9,19]. (b) Snapshot of the leaderboard for an image in the ReefnFish dataset.

Evaluation results can be displayed either as the average of all processed images in a dataset or as individual scores for each image. Moreover, original and processed images are shown to enable visual comparison.

As example, we uploaded the results of two published methods [9,19] generated from their implementations and one of our previous works [7]. An anonymous submission is also included. Figure 5(a) reports a snapshot of this leaderboard and Fig. 5(b) the evaluation of an individual image, both from the Reefn-Fish dataset.

5   Conclusion

We presented PUIQE, the first online platform for underwater image quality evaluation. PUIQE supports the development of underwater image processing algorithms by facilitating their comparisons, with results presented in the form of a leaderboard. PUIQE allows an easy access to images frequently used in publications and provides a simple-to-use evaluation with existing performance measures. We expect that the proposed platform will boost the development of new algorithms and the convergence towards standardised procedures for underwater image quality evaluation.

References

1. Horgan, J., Daniel T.: Computer Vision Applications in the Navigation of Unmanned Underwater Vehicles. Underwater Vehicles (2012)
2. Strachan, N.: Recognition of fish species by colour and shape. Image Vis. Comput. **11**, 2–10 (1993)
3. Emberton, S., Chittka, L., Cavallaro, A.: Hierarchical rank-based veiling light estimation for underwater dehazing. In: British Machine Vision Conference (2015)
4. Emberton, S., Chittka, L., Cavallaro, A.: Underwater image and video dehazing with pure haze region segmentation. Comput. Vis. Image Underst. **168**, 145–156 (2018)
5. Galdran, A., Pardo, D., Picn, A., Alvarez-Gila, A.: Automatic red-channel underwater image restoration. J. Vis. Commun. Image Represent. **26**, 132–145 (2015)
6. Peng, Y., Cosman, P.: Underwater image restoration based on image blurriness and light absorption. IEEE Trans. Image Process. **26**, 1579–1594 (2017)
7. Li, C. Y., Cavallaro, A.: Background light estimation for depth-dependent underwater image restoration. In: IEEE International Conference on Image Processing (2018)
8. Ancuti, C., Ancuti, C., De Vleeschouwer, C., Bekaert, P.: Color balance and fusion for underwater image enhancement. IEEE Trans. Image Process. **27**, 379–393 (2018)
9. Berman, D., Treibitz, T., Avidan, S.: Diving into haze-lines: color restoration of underwater images. In: British Machine Vision Conference (2017)
10. Chiang, J., Chen, Y.: Underwater image enhancement by wavelength compensation and dehazing. IEEE Trans. Image Process. **21**, 1756–1769 (2012)
11. The Middlebury Computer Vision Pages. http://vision.middlebury.edu/flow/. Accessed June 2018

12. Multiple Object Tracking Benchmark. https://motchallenge.net/. Accessed June 2018
13. Yang, M., Sowmya, A.: An underwater color image quality evaluation metric. IEEE Trans. Image Process. **24**, 6062–6071 (2015)
14. Panetta, K., Gao, C., Agaian, S.: Human-visual-system-inspired underwater image quality measures. IEEE J. Oceanic Eng. **41**, 541–551 (2016)
15. Hasler, D., Suesstrunk, S.: Measuring colorfulness in natural images. In: SPIE, pp. 87–95 (2003)
16. Panetta, K., Agaian, S., Zhou, Y., Wharton, E.: Parameterized logarithmic framework for image enhancement. IEEE Trans. Syst. Man Cybern. Part B (Cybern.) **41**, 460–473 (2011)
17. BubbleVision Youtube Channel. https://www.youtube.com/user/bubblevision. Accessed June 2018
18. Bins, J., Draper, B., Bohm, W., Najjar, W.: Precision vs. error in JPEG compression. In: SPIE, vol. 3817 (1999)
19. He, K., Sun, J., Tang, X.: Single image haze removal using dark channel prior. IEEE Trans. Pattern Anal. Mach. Intell. **33**, 2341–2353 (2011)

Tracking Sponge Size and Behaviour with Fixed Underwater Observatories

Torben Möller[1]([✉]), Ingunn Nilssen[2], and Tim Wilhelm Nattkemper[1]

[1] Biodata Mining Group, Bielefeld University, 33615 Bielefeld, Germany
tmoeller@cebitec.uni-bielefeld.de, tim.nattkemper@uni-bielefeld.de
[2] Equinor, Research and Technology, 7005 Trondheim, Norway
innil@equinor.com

Abstract. More and more fixed underwater observatories (FUO) are being used for high temporal coverage and resolution monitoring of specific areas of interest, such as coral reefs. FUOs equipped with fixed HD cameras and other sensors make it possible to relate visual characteristics of a species to characteristics of its environment.

The aim of this study is to demonstrate how changes in size of sponges can be tracked automatically over time and to investigate to what extent various environmental parameters might influence the behaviour. Both gradual long-term changes and major short-term changes of the sponge size should be taken into consideration. This is the first study that estimates sponge sizes over a long time period.

We present and evaluate an automated process based on a convolutional network (the U-Net) to automatically generate a series of sponge sizes from an image series showing one sponge over a time-interval of 9 month. Further, we analyze the resulting time series together with additional data of the sponge habitat. Our experiments show that our work-flow produces a reliable segmentation of the sponge that can be used for further analysis of the sponge behaviour. Moreover, our results indicate that an increased salinity of the surrounding water is associated to a more frequent *pumping activity* of the sponge.

Keywords: Marine environmental monitoring · Sponge Segmentation · CNN

1 Introduction

Sponges are sessile, filter feeding [18] organisms. They are therefore described as key organisms that draw water to themselves by *pumps*, filter organic matter form the water and bring it to the benthic community [11]. Due to this behaviour and the high volumes of water that can be pumped through the sponges, they are expected to play an important role in the marine carbon circle [7].

The increased numbers of Fixed Underwater observatories (FUO) deployed in recent years [2,4,5,8,19], enable observations of sponge and other organisms with high temporal resolution and coverage. Images allow the quantitative and

Z. Zhang et al. (Eds.): ICPR 2018 Workshops, LNCS 11188, pp. 45–54, 2019.
https://doi.org/10.1007/978-3-030-05792-3_5

qualitative estimation of species, e.g. monitoring of coral polyp activity [12] and coral color [14], and estimation of shrimp, eelpout, crab or snail count [1,13]. One of the most interesting species to monitor is the sponge which is monitored in this study. To generate a time-series of sponge sizes it is necessary to segment the sponge in the images of the FUO. In order not to miss any of the usually short-term pumping activities, the sponge must be segmented in each of the images in the analyzed period. Due do the high amount of images created by FUOs, a manual segmentation would be extremely time consuming. An automated approach to create a reliable time-series of sponge sizes is needed.

There are only few publications describing (semi-) automated segmentation of sponge. In [17] the tool *Seascape* is introduced and used for semi-automatic segmentation of sponge (and other marine organisms). Seascape allows to segment an image with an dynamically adaptable segmentation level. However, after the segmentation, all segments belonging to the sponge have to be labeled manually. In [3] the performance of a method referred to as the *automatic color segmentation method* is evaluated in the context of image analysis at benthic sites, including sponge segmentation. Given an *initial* pixel of the sponge, the method defines nearby pixels with a similar color to be sponge. This method still requires user interaction by selecting the initial pixel. Moreover the authors of [3] conclude that small variations of color in the image lead to poor performance of the method. To the best of our knowledge, no automatic segmentation of sponge has been published yet.

In this study, we propose a work-flow for the extraction of a time-series of sponge sizes from an image series of sponges. The segmentation is highly based on the U-Net, as it produces good segmentation results with a reasonable amount of training data as shown in Sect. 4. Moreover, the generated time-series is analyzed in order to investigate sponge behaviour and possible impact on this by various parameters in the ambient environment.

2   Material

In this paper, we analyze one sponge that is monitored by the fixed underwater observatory *LoVe* (Lofoten Vesterålen Ocean Observatory [5]). Love is located in a coral reef area 22 km off the cost of Northern Norway at (N 68° 54.474′, E 15° 23.145′) in a water depth of approximately 260 m.

LoVe is equipped with an HD camera taking images with a size of 5184 × 3456 pixels. The analyzed image sequence covers a period of approximately 9 month from 1st of October 2013 14:30 to 18th of June 2014 07:17. The images were taken in 60 min intervals, except for a small number of images missing due to technical dysfunctions. This results in a total number of 5701 analyzed images. After affine registration of the LoVe images, we manually selected an area for this study, 384 pixels wide and 450 pixels high, showing the monitored sponge. See Fig. 1 for an example image from the LoVe-Observatory.

Fig. 1. A sample image of the LoVe-Observatory with a sample frame of the monitored sponge at the top right.

In addition to the HD images, the following data from LoVe is used in this study: Chlorophyll, Conductivity, Depth, Salinity and Temperature. All images and data collected at the LoVe-observatory are publicly available online[1].

3 Methods

The workflow, measuring behaviour of the sponge from the image series, consists of several successive steps: First, the sponge is automatically segmented in each image. Second, the segmentation is improved by taking advantage of the fact that the sponge is one-piece. The number of pixels segmented as sponge is then considered as the *size* of the sponge. Next, outlier detection is applied to the series of sponge sizes to sort out the few images where the segmentation is poor due to objects interfering with the sponge or the camera being out of position due to strong currents. The resulting time series can then be used to detect *sponge pumping* and to relate the sponge data to other sensor data.

3.1 Segmentation

The U-Net [15] is a convolutional deep learning architecture designed for image segmentation. The U-Net computes features at different levels of resolution to be used for the segmentation. To do so, the basic U-Net architecture consist of a

---

[1] http://love.statoil.com.

downsampling path followed by an upsampling path (see **Fig. 2**). The downsampling path consists of N convolutional layers C_i, each followed by a (downsampling) pooling layer. The final layer of the downsampling path is then upscaled in the upsampling path. The upsampling path consists of N convolutional layers each followed by an upsampling layer U_i. The layer C_{N-i} has the same shape as the layer U_i and is concatenated to U_i during the upsampling to obtain features from the different scales of resolution. An output layer is generated from the last convolutional layer of the upsampling path by first applying two convolutional layers, followed by a dropout and another convolution layer. In this work, the number of pooling layers and their strides have been chosen to match the prime factors of the width and height of the input patches (450 and 384, respectively). Figure 2 shows the strides and all other (not trainable) network parameters used in this work.

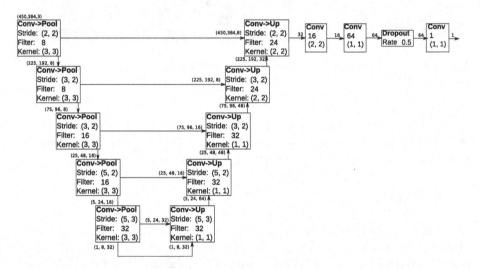

Fig. 2. The structure of the U-Net. A block named *Conv-> Pool* consist of a convolutional layer followed by a maximum pooling layer. The values given inside the *Conv-> Pool*-blocks represent the number of filters and the kernel size of the convolutional layer as well as the stride of the pooling layer in x- and y directions. A block named *Conv->Up* consists of a convolutional layer followed by an upscaling layer and a concatenation layer. The values given inside the *Conv->up*-blocks represent the number of filters and the kernel size of the convolutional layer as well as the upscaling factor of the pooling layer in x- and y directions.

To train the network, 159 sponge patches have been labeled manually using the online annotation tool Biigle [10]. Biigle is available online[2] and allows, among other things, manual segmentation of an object at pixel level. The training samples have been selected so that each third of the time series contains the

---

[2] https://biigle.de.

same number of training samples. This was done to take account of changes in the optical properties of the water over time and the growing biofouling on the camera housing. For each sample its rotation through 180 degrees and its mirror image (for a reflection with respect to the vertical axis) was computed. For each original sample, each rotated sample and each mirror image, two copies with additional Gaussian noise where made to increase the size of the trainings set by a factor of nine. The net was then trained with the resulting 1431 training samples using a train-test split with 10% test samples. The Adam optimizer [9] was used to minimize the binary cross entropy for 100 epochs.

3.2   Post-processing

The trained U-net predicts for each input sample p_i taken by the observatory at a timepoint t_i a binary 1-channel mask of the same shape as the input samples. A binary pixel value is $f(x,y) = 1$ if it belongs to the sponge and $f(x,y) = 0$ otherwise. A morphological opening with a 5×5 square as the structuring element is applied to the predicted masks for 8 iterations.

The final step ensures that each resulting mask m_i contains only one connected component, i. e. a connected subset of pixels with value 1. To do so, all connected components are detected in each mask and only sponge pixels in the largest connected region are considered to belong to the sponge. The size (i. e. the number of pixels) of the largest region is then considered the sponge size s_i of the sponge at timepoint t_i. With $D = \{(t_1, s_1), \ldots, (t_M, s_M)\}$ we denote the set of all pairs of timepoints and corresponding sponge sizes.

3.3   Outlier-Detection

The segmentation can still give poor results when the camera is out of position or an object blocks the view. A Grubbs' test for outliers [6] is performed on the set S of all predicted sponge sizes in D to remove the images that are segmented poorly. The Grubbs' test for outliers at significance level α performs a t-test at significance level α on the test statistic

$$G = \frac{\max_{s \in S} |s - \bar{S}|}{\sigma}, \tag{1}$$

where $\bar{S}$ and σ are the mean and standard deviation of S respectively. If the t-test is positive, $\arg\max_{s \in S}$ is removed from S and the whole procedure is repeated iteratively until the t-test is negative. In this study, we applied a t-test at significance level $\alpha = 0.05$ to S. As the outliers are not considered anymore in what follows, the set of sizes that are not removed from S during Grubbs' test are denoted (by abuse of notation) as $S = \{s_1, \ldots, s_N\}$. With $D = \{(t_i, s_i) | s_i \in S\}$ we denote the set of all pairs of timepoints with corresponding sponge sizes that are not considered an outlier. Without loss of generality let $t_{i+1} > t_i$.

3.4   Time-Series Analysis

The analysis is divided into an analysis of long-term and short-term changes of the sponge size. For several sensors (Chlorophyll, Conductivity, Depth, Salinity and Temperature), data are available in the form $(\tau_0, y_0), \dots (\tau_{N'}, y_{N'})$ where y_j denotes the value of a sensor at timepoint τ_j. All the values are from the same time period as the sponge sizes and have the same temporal resolution of one value per hour. However, a few measurement from both the camera and the other sensors failed due to technical dysfunction. To account for this, we denote for $i \in \{1 \dots N'\}$ the index of the measurement with the smallest time gap to t_i by $\hat{i} = \arg\min_{j\in\{1,\dots,N'\}} (|\tau_j - t_i|)$. This makes it straightforward to use the Spearman's-ρ [16], defined by

$$\rho = \frac{\sum_{i=1}^{N} (s_i - \bar{s})(y_{\hat{i}} - \bar{y})}{\sqrt{\sum_{i=1}^{N} (s_i - \bar{s})^2 \sum_{i=1}^{N} (y_{\hat{i}} - \bar{y})^2}}, \tag{2}$$

to analyze the correlation between the sponge data and other sensor data. In order to account for short term variations of the sponge size and inaccuracies in the sensor measurements, the sponge sizes as well as the sensor data is filtered with a Gaussian kernel, before applying Spearman's-ρ.

Sponge Pumping. The analysis of short-term changes in sponge size is aimed at (i) finding spikes where the sponge changes its size significantly for a short period of time and at (ii) relating the occurrence of these events to other sensor data. To ensure that there is always approximately 1 h time gap between two measurements, all sponge sizes were removed from the series that have a time interval of less than 50 min from the preceding measurement. For each pair of subsequent measurements more than 70 min apart, the time series is split into two sub-series. Series containing less than 9 measurements are ignored in what follows. In the end, the series is split into 40 sub-series containing a total of 5493 measurements.

To find spikes, each sub-series is analyzed independently from all other time-series. Let $\left((t_1^j, s_1^j), \dots, (t_{N^j}^j, s_{N^j}^j)\right)$ denote the pairs of timepoints and corresponding sponge sizes for one of the sub-series j. For $1 \leq j \leq 40$ and $0 \leq i \leq N^j$ let

$$\bar{s}_i^j = \frac{1}{\min(i+5, N^j) - \max(i-5, 0)} \cdot \sum_{\substack{k=\max(i-5,0) \\ k \neq i}}^{\min(i+5, N^j)} s_k^j \tag{3}$$

denote the mean of the 5 sponge sizes measured before and 5 sizes measured after s_i^j. Moreover, denote by $p_i^j = s_i^j / \bar{s}_i^j$ the sponge size at timepoint t_i relative to its size at the timepoints before and after t_i. In what follows, we say the sponge *pumps* at timepoint t_i^j if and only if $p_i^j < 0.9$. This is motivated by the fact that the number of relative sponge sizes larger than a given fraction p, denoted by $n(p) = \bigcup_p \left| \left\{ 1 \leq i \leq N_j \text{ with } p \leq p_i^j \leq 1 \right\} \right|$, decreases rapidly around 0.9.

In order to relate the frequency of sponge pumping to other sensor data, the sensor data is split into two subsets as follows: Let P denote the set of all timepoints (in minutes) where the sponge is pumping. We denote by

$$Y^p = \{ y_i \,|\, \exists k \in P \text{ such that } 0 < t_k - \tau_i < 60 \} \tag{4}$$

the set of all sensor data that are measured 1 h or less before the sponge pumps. By $\overline{Y^p}$ we denote all other sensor data. The Welch's t-test [20], which is a non-parametric alternative to the t-test, can then be applied to test if there is a significant difference between the measurements Y^p that are associated with sponge pumping and the measurements $\overline{Y^p}$ which are not associated with sponge pumping.

4 Results

The performance of the segmentation has to be evaluated to make sure that the time-series of sponge sizes is suitable for further analysis. We manually segmented twelve sponge images to compare them to the predicted contours. None of the images has been used during the training of the network. Also, we made sure that (i) four images are included from each third of the time period and (ii) the images show the sponge while it is pumping as well as while it is not pumping. A visual impression of the segmentation is shown in Fig. 3 where the predicted contours are shown in the image along with the manually drawn ground-truth contours.

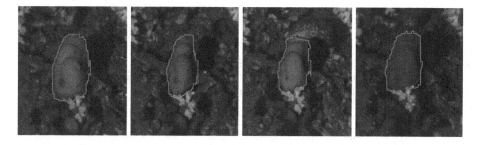

Fig. 3. Predicted and ground-truth contours. Blue: ground-truth, Red: automatically predicted contours. (Color figure online)

In order to compute performance measures for the segmentation let

TP The number of pixels in all test images that are correctly detected as sponge
FP The number of pixels in all test images that are incorrectly detected as sponge

FN The number of sponge-pixels that are not detected as sponge

Computation of precision, recall and F1-score results in

$$P = \frac{TP}{TP + FP} = 0.89, \qquad R = \frac{TP}{TP + FN} = 0.97, \qquad F1 = \frac{2 \cdot P \cdot R}{P + R} = 0.93 \quad (5)$$

respectively.

The few misclassified pixels might only become a problem if the error of the segmentation is large compared to the actual change of the sponge size. To check if that is the case, a linear regression of the predicted size on the true sizes was computed. The linear regression results in a Pearson's r of $r = 0.98$ and a coefficient of determination of $r^2 = 0.96$. This shows that the computed time-series of sponge sizes is reliable and suitable for further analysis. The computed time series of sponge sizes is shown in Fig. 4.

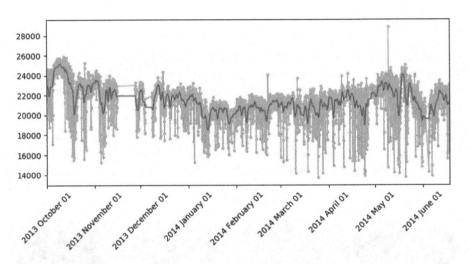

Fig. 4. The sponge size expressed as pixels. Light blue: the automatically computed sponge sizes. Dark blue: the automatically computed sponge sizes after applying a Gaussian filter with $\sigma = 10$. (Color figure online)

For analysis of long term changes, the time series of sponge sizes was compared to time series of other sensor data as described in Sect. 3.4. See Table 1 for the resulting values of Spearman's-ρ. Except for a weak correlation of chlorophyll to sponge size, the table does not show correlations of the sponge size to any of the sensor data. This is further discussed in Sect. 5.

To relate the sponge pumping to other sensor data, t-tests were conducted as described in Sect. 3.4 (Sponge Pumping). The resulting p-values are listed in Table 2. The results indicate that the salinity and the conductivity has been higher at the timepoints before the sponge retracts (compared to full size). These findings are further discussed in the next section.

Table 1. Rank correlation between the sponge size and other sensor data. Left: Type of data compared to sponge size. Right: The corresponding Spearman's-ρ

Sensor	Spearman's-ρ
Chlorophyll	−0.45
Conductivity	0.20
Depth	−0.25
Salinity	0.16
Temperature	0.29

Table 2. Results of the Welch's-test as described in Sect. 3.4. Left: type of data compared to sponge pumping. Right: p-value of the corresponding Welch's test.

Sensor	p-value
Chlorophyll	0.2501
Conductivity	0.0597
Depth	0.8346
Salinity	0.0388
Temperature	0.4867

5   Discussion and Conclusion

We have demonstrated that the size of a sponge can be tracked successfully with the proposed workflow. Moreover, we have used the generated time series of sponge sizes to investigate to what extent various environmental parameters might influence the behaviour. There was no long-term correlation found between the sponge sizes to any of the other sensors (Chlorophyll, Conductivity, Depth, Salinity, Temperature). However, from Fig. 4, one might assume that the overall size of the sponge is smaller from January to April. This might indicate a seasonal (potentially delayed) change of the sponge size. This should be analyzed in future work, when more data is available.

Regarding the sponge pumping, based on the Welch's test, change both in salinity and conductivity seem to correlate with increased pumping activity (p-values 0.0388 and 0.0597 respectively). The result of the Welch's test regarding conductivity is expected after considering the result of the Welch's test regarding salinity, as conductivity is used to compute salinity. Change in salinity might be an indication of change in water masses. Potentially, change in salinity can also indicate access to more nutrient rich water and potentially explain the increased sponge pumping. The current study has been performed to demonstrate the potential of the methodology in detection of natural variations in sponge behaviour given specific ambient conditions. Further work will also include other data, such as current speed and direction. Moreover, a supporting study over a short time period with a high temporal resolution might be done to estimate how many short sponge pumps occur in the period of one hour between two images.

Acknowledgments. We thank Equinor for the financial support and for providing image and sensor data as well as NVIDIA Corporation for donating the GPU used in this project. We thank Jens Plettemeier for conducting experiments.

References

1. Aguzzi, J., Costa, C., et al.: Behavioral rhythms of hydrocarbon seep fauna in relation to internal tides. Mar. Ecol. Prog. Ser. **418**, 47–56 (2010)
2. Aguzzi, J., et al.: The new seafloor observatory (OBSEA) for remote and long-term coastal ecosystem monitoring. Sensors **11**(6), 5850–5872 (2011)
3. Bernhardt, S.P., Griffing, L.R.: An evaluation of image analysis at benthic sites based on color segmentation. Bull. Mar. Sci. **69**(2), 639–653 (2001)
4. Ocean Networks Canada: NEPTUNE in the NE Pacific (2014). http://oceannetworks.ca/installations/observatories/neptune-ne-pacific/
5. Godø, O.R., Johnson, S., Torkelsen, T.: The LoVe ocean observatory is in operation. Mar. Technol. Soc. J. **48**(2), 24–30 (2014)
6. Grubbs, F.E.: Sample criteria for testing outlying observations. Ann. Math. Statist. **21**(1), 27–58 (1950)
7. Hoer, D.R.: The role of marine sponges in carbon and nitrogen cycles of coral reef and nearshore environments. Ph.D. thesis, The University of North Carolina at Chapel Hill (2015)
8. Kawabata, K., et al.: Underwater image gathering by utilizing stationary and movable sensor nodes: towards observation of symbiosis system in the coral reef of Okinawa. Int. J. Distrib. Sens. Netw. **10**(7) (2014)
9. Kingma, D.P., Ba, J.: Adam: a method for stochastic optimization. arXiv preprint arXiv:1412.6980 (2014)
10. Langenkämper, D., Zurowietz, M., Schoening, T., Nattkemper, T.W.: BIIGLE 2.0 - browsing and annotating large marine image collections. Front. Mar. Sci. **4**, 83 (2017)
11. Leys, S.P., Yahel, G., Reidenbach, M.A., Tunnicliffe, V., Shavit, U., Reiswig, H.M.: The sponge pump: the role of current induced flow in the design of the sponge body plan. PLOS ONE **6**(12), 1–17 (2011)
12. Osterloff, J., Nilssen, I., Järnegren, J., Buhl-Mortensen, P., Nattkemper, T.W.: Polyp activity estimation and monitoring for cold water corals with a deep learning approach. In: 2016 ICPR 2nd Workshop on Computer Vision for Analysis of Underwater Imagery (CVAUI), pp. 1–6. IEEE (2016)
13. Osterloff, J., Nilssen, I., Nattkemper, T.W.: A computer vision approach for monitoring the spatial and temporal shrimp distribution at the love observatory. Methods Oceanogr. **15**, 114–128 (2016)
14. Osterloff, J., Nilssen, I., Nattkemper, T.W.: Computational coral feature monitoring for the fixed underwater observatory LoVe. In: Proceedings of IEEE OCEANS 2016 (2016)
15. Ronneberger, O., Fischer, P., Brox, T.: U-Net: convolutional networks for biomedical image segmentation. CoRR abs/1505.04597 (2015)
16. Spearman, C.: The proof and measurement of association between two things. Am. J. Psychol. **15**(1), 72–101 (1904)
17. Teixidó, N., Albajes-Eizagirre, A., et al.: Hierarchical segmentation-based software for cover classification analyses of seabed images (Seascape). Mar. Ecol. Prog. Ser. **431**, 45–53 (2011)
18. Riisgaard, H.U., Larsen, P.S.: Filter feeding in marine macro invertebrates: pump characteristics, modelling and energy cost. Biol. Rev. **70**(1), 67–106 (1995)
19. Vardaro, et al.: A Southeast Atlantic deep-ocean observatory: first experiences and results. Limnol. Oceanogr.: Methods **11**, 304–315 (2013)
20. Welch, B.L.: The generalization of 'student's' problem when several different population variances are involved. Biometrika **34**(1/2), 28–35 (1947)

Enhancement of Low-Lighting Underwater Images Using Dark Channel Prior and Fast Guided Filters

Tunai Porto Marques[1(✉)], Alexandra Branzan Albu[1(✉)],
and Maia Hoeberechts[2(✉)]

[1] University of Victoria, Victoria, BC V8P5C2, Canada
{tunaip,aalbu}@uvic.ca
[2] Ocean Networks Canada, Victoria, BC V8P5C2, Canada
maiah@uvic.ca

Abstract. Low levels of lighting in images and videos may lead to poor results in segmentation, detection, tracking, among numerous other computer vision tasks. Deep-sea camera systems, such as those deployed on the Ocean Networks Canada (ONC) cabled ocean observatories, use artificial lighting to illuminate and capture videos of deep-water biological environments. When these lighting systems fail, the resulting images become hard to interpret or even completely useless because of their lighting levels. This paper proposes an effective framework to enhance the lighting levels of underwater images, increasing the number of visible, meaningful features. The process involves the dehazing of images using a dark channel prior and fast guided filters.

Keywords: Image dehazing · Low-lighting underwater imagery
Dark channel prior · Transmission map refinement · Fast guided filter

1 Introduction

Low-lighting images present a hard challenge for a number of computer vision algorithms. Since the contrast in such images is lower than ideal, it becomes harder to detect edges, corners, and saliences in general on them. Without this capacity, higher level tasks such as shape detection, matching, motion estimation, might be difficult to perform. While simple methods can be used to enhance the overall lighting level of an image (e.g. changing the "value" channel on HSV images), these simplified approaches will affect all regions of an image homogeneously. Regions that were originally bright might experience an over-compensation in lighting. Other methods, as the one proposed in [1], look for specific regions of the image where "darkness" is present, and then attempt to enhance these particular regions.

Ocean Networks Canada (ONC), an initiative of the University of Victoria, Canada, operates cabled ocean observatories which host a multitude of ocean sensors to gather physical, geological and biological data over long time intervals. Among these sensors are video cameras that have been recording the seabed and similar environments for years. Since these cameras are usually deployed in deep depths, no sunlight is present at these locations. Thus, artificial lighting is used to illuminate the monitored sites.

© Springer Nature Switzerland AG 2019
Z. Zhang et al. (Eds.): ICPR 2018 Workshops, LNCS 11188, pp. 55–65, 2019.
https://doi.org/10.1007/978-3-030-05792-3_6

Since it is impossible to uniformly illuminate the whole scene and sometimes the light systems fail, videos with significant dark regions are created. These regions might compromise the visual analysis (either automated or manual) of the data.

This paper proposes a new approach for enhancing the visibility of low-lighting underwater imagery, which integrates a dehazing algorithm and image filtering. The remainder of the paper is structured as follows. Section 2 presents related work, while Sect. 3 describes the proposed approach. Experimental results are discussed in Sect. 4, while Sect. 5 draws conclusions.

2   Related Work

A central part of the proposed approach involves the dehazing of images. Several different approaches have been used to achieve this goal, but most of them need multiple inputs. Polarization-based methods, which consider scattering properties of two or more images to retrieve depth information and remove haze were proposed in [2]. Approaches that used multiple images of the same scenario under different weather conditions were presented in [3]. However, the basic disadvantage of these methods is that more often than not, only one image of the hazy scene is available. Therefore, methods that use only one hazy image as input and retrieve its haze-less version are needed. In 2010, He et al. [4] proposed a single-image dehazing method. It is based on an assumption called *dark channel prior* (DCP) that states the following: "non-sky regions in an image have, inside a patch of given size, at least one pixel with very low intensity in one of the color channels". He's dehazing method received a lot of attention and was used and modified by numerous researchers.

Other relevant single-image techniques that addressed the dehazing task are: Tarel and Hautiere [5], Meng et al. [6] and Fattal [7]. However, comparative results in multiple articles [8–10] show that the DCP-based dehazing technique of [4] is still one of the best options to choose from in terms of performance and accuracy.

In order to enhance the lighting level of video frames, [1] uses the DCP-based dehazing algorithm of [4] with the addition of a very simple observation: the dark parts of low-lighting images look like haze in their inverted versions.

3   Proposed Approach

The proposed low-lighting enhancement framework shown in Fig. 1 consists of a computational pipeline using inversion, a DCP-based dehazing algorithm [4] and a guided image filter [11].

Fig. 1. Low-lighting image enhancement framework.

The framework is based on the observation from [1] that "*darkness looks like haze in inverted images*". Hence, in order to attenuate such dark regions, the image must be inverted, dehazed (using the DCP-based method of [4]), and then once again inverted. The original "*tmap refinement*" step (discussed further in detail) from [4] is performed differently in our proposed approach: three distinct filters (Gaussian, bilateral and guided) are evaluated and discussed to that end.

3.1 Image Dehazing Using the Dark Channel Prior

A hazy image can be mathematically modeled as follows [4]:

$$I(x) = J(x)t(x) + A(1 - t(x)) \tag{1}$$

where I is the observed intensity (hazy image), J is the scene radiance (haze-less image), A is the atmospheric light, and t represents the light that reaches the camera without scattering (medium transmission). The goal of the dehazing method is to find J, the haze-less version of the image, by calculating A and t given the input image I. The first step in the dehazing process is to calculate the *dark channel*. The dark channel is a one-layered image that is populated by the pixel with the lowest intensity among a square patch Ω of given size, considering all three (RGB) channels of the hazy image, as described in Eq. (2):

$$J^{dark}(x) = \min_{y \in \Omega(x)} \left(\min_{c \in \Omega\{r,g,b\}} J^c(y) \right) \tag{2}$$

The *dark channel prior* (DCP) is based on the observation that for non-sky regions, at least one pixel intensity in one of the three color channels is going to be significantly low. This particular region of the dark channel will tend to zero $(J^{dark} \rightarrow 0)$. The atmospheric light A is calculated in [4] by initially choosing the 0.1% brightest pixels of the dark channel (equivalent to the most haze-opaque regions of the hazy image). Then, the pixels in these same locations in the *hazy* image are retrieved. The next step involves calculating the mean of this group of pixels, or simply selecting the intensities in R,G and B of the brightest one as the atmospheric light (the latter is done in this paper).

He et al. [4] uses the dark channel prior to derive a simplified equation for the transmission map using the initial hazy image equation (Eq. (1)). The matrix $t(x)$ represents the light that is captured by the camera.

$$t(x) = 1 - w \min_{y \in \Omega(x)} \left(\min_c \frac{I^c(y)}{A^c} \right) \tag{3}$$

where A^c is the atmospheric light in each color channel for images with pixel intensities valued between [0, 1]. A phenomenon called *aerial perspective* states that the haze formed by particles in the air is important for allowing distance perception. Therefore, the constant $w(0 < w < 1)$ is introduced to preserve some haze and create more realistic dehazed images. The scene radiance can be recovered using the calculated atmospheric light and transmission map using the following:

$$J(x) = \frac{I(x) - A}{\max(t(x), t0)} + A \qquad (4)$$

The recovered scene radiance (haze-less image) is prone to noise in very haze-dense regions, where the denominator in Eq. (4) is close to zero. A constant $t0$ is then introduced to limit the lower value of this denominator. The $t0$ parameter preserves some haze, similarly to what is done by parameter w of Eq. (3).

Transmission Map Refinement. Recovering the scene radiance using the unfiltered transmission maps obtained with Eq. (3) could lead to undesired dehazing artifacts, such as halos or "pixel blocks" [4]. This phenomenon happens because the transmission profile of the image is not always constant inside the patch Ω chosen (in particular for bigger patches). In order to mitigate this effect, the transmission map is refined (filtered) before its use in the radiance recovery phase. This refinement plays an important role on the quality of the dehazed image, given that the scene radiance is recovered directly from the transmission map and the atmospheric light. Different filters are commonly used to perform the refinement, most noticeably: Gaussian filters, bilateral filters [12] and fast guided filters [11, 13]. These three refinement options are tested (similarly to the procedure in [14]) and the results are reported in the next section.

Gaussian Filter. The Gaussian filter uses a 2-D gaussian function (G_{σ_s}) with standard deviation σ_s to filter the image. The resulting transmission map $\hat{t}(y)$ can be obtained with the following [10]:

$$\hat{t}(y) = \frac{1}{\sum_{y \in \Omega(x)} G_{\sigma_s}(||x - y||)} \sum_{y \in \Omega(x)} G_{\sigma_s}(||x - y||)t(y) \qquad (5)$$

Bilateral Filter. The bilateral filter is a popular edge-preserving, noise-reducing filtering option [12]. In this filtering process, each pixel of the image is replaced by a weighted average of its neighboring pixels. The weights of each neighbor pixel are based not only on their distances to the central pixel, but also on radiometric differences (e.g. color intensity, depth distance). The filtered transmission map can be obtained as [12, 14]:

$$\hat{t}(y) = \frac{1}{G_{\sigma_s}(||x - y||)G_{\sigma_r}(||I(x) - I(y)||)} \sum_{y \in \Omega(x)} G_{\sigma_s}(||x - y||)G_{\sigma_r}(||I(x) - I(y)||)t(y) \qquad (6)$$

where G_{σ_r} is the function with range kernel σ_r responsible smoothing with respect to radiometric differences, and the function G_{σ_s} with spatial range σ_s smooths the image around the neighboring pixels based on their coordinate distances.

Fast Guided Filter. A filtered output image q can be calculated in terms of a guidance image I and a filtering input image p using the following:

$$q_i = a_k I_i + b_k, \forall i \in w_k \tag{7}$$

where i is the pixel's index and w_k refers to a square window of radius r. After minimizing the reconstruction error, [11] offers Eqs. (8) and (9) to calculate a_k and b_k:

$$a_k = \frac{\frac{1}{|w|}\sum_{i \in w_k} I_i p_i - \mu_k \bar{p}_k}{\sigma_k^2 + \epsilon} \tag{8}$$

$$b_k = \bar{p}_k - a_k \mu_k \tag{9}$$

where μ_k and σ_k are, respectively, the values of mean and variance inside the window w in the input image. ϵ controls the degree of smoothness of the filtered image.

4   Experimental Results

This section presents results of a comparison between different techniques for transmission map refinement, dehazing of images and enhancement of low-lighting frames in underwater videos. It also describes the synthesis process of a dataset of 100 hazy images used in the experiments. Data used in this work were provided by Ocean Networks Canada.

4.1   Transmission Map Refinement

A reference (ground truth) transmission map is necessary to evaluate and determine the most efficient refinement method. The transmission map of a single image is estimated using the atmospheric light A and the DCP (Eq. (3)). However, if the depth map of an image is available and the atmosphere is considered to be homogeneous, the ground truth transmission map can be alternatively calculated as:

$$t(x) = e^{-\beta d(x)} \tag{10}$$

where β is the scattering coefficient of the atmosphere and d is the scene depth. An image without any haze has a scattering coefficient of zero.

Synthesis of Hazy Images Using Depth Maps.   There are several datasets that provide pairs of images and their depth maps. Popular examples are: FRIDA [15], Middlebury Stereo Datasets [16] and NYU-Depth V2 [17] (formed by 1449 640 × 480 pixels images and their depth maps). In order to estimate the transmission map to be compared with the ground truth calculated, a *hazy* version of the image must be synthesized first. The following equation, a combination of Eqs. (1) and (10), is used to do that:

$$I(x) = J(x)e^{-\beta d(x)} + A\left(1 - e^{-\beta d(x)}\right) \tag{11}$$

With the NYU-Depth V2 dataset, J and d are known. For this project, 100 images from this dataset are used to synthesize 100 hazy images using Eq. (11). In this process, β and A are set to 0.01 and [1 1 1], respectively. Figure 2 presents an example of a synthesized hazy image and its transmission maps (estimated and ground truth).

Fig. 2. Synthesized images and transmission maps. (a) Original image from [17]. (b) Depth map. (c) Generated hazy image using $\beta = 0.01$ and $A = [111]$. (d) Calculated ground truth transmission map. (e) Estimated transmission map (unfiltered).

Comparison of Transmission Map Refinement Methods. Three different filters are evaluated for the refinement of the transmission map: Gaussian, bilateral, and fast guided filter. Additionally, the unfiltered version of the estimated transmission map is also analyzed. The methods used to compare the estimated maps with the ground truth were two full-reference quality metrics: Structural Similarity Index (SSIM) and Root Mean-Squared Error (RMSE). In the experiments, the ground truth transmission maps of all 100 images were compared with the estimated transmission maps of the synthetic hazy images. The results shown below are the average of these 100 comparisons.

Unfiltered Transmission Map. This version of the transmission map is the one obtained directly from Eq. (3), considering $w = 0.98$ (minimal levels of haze preserved). This value of w is chosen because the provided depth map refers to the haze-less version of the original image, so a higher value of w will better represent it in Eq. (3).

Figure 3 shows that larger patch sizes led to better results (lower RMSE and higher SSIM). Results for patch sizes larger than 19×19 were virtually the same. The trade-off between results and processing time plays an important factor: transmission maps calculated using patches sized 15×15 took on average 1 s to be calculated, whereas 19×19 sized patches increased that time in approximately 50%. Figure 3(c)–(d) shows that values higher than 0.85 for parameter w will increase the RMSE and decrease the SSIM. Table 1 presents the best combination of parameters observed for the unfiltered transmission maps.

Gaussian Filter. The sole controlling parameter exclusive to the Gaussian filter is its standard deviation σ_s. In the following experiments, w is set to $= 0.85$ and different patch sizes and σ_s ("sigma") are tested.

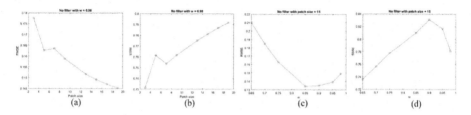

Fig. 3. Difference between unfiltered estimated transmission maps and ground truth. (a)–(b) RMSE and SSIM for varying patch size. (c)–(d) RMSE and SSIM for varying w.

Unlike the case of the unfiltered version, the 19×19 sized patches did not produce the best refinement results (Fig. 4). σ_s values higher than 5 were virtually uninfluential to the results. The Gaussian filter is efficient in eliminating color textures that might result from bigger patches Ω because of its blurring effect. However, this filter does not preserve the edges in the output image, which might negatively affect posterior processing.

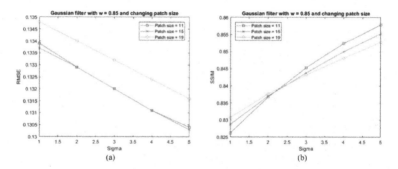

Fig. 4. Difference between gaussian-filtered transmission map and ground truth. (a) RMSE for varying patch size and sigma. (b) SSIM for varying patch size and sigma.

Bilateral Filter. This filter is controlled by two parameters: range kernel σ_r and spatial range σ_s. However, in the experiments where those varied, the changes in the results were almost unnoticeable. Instead, changes in the patch size used to calculate the transmission map effectively changed the values of RMSE and SSIM. Thus, σ_r, σ_s and w were set to 0.05, 15 and 0.85, respectively (while the patch size varies).

Increases in patch size after 23 were not able to significantly improve the results (Fig. 5). Since the bilateral filter awards higher weights to similarly colored pixels to the central one, the edges are preserved. That leads to sharper filtered transmission maps.

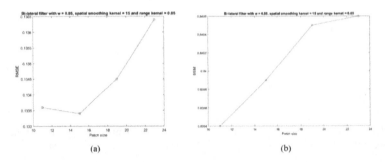

Fig. 5. Difference between the transmission maps refined with the bilateral filter and ground truth. (a) RMSE for varying patch size. (b) SSIM for varying patch size.

Fast Guided Filter. The fast guided filter is controlled by three parameters: subsampling ratio s, square window radius r and smoothing degree ϵ. The results below were obtained with a fixed patch size of 15 and $w = 0.85$ (Fig. 6).

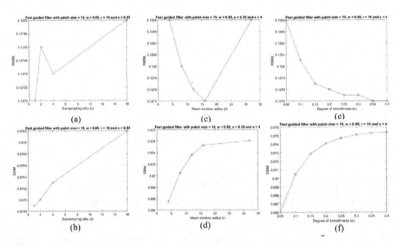

Fig. 6. RMSE and SSIM for transmission map and ground truth using the fast guided filter. (a)–(b) Varying subsampling ratio s. (c)–(d) Varying window radius r. (e)–(f) Varying ϵ.

The increase in s caused the RMSE to grow, however it also boosted the SSIM (Fig. 7(a) and (b)). Window radiuses bigger than 16 increased the RMSE and did not change significantly the SSIM. Changes in the degree of smoothness ϵ produced the most desirable results (decreasing RMSE and an increasing SSIM). For this parameter, values higher than 0.35 generated only small changes in the output. Table 1 shows that the combination of patch size, w, s, r and ϵ of 15, 0.85, 4, 16 and 0.4, respectively, yields the best refinement result observed in the experiments with the fast guided filter.

Table 1. Best combination of parameters for the refinement methods evaluated.

Filter	Patch size	w	σ_s (sigma)	σ_r	σ_s (r. kernel)	s	r	ϵ	SSIM	RMSE
Unfiltered	15	0.9	N/A	N/A	N/A	N/A	N/A	N/A	0.8308	0.1351
Gaussian	11	0.85	5	N/A	N/A	N/A	N/A	N/A	0.8579	0.1304
Bilateral	19	0.85	N/A	0.05	5	N/A	N/A	N/A	0.8405	0.1345
Fast guided	15	0.85	N/A	N/A	N/A	4	16	0.4	**0.8754**	**0.1274**

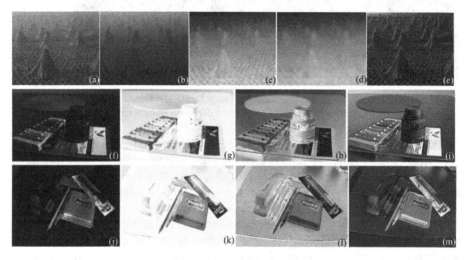

Fig. 7. (a) Hazy image. (b) Dark channel. (c) Transmission map. (d) Filtered transmission map. (e) Dehazed image. (f)–(m) Low-lighting images from [19], their complements, the dehazed version of the complements and the final, enhanced image.

Dehazing and Low-Lighting Enhancement. Given the results summarized in Table 1, the fast guided filter is chosen to refine the transmission maps estimated in the framework. Figure 7 shows the complete process of inverting, dehazing, and then inverting the image once again. Figure 7(a)–(e) illustrates the dehazing process. Note in Fig. 7(d) that the transmission map is filtered, but the edges are still visible. The dehazed image in Fig. 7(e) is virtually free of haze (except that preserved using w and $t0$). Figure 7(f)–(m) illustrates the low-lighting enhancement process. The enhanced images allow for an easier perception of details (edges and corners), as discussed below.

The Canny edge detection algorithm [18] is used to measure the increase in number of detected edges before and after the lighting enhancement. This metric is commonly used to assess the quality of dehazing processes [14]. The parameters (standard deviation of the Gaussian filter σ_s, strong threshold s_t and weak threshold w_t) used in this experiment are: $\sigma_s = 1.41$, $s_t = 0.3$, $w_t = 0.02$. The ratio between the number of edges before and after enhancement is 2.14 for the lens in Fig. 8(a) and (d), 2.05 for the office supplies in Fig. 8(b) and (e) and 3.5 for ONC's underwater image in Fig. 8(c) and (f).

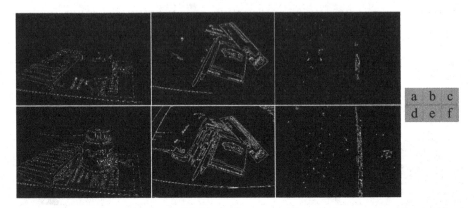

Fig. 8. (a)–(c). Edges found in low-lighting images. (d)–(f) Edges found in the lighting enhanced versions of the images (same Canny edge detection parameters).

The edge detection experiment was also performed on 710 frames of an underwater video from ONC. The overall ratio of increase calculated was 3.95 (in this experiment, the parameters used were $\sigma_s = 1.41$, $s_t = 0.44$, $w_t = 0.04$). It is important to notice that not *all* the new edges observed after the enhancement might be considered as enhancements, as they may be, for example, noise created by the enhancement process.

The enhanced images on Fig. 9 presents significantly more detail (visible edges) and overall information that was not visible in their original counterparts. The time to process each high-resolution frame (2560×1920 pixels) is 5 s when using a computer equipped with an Intel Core i7-6700HQ processor and 16 GB of RAM memory.

Fig. 9. ONC underwater images before ((a), (c)) and after ((b), (d)) lighting enhancement.

5 Conclusion

This paper describes the synthesis of hazy scenes out of an *image/depth map* dataset, the thorough analysis of three refinement methods for transmission maps, the use of a DCP-based dehazing algorithm [4] in addition with a lighting enhancement method [1] and proposes an efficient approach for the enhancement of low-lighting underwater imagery. As a result, it determined a strong candidate for the refinement of transmission maps, and the enhancement framework produced images with a significantly higher number of useful features (edges) and overall better visibility (brightness). Future improvements in the framework should address limitations related to the processing time and color preservation.

References

1. Dong, X., et al.: Fast efficient algorithm for enhancement of low lighting video. In: 2011 IEEE International Conference on Multimedia and Expo, Barcelona, pp. 1–6 (2011)
2. Schechnner, Y.Y., Narasimhan, S.G., Nayar, S.K.: Polarization-based vision through haze. Appl. Optics **42**(3), 511–525 (2003)
3. Narasimhan, S.G., Nayar, S.K.: Contrast restoration of weather degraded images. IEEE Trans. Pattern Anal. Mach. Intell. **25**(6), 713–724 (2003)
4. He, K., Sun, J., Tang, X.: Single image haze removal using dark channel prior. IEEE Trans. Pattern Anal. Mach. Intell. **33**(12), 2341–2353 (2011)
5. Tarel, J.P., Hautière, N.: Fast visibility restoration from a single color or gray level image. In: 2009 IEEE 12th International Conference on Computer Vision, Kyoto (2009)
6. Meng, G., Wang, Y., Duan, J., Xiang, S., Pan, C.: Efficient image dehazing with boundary constraint and contextual regularization. In: 2013 IEEE International Conference on Computer Vision, Sydney, NSW, pp. 617–624 (2013)
7. Fattal, R.: Dehazing using color lines. ACM Trans. Graph. **34**, 1–14 (2014)
8. Ancuti, C., Ancuti, C.O., Vleeschouwer, C.: D-Hazy: a dataset to evaluate quantitatively dehazing algorithms. In: 2016 IEEE International Conf. on Image Processing (2016)
9. Ren, W., Liu, S., Zhang, H., Pan, J., Cao, X., Yang, M.: Single image dehazing via multi-scale convolutional neural networks. In: European Conference on Computer Vision – ECCV 2016, pp 154–169, September 2016
10. Alharbi, E.B., Ge, P., Wang, H.: A research on single image dehazing algorithms based on dark channel prior. J. Comput. Commun. **4**, 47–55 (2016)
11. He, K., Sun, J., Tang, X.: Guided image filtering. IEEE Trans. Pattern Anal. Mach. Intell. **35**(6), 1397–1409 (2013)
12. Tomasi, C., Manduchi, R.: Bilateral filtering for gray and color images. In: Sixth International Conference on Computer Vision, pp. 839–846 (1988)
13. He, K., Sun, J.: Fast Guided Filter. eprint arXiv:1505.00996. Bibliographic code: 2015arXiv150500996H, May 2015
14. Lee, S., Yun, S., Nam, J., Won, C.S., Jung, S.: A review on dark channel prior based image dehazing algorithms. EURASIP J. Image Video Process. **2016**, 4 (2016)
15. Tarel, J.-P., et al.: Vision enhancement in homogeneous and heterogeneous fog. IEEE Intell. Transp. Syst. Mag. **4**(2), 6–20 (2012)
16. Scharstein, D., et al.: High-resolution stereo datasets with subpixel-accurate ground truth. In: Jiang, X., Hornegger, J., Koch, R. (eds.) GCPR 2014. LNCS, vol. 8753, pp. 31–42. Springer, Cham (2014). https://doi.org/10.1007/978-3-319-11752-2_3
17. Silberman, N., Hoiem, D., Kohli, P., Fergus, R.: Indoor segmentation and support inference from RGBD images. In: Fitzgibbon, A., Lazebnik, S., Perona, P., Sato, Y., Schmid, C. (eds.) ECCV 2012. LNCS, vol. 7576, pp. 746–760. Springer, Heidelberg (2012). https://doi.org/10.1007/978-3-642-33715-4_54
18. Canny, J.: A computational approach to edge detection. IEEE Trans. Pattern Anal. Mach. Intell. **PAMI-8**(6), 679–698 (1986)
19. Anaya, J., Barbu, A.: RENOIR – a dataset for real low-light image noise reduction. J. Vis. Commun. Image Represent. **51**(2), 144–154 (2018)

Underwater-GAN: Underwater Image Restoration via Conditional Generative Adversarial Network

Xiaoli Yu, Yanyun Qu$^{(\boxtimes)}$, and Ming Hong

School of Information Science and Engineering, Xiamen University, Xiamen, China
yuxli@foxmail.com, yyqu@xmu.edu.cn, 1184307675@qq.com

Abstract. Underwater image restoration is still a challenging task until now, because underwater images are degenerated due to the complex underwater imaging environment and poor light condition. The image degeneration includes color distortion, low contrast, and blur. In this paper, we propose Underwater-GAN, a conditional generative adversarial network for underwater image restoration. In Underwater-GAN, we use Wasserstein GAN with gradient penalty term as the backbone network. We design the loss function as the sum of the loss of generative adversarial network and the perceptual loss. In the discriminator of Underwater-GAN, we use a convolution patchGAN classifier to learn a structural loss instead of the image-level loss or pixel-wise loss. Moreover, we construct an underwater image dataset by simulating to generate underwater images according to the underwater imaging model. We train our model with these simulated underwater dataset. The results of our experiments show that the proposed method produces better visual qualitative and quantitative indicators than existing methods.

Keywords: Underwater image restoration
Generative adversarial network · Perceptual loss

1 Introduction

Recently, underwater images and videos have played an increasingly important role in marine military, marine engineering and marine research. Therefore, it's particularly important to obtain high-quality images from the deep ocean for the marine exploration. But disappointedly, very little analysis was performed on underwater image processing. Underwater image restoration is still a challenging task because underwater images are degenerated due to the complex underwater imaging environment and poor light condition. Concretely, light rays decay exponentially as they pass through water, which makes underwater images lower contrast and blurred. And different color wavelengths have different attenuation rates when they pass through water, which results in the color distortion of the underwater images. Moreover, fine particles dissolved in water may make underwater image noisy. Thus, the poor visibility of underwater images

© Springer Nature Switzerland AG 2019
Z. Zhang et al. (Eds.): ICPR 2018 Workshops, LNCS 11188, pp. 66–75, 2019.
https://doi.org/10.1007/978-3-030-05792-3_7

make it difficult for the subsequent operation such as object recognition, image understanding and analysis in the application scenario of marine military, ocean engineering, and marine research.

Traditional image restoration methods were often directly applied to underwater image processing, such as histogram equalization [1] and white balance [2], all of which can improve the visual quality of underwater images to some extent, but there are still unsolved issues such as amplification of noise, artificial artifacts, and color distortion. Recently, special image restoration methods for underwater images emerged. Henke et al. [3] applied the classic color constancy algorithm to underwater images and proposed a color-constant algorithm based on features to fix color distortion of underwater images. Galdran et al. [4] proposed a red channel method to process underwater images based on the classic dark channel image dehazing method [10]. Li et al. [5] also uses the dark channel method to process the blue-green channel of underwater images. In a word, lots of methods are based on some prior knowledge of underwater imaging to solve the underwater image restoration problem. However, these methods still have limitations in underwater image restoration. The above mentioned methods can not restore the image well, because the original assumption is invalid with the changes of water turbidity and illumination.

With the development of deep neural networks [6], the generative adversarial networks (GANs) [7] are increasingly implemented on image restoration and achieve promising visual effect. For example, SRGAN [9] is a super-resolution method which uses GAN for super-resolution, and the SR images have more clear details and better visual qualities. Most importantly, the generative adversarial networks can learn the distribution of the target samples, thus they processes the data with greater robustness. Though it is an end-to-end underwater image restoration method which requires few interference by hand, the underwater image dataset is very difficult to build. In order to solve the problem of training data, WaterGAN [13] uses GAN to generate the underwater image. The latest work for underwater image restoration is [22], which uses CycleGAN to generate the realistic underwater image and then implements Wasserstein GAN [14] to restore underwater images. Different from the two mentioned methods, we use a physical simulator to generate multiple underwater images from an underwater image which is modeled according to underwater physical imaging theory [11,12]. We design a conditional GAN, named Underwater-GAN, for underwater image restoration. We treat Wasserstein GAN as the backbone of our neural network in which the perceptual loss is added to the GAN loss function. Moreover, the structural loss rather than the pixel-wise or image-level loss is used in the discriminator of Underwater-GAN. Our experimental results show that our method is better than existing underwater images recovery methods, both in visual qualities and in quantitative indicators for underwater images.

2 Underwater Image Simulator

2.1 Underwater Imaging Model

Usually light passing through the underwater will undergo different degrees of attenuation with the increasing depth of the underwater. Considering the attenuation of lights, the modified Koschmieder model [12] is applied to underwater lighting conditions. The degeneration of underwater images can be formulated as follows:

$$I_U^c(x) = I_R^c(x) e^{-\eta d(x)} + \beta^c(x)(1 - e^{-\eta d(x)}), c \in \{r, g, b\}, \tag{1}$$

where $I_U^c(x)$ is the degraded underwater image, $I_R^c(x)$ is the real scene in the water, η is the scattering coefficient related to the wavelength, $\beta^c(x)$ is a parameter dependent on wavelength, and $d(x)$ is the distance from the scene point to the camera.

2.2 Underwater Image Generation

Based on the underwater imaging model above, we implement a model-based turbidity simulator to simulate the distorted underwater images to train our network. The first term of (1), denoted by S_1, is modeled for the attenuation of light:

$$S_1 = I_R^c(x) e^{-\eta d(x)}. \tag{2}$$

If we can collect a dataset which includes real images and the corresponding depth maps, S_1 can be easily obtained by randomly selecting scattering coefficient η. However, there is no underwater image dataset with depth maps, we only can get the real underwater images but without depth maps. In order to solve the problem, we simulate multiple underwater images from turbidity images. For a real underwater image without the depth map, we randomly generate a value from [0,1] as the distance $d(x)$. And then we use the turbidity image to get the scattering coefficient η

$$\eta^c = \frac{1}{M \times N} \sum_{x=1}^{M} \sum_{y=1}^{N} (-log \frac{T^c(x, y)}{l \times t \times I_0}), c \in \{r, g, b\}, \tag{3}$$

where $T^c(x, y)$ is the turbidity image with the size $M \times N$, and l, t and I_0 are all constants, which are set as 1, 1.06, 1.0, respectively.

As light travels through the water, it is also subjected to scattering. In our turbidity simulator, the scattering parameter β^c is calculated as

$$\beta^c = l \times t \times I_0 \times e^{-\eta^c max(T^c)}, c \in \{r, g, b\}. \tag{4}$$

The second term of (1) can be performed as a turbidity mask:

$$M_2 = \beta^c(1 - e^{-\eta^c d(x)}), c \in \{r, g, b\}. \tag{5}$$

The final degraded underwater image is the sum of S_1 and the mask M_2:

$$I_U = S_1 + M_2. \tag{6}$$

Figure 1 shows some simulating degraded underwater images and the corresponding turbidity images used to synthesize them. Using one clear image, the different turbidity images can simulate different degraded underwater images.

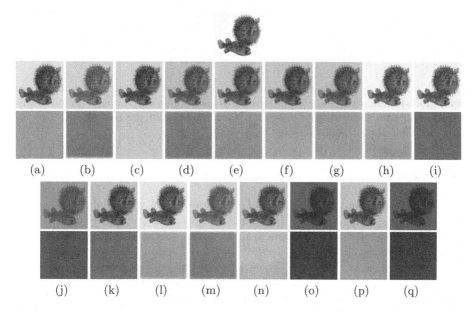

(a)   (b)   (c)   (d)   (e)   (f)   (g)   (h)   (i)

(j)   (k)   (l)   (m)   (n)   (o)   (p)   (q)

Fig. 1. We totally use 17 different turbidity images to simulate the diverse underwater conditions. The first image is one original clear underwater image, and the others are 17 image pairs of degenerate underwater images and the corresponding turbid blocks used to generate them.

3   The Architecture of Underwater-GAN

In this paper, we detail the architecture of Underwater-GAN. In addition, we use the sum of the adversarial loss and perceptual loss as the generator loss. The Underwater-GAN architecture is shown in Fig. 2. The generator aims at obtaining the clear underwater images. In the training stage, the generated clear images is fed into discriminator and the prediction is estimated by the distance between the real clear underwater image and the restored underwater image. In the testing stage, we only use the generator network to produce the clear underwater images.

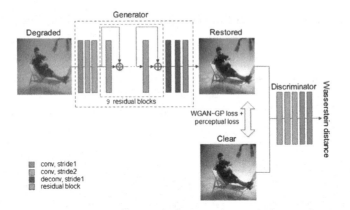

Fig. 2. Underwater-GAN for underwater image restoration. Generator network obtains the degraded underwater images and generates clear underwater images. While training, discriminator network gets generated clear images and the real clear images as inputs and estimates the distance between them.

3.1 Loss Function

For the degraded underwater image I_U without other useful information, we aim to recover a clear image $\hat{I}_R$. Here we employ a conditional generative adversarial network whose generator can transform the degraded underwater images to the clear images. Both the generator and the discriminator use the convolutional neural network. The adversarial loss estimate the quality of the restored image and the generator can produce images that are close to real images. It is recognized that the combination of the adversarial loss and the content loss is effective in image restoration [15,16]. In this paper we use perceptual loss [17] as the content loss. Thus we define the loss function as the sum of adversarial loss and perceptual loss:

$$L = L_{GAN} + \lambda_p L_p, \tag{7}$$

where L_{GAN} is the adversarial loss, L_P represents the perceptual loss and λ_p is the weight which trades off the adversarial loss and the perceptual loss.

Considering that the original GAN [7] is unstable, easily suffering from mode collapse, exploding or vanishing gradient, we use the conditional version [8] of WGAN-GP [14] as the critical function. The adversarial loss can be expressed as follows:

$$L_{GAN} = E[D_{\theta_D}(I_R)] - E[D(G_{\theta_G}(I_U))] - \lambda E_{\hat{x} \sim p_{\hat{x}}}[(\| \nabla_{\hat{x}} D(\hat{x}) \|_2 - 1)^2], \tag{8}$$

where I_U is an degraded underwater image, I_R is the corresponding clear underwater image, G_{θ_G} is the generator, D_{θ_D} is the discriminator, $p_{\hat{x}}$ is sampled uniformly along straight lines between pairs of points sampled from the data distribution and the generator distribution and λ is a weight of the gradient penalty term.

The perceptual loss calculates the feature map distances between the generated and the target images and it can be formulated as follows:

$$L_P = \sum_{j=1}^{n} \frac{1}{C_j H_j W_j} \parallel \phi_j(G_{\theta_G}(I_U)) - \phi_j(I_R) \parallel_2^2, \tag{9}$$

where j denotes the j-th convolutional layer, ϕ_j is the feature map in the j-th convolutional layer with the size of $C_j \times H_j \times W_j$. We use VGG-19 [23] as the feature map extraction network.

3.2   Network Architecture

The generator architecture is a fully convolutional network, similar to [17]. The whole generator network is stacked sequentially by a convolution layer with kernel size 7×7, two convolution layers with kernel size 3×3 and stride 2, nine residual blocks, two deconvolution layers with stride 2, and a convolutional layer with kernel size 7×7. Each of residual blocks is built up with two convolutional layers with kernel size 3×3 and the first convolutional layer is followed by an instance normalization layer and a ReLU activation layer. In each residual block, the dropout regularization is added behind the first convolutional layer and the probability is 0.5. In addition to residual blocks, every convolutional layer except the last layer is also followed by an instance normalization layer and ReLU activation layer. We apply a tangent activation function after the last convolutional layer.

Our fully convolutional discriminator network based on WGAN-GP is modeled as a PatchGAN [15] with patch size 8. The discriminator network consists of five convolutional layers with kernel size 4×4. The first convolutional layer is with stride 2, followed by a Leaky ReLU layer with slope 0.2. The next two convolutional layers is with stride 2, each of which, an instance normalization layer and a Leaky ReLU layer with slope 0.2 follow. The fourth convolutional layer is with stride 1, followed by an instance normalization layer and a Leaky ReLU activation layer too. The last convolution layer uses stride 1, followed by a Sigmoid activation layer.

4   Experimental Results

4.1   Underwater Image Dataset

There are not existing dataset which contains pairs of clear images and their corresponding degraded underwater images for training, therefore, based on the physical imaging model (1) for underwater images, we only use the clear images without other extra information to simulate the underwater images with different light attenuation. We generate multiple images with different turbidity images and Fig. 1 shows that we totally use 17 different turbidity images to diversely simulate the underwater conditions.

We collect three thousand clear underwater images from Internet as the Ground Truth. For each clear underwater image, we generate 17 degraded underwater images using the underwater image simulator with 17 different turbidity images, and then we randomly select nine of the seventeen for training. So, totally, we simulate 27000 image pairs of clear underwater images and corresponding degraded underwater images for training. In the testing stage, we find other 667 clear underwater images which are total different from training data, and in the same way, for each of them, we produce two different degraded underwater images for a testing underwater image, thus, we have 1334 images for testing. Figure 3 shows some samples of clear underwater images and the corresponding generated degraded underwater images.

Fig. 3. Some pairs of the clear underwater images and the synthesized degraded underwater images.

4.2   Training

It is worth noting that we do not apply the conditional version in the training stage, because we don't need to punish the mismatch of the input images and the output images.

We train the Underwater-GAN on the image pairs whose degraded underwater images are generated by underwater simulator. The training underwater images and testing images are both of size $400 \times 400 \times 3$. The inputs of the generator are underwater images and appropriate weights of the generator are learned to produce restored underwater images by minimizing the adversarial loss and perceptual loss between the restored and the clear one. At the meantime, the discriminator computes the Wasserstein distance between the generated clear underwater images by generator and the real clear underwater images to coach the generator for training.

In our experiments, we set the weight of the gradient penalty term λ as 10, the weight of the perceptual loss term λ_p as 100, batch size as 1 and use the ADAM optimizer to train our model. The discriminator network is updated five times when the generator is updated one time.

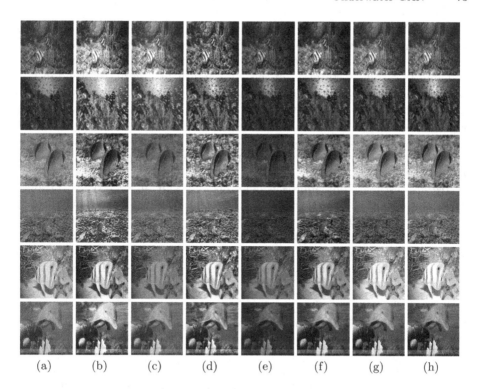

(a)   (b)   (c)   (d)   (e)   (f)   (g)   (h)

Fig. 4. Different methods for underwater images restoration. From the first column to the last column: (a) Original, (b) HE, (c) GW, (d) Fusion, (e) SUIR, (f) UGAN-P, (g) ours, (h) GT (Ground Truth).

4.3   Evaluation

A blue or green hue exists in many of the degraded underwater images, but sometimes, due to different color wavelength attenuation, there may be a yellow hue or haze on the underwater images. Figure 4 shows some underwater images and corresponding recovered underwater images which are restored by several state-of-the art restoration approaches, including histogram equalization (HE) [19], gray World (GW) [20], Fusion [21], SUIR [5] and UGAN-GP [22]. WaterGAN [13] requires depth images for the training, so we don't use it for comparison. In our experiments, the test images were obtained under varying underwater scenes with different color wavelength attenuations on the images. The experiment results show that even though under different illuminations, the proposed method can achieve good visual effects for the testing images. As we can see in Fig. 4, the degraded underwater images always have distorted colors, blurred surfaces and low contrasts. We found that all of these methods can correct the color to some extent when there is color wavelength distortion on the image, but their correction effects are obviously different. For example, histogram equalization (HE) may make the images too sharp and lose the original information. GW is a often used color balance algorithm, and as we can see, it can make the images have better visual effects, but sometimes the images it recovers have haze and SUIR is only valid for some specific images. As for Fusion [21], we found that some restoration images also appear too sharp, resulting in bad visual effect. In addition, the images recovered by UGAN-P have a lower brightness. Comparatively, it is observed obviously that our proposed method have a better performance. Although different color wavelength attenuation exists in these degraded underwater images, our method can correct their color and the clear underwater images got by our approach are very close to the real clear underwater images.

We also estimate our approach in terms of PSNR and SSIM [24]. Table 1 shows the PSNR and SSIM results of the degraded underwater images and the restored images from different method. Comparing with other methods, the experimental results shows that our method can achieve the best results on quantitative evaluation indicators in both PSNR and SSIM. Our approach achieve the breakthough gain of (4.616, 0.100) compared with UGAN-P. It demonstrates that our approach is effective.

Table 1. Comparison of underwater image restoration methods in terms of PSNR and SSIM on the testing image dataset.

Method	Degraded	HE	GW	Fusion	SUIR	UGAN-P	Ours
PSNR	17.389	13.828	15.745	17.928	14.214	18.983	**23.799**
SSIM	0.741	0.616	0.663	0.662	0.683	0.760	**0.860**

5   Conclusions

In this paper, we aim at solving the problem of underwater image restoration. We propose Underwater-GAN based on WGAN-GP for underwater image restoration. We construct an underwater image dataset by a simulator which is modeled according to the underwater imaging theory. The experimental results demonstrate that Underwater-GAN is effective and superior to other state-of-the-art underwater image restoration methods in both quantitative estimation and visual effects.

References

1. Hummel, R.: Image enhancement by histogram transformation. Comput. Graph. Image Process. **6**, 184–195 (1977)
2. Liu, Y.C., Chan, W.H., Chen, Y.Q.: Automatic white balance for digital still camera. IEEE Trans. Consum. Electron. **41**, 460–466 (1995)
3. Henke, B., Vahl, M., Zhou, Z.: Removing color cast of underwater images through non-constant color constancy hypothesis. In: IEEE International Symposium on Image and Signal Processing and Analysis (2013)

4. Galdran, A., Pardo, D., et al.: Automatic red-channel underwater image restoration. J. Vis. Commun. Image Represent. (JVCIR) **26**, 132–145 (2014)
5. Li, C., Guo, J., Pang, Y., Chen, S., Wang, J.: Single underwater image restoration by blue-green channels dehazing and red channel correction. In: IEEE International Conference on Acoustics, Speech and Signal Processing (ICASSP) (2016)
6. Goodfellow, I., Bengio, Y., Courville, A.: Deep Learning. MIT Press, Cambridge (2016)
7. Goodfellow, I., et al.: Generative adversarial nets. In: Conference on Neural Information Processing Systems (NIPS) (2014)
8. Mirza, M., Osindero, S.: Conditional generative adversarial nets. arXiv: 1411.1784
9. Ledig, C., Theis, L., et al.: Photo-realistic single image super-resolution using a generative adversarial network. In: IEEE Conference on Computer Vision and Pattern Recognition (CVPR) (2017)
10. He, K., Sun, J., Tang, X.: Single image haze removal using dark channel prior. IEEE Trans. Pattern Anal. Mach. Intell. (T-PAMI) **33**, 2341–2353 (2011)
11. Jaffe, J.S.: Computer modeling and the design of optimal underwater imaging systems. IEEE J. Ocean. Eng. **15**, 101–111 (1990)
12. Koschmieder, H.: Theorie der horizontalen Sichtweite. In: Beitrage zur Physik der freien. Atmosphare (1924)
13. Li, J., Skinner, K.A., et al.: WaterGAN: unsupervised generative network to enable real-time color correction of monocular underwater images. arXiv: 1701.07875
14. Gulrajani, I., Ahmed, F., Arjovsky, M., Dumoulin, V., Courville, A.: Improved training of wasserstein GANs. arXiv: 1704.00028
15. Isola, P., Zhu, J.Y., Zhou, T., Efros, A.A.: Image-to-image translation with conditional adversarial networks. In: CVPR (2017)
16. Pathak, D., Krahenbuhl, P., Donahue, J., Darrell, T., Efros, A.A.: Context encoders: feature learning by inpainting. In: CVPR (2016)
17. Johnson, J., Alahi, A., Li, F.: Perceptual losses for real-time style transfer and super-resolution. In: European Conference on Computer Vision (ECCV) (2016)
18. Kupyn, O., Budzan, V., Mykhailych, M.: DeblurGAN: blind motion deblurring using conditional adversarial networks. arXiv:1711.07064
19. Gonzalez, R., Woods, R.: Digital Image Processing. Addison-Wesley Publishing Company, Boston (1992). Chapter 4
20. Johnson-Roberson, M., Bryson, M., et al.: High-resolution underwater robotic vision-based mapping and 3D reconstruction for archaeology. Field Robot. **34**, 625–643 (2016)
21. Bekaert, P., Haber, T., et al.: Enhancing underwater images and videos by fusion. In: IEEE Conference on Computer Vision and Pattern Recognition (CVPR) (2012)
22. Fabbri, C., Islam, M.J., et al.: Enhancing underwater imagery using generative adversarial networks. In: IEEE Conference on Robotics and Automation (ICRA) (2018)
23. Simonyan, K., Zisserman, A.: Very deep convolutional networks for large-scale image recognition. In: International Conference on Learning Representations (ICLR) (2015)
24. Wang, Z., Bovik, A.C., Sheikh, H.R., Simoncelli, E.P.: Image quality assessment: from error visibility to structural similarity. IEEE Trans. Image Process. **13**(11), 600–612 (2004)

Single Image Plankton 3D Reconstruction from Extended Depth of Field Shadowgraph

Claudius Zelenka$^{(\boxtimes)}$ and Reinhard Koch

Department of Computer Science, Kiel University, Kiel, Germany
{cze,rk}@informatik.uni-kiel.de

Abstract. Marine plankton occurs in the ocean with strongly varying degrees of sparsity. For in-situ plankton measurements the shadowgraph has been established as the observation device of choice in recent years. In this paper a novel depth from defocus based approach to partially coherent 3D reconstruction of marine plankton volumes is presented. With a combination of recent advances in coherent image restoration and deep learning, we create a 3D view of the shadowgraph observation volume. For the selection of in-focus images we develop a novel training data generation technique. This kind of reconstruction was previously only possible with holographic imaging systems, which require laser illumination with high coherence, which often causes parasitic interferences on optical components and speckles. The new 3D visualization gives easily manageable data by resulting in a sharp view of each plankton together with its depth and position. Moreover, this approach allows the creation of all-in-focus images of larger observation volumes, which is otherwise impossible due to the physically limited depth of field. We show an effective increase in depth of field by a factor of 7, which allows marine researchers to use larger observation volumes and thus a much more effective observation of marine plankton.

Keywords: Marine plankton · Shadowgraph · Image restoration

1 Introduction

Plankton observation and measurement is of very high importance foremost for marine biology [6], because plankton has impact on the entire marine habitat. The density of the plankton in the ocean is usually low, hence the volume and depth of our observation volume should be as large as possible. Furthermore, for practical reasons the observation should be performed with single images, because both plankton and the imaging device are constantly moving [3]. Another important demand is a simple and robust illumination to allow in situ measurements.

With a limited depth of field, in an image of a 3D volume not all objects are in focus. In a shadowgraph system [16] this may apply to most objects, as the

© Springer Nature Switzerland AG 2019
Z. Zhang et al. (Eds.): ICPR 2018 Workshops, LNCS 11188, pp. 76–85, 2019.
https://doi.org/10.1007/978-3-030-05792-3_8

requirements on light and resolution set optical limits on the depth of the field. Due to the low coherence, the recorded image contains amplitude information only and the fine structures of a hologram are not visible. The holographic methods are therefore not applicable.

The research objective of this paper is a novel reconstruction method using a light source with low coherence, which can achieve results similar to holographic imaging. A key detriment of holographic methods is a low field of view [2]. We provide a brief introduction into both the shadowgraph and holography in Sect. 2. In this paper we will show that this objective can be achieved by using recent iterative image restoration algorithms. This allows us to increase the effective depth of field of the shadowgraph due to the ability to refocus (Sect. 3).

The success of deep learning in dense depth estimation from natural images [5], motivates our choice to train a deep classifier to estimate 3D information in a depth from defocus approach. We do not need to reconstruct a dense 3D volume for 3D volume segmentation as in holographic methods, but instead only require a reconstruction stack of low density, in which we then apply the classifier (Sect. 4) to find the in-focus image. To facilitate the training of the classifier, we will demonstrate a convenient technique to generate large amounts of training data with little effort.

Besides refocusing and 3D visualization (Sect. 6), another contribution of this paper is the generation of all-in-focus images (Sect. 5) from a single image.

2   Related Work

In this section we give a short overview of related works about the shadowgraph and holography.

2.1   Shadowgraph

For a detailed introduction into shadowgraph systems we refer to [11]. In general, the focused shadowgraph is an imaging concept meant for the observation of small opaque or semitransparent objects [16].

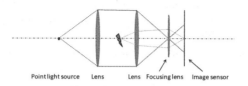

Point light source   Lens   Lens Focusing lens   Image sensor

Fig. 1. Optical drawing of the focused shadowgraph. Black dots show the illumination edge rays, blue the rays from the objects projection onto the camera sensor. Shown is an adaptation of a drawing from [16]. (Color figure online)

An optical drawing of a focused shadowgraph principle is shown in Fig. 1. A typical focused shadowgraph is composed of the following elements. Light of a point light source is converted with a condensation lens into parallel light. This light is used to illuminate the target of observation at which point the opaqueness of the target creates an image of light and shadow. With a second condensation lens this light is focused into the focusing lens. The focusing lens has the purpose of selecting a plane of focus. It projects the light and shadow image from the target onto the image sensor.

A focused shadowgraph system for plankton observation called 'In situ ichthyoplankton imaging system' ISIIS is presented in [4]. It uses a collimated pin hole LED illumination inside a stainless steel tube housing and a camera in a second tube housing. Both tubes are axially arranged and plankton is observed by projecting light from the illumination tube towards the camera tube. In [13] a similar system is compared to physical sampling methods in a field application with good results.

2.2 Holography

As [8] explains, 'the hologram is a record of interference between light diffracted from object illuminated by a coherent light and a known reference beam', furthermore 'a hologram contains both the amplitude and phase of the diffracted wave'. For the observation of the interference between the diffracted beam and the reference beam a very high resolution is needed. Additionally, there is a stringent requirement on the coherence of the light source, which may be difficult to achieve. In magnified images of holograms we see streaks, which are caused by these interferences and from which the phase information can be extracted.

The required coherence length is typically achieved with lasers [8], or with a LED in combination with a very small aperture of $10\,\mu$m for the observation of $10\,\mu$m objects [14]. Larger objects would require an even smaller aperture. In this case the available light power is drastically reduced. [1] compares laser and LED illumination and reports a strong deterioration in quality for LED illumination, so that 'only the overall shape of the sample is visible'.

An extension of the depth of field and 3D reconstruction of a microscopical volume is possible with holography, for example with digital inline holographic microscopy (DIHM) [8]. Many works apply these methods, e.g. [2] on microalgae.

We conclude that holographic plankton observation is a well established field of research, however the limitation of holography in resolution, field of view and light source apply. The key difference between the two imaging concepts introduced in this section is that the shadowgraph lacks phase information.

3   Restoration of Shadowgraph Images

In the previous section we saw that holographic methods rely on the extraction of amplitude and phase information from the recorded hologram with subsequent reconstruction of the 3D volume. In this section we want to develop a method which can restore an image from a shadowgraph.

For our shadowgraph we use a setup as in Fig. 1, where an LED is used as illumination. In our setting we use a 1 mm aperture in front of a green LED, which emits light with partial coherence. For this scope of imaging, it can be considered as a coherent light source. The camera has an resolution of 11 *pixel* per mm. Therefore an imaging model, which obeys the physical laws of coherent imaging, must be used.

This means that other approaches in deconvolution [10] and depth from defocus [5] are not applicable, because they are designed for incoherent illumination.

Coherent imaging preserves distinct properties of the object, which is an essential advantage compared to the incoherent case. Defocus means that image and focus plane are not identical, which in coherent optics can be modeled as a spherical wave front deformation. Using the coherent imaging model and the WFC (Wavefront correction)-algorithms of [18], we want to compensate the defocus even in very noisy and non-ideal conditions such as a shadowgraph. The WFC-algorithm we choose is the WFC-FISTA (fast iterative shrinkage thresholding algorithm), which includes an L_1 gradient prior for additional noise resilience [18].

The input of the algorithm is the captured intensity image from the image plane of the shadowgraph plus the spherical wavefront deformation of the defocus, which we want to compensate. From the target focus plane light distribution $x \in \mathbb{C}^{m \times n}$ we demand two properties. First, that transforming the focus plane via the Fourier plane and spherical wavefront deformation p_d into the focus plane yields the amplitude of the image plane o_0, which is calculated by the square root of the shadowgraph intensity image s. Simplified, this means that reblurring the in-focus image must result in the input shadowgraph image. Second, that due to the linearity of the optical system the in-focus phase is planar. Neglecting constant offset we can set it to zero, which means x is real and positive [18].

With the transform in the last paragraph from focus plane x via Fourier plane to the image plane o_0 described by function W_f, where matrix F applies the Fourier transform by left multiplication, the first property can be expressed as:

$$o_0 = W_f(x) = ||F^{-1}(F \otimes p_d)x||_2. \tag{1}$$

To convert this relation into an optimization, the mean squared error is considered. The optimization target variable is the complex distribution in the focus plane x which must have a planar wavefront and hence be in $\mathbb{R}_+^{m \times n}$,

$$\underset{x}{\arg\min}||(W_f(x) - o_0)||_2^2 + \lambda ||\nabla x||_1$$
$$\text{subject to: } x \in \mathbb{R}_+^{m \times n}, \tag{2}$$

where $\lambda \in \mathbb{R}$ denotes a weighting parameter to control the strength of the regularization on image gradients. We use $\lambda = 0.005$ in all experiments. Solving this optimization problem results in the focus plane amplitude x with intensity $||x||^2$, the focused image. For a more detailed explanation and an evaluation of WFC-FISTA compared to other approaches, see [18].

The result of our restoration is shown in Fig. 2. The sharp contours of the plankton and its antennas are clearly recovered. The advantage of using this restoration is that a sharp 2D image is reconstructed, even though we lack the phase information, which is available in holographic imaging. For this refocusing through restoration the strength of the defocus is a necessary parameter. The estimation of the appropriate defocus is subject of the following section.

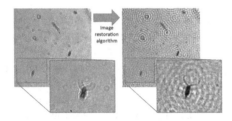

Fig. 2. Restoration results on shadowgraph images.

4   Focus Estimation

While restoring the images with the WFC-algorithm, we compensate the defocus with a spherical wavefront deformation, which has the same effect as if we used a physical spherical lens of suitable radius. Together with the input image, the WFC-algorithm produces a result image, in which objects for which the defocus is correctly compensated, are sharp. Images of the shadowgraph are shown in Fig. 3.

The defocus depends on the distance to the lens, which means we can estimate the distance of objects, by inverting this relationship and finding the sharpest image.

An automatic determination of focus requires a classifier, which is able to distinguish between sharp and unsharp images. Evaluating a gradient or variance based term is good enough for incoherent images, however such an approach fails for real coherent images, where it is unclear if large gradients are caused by

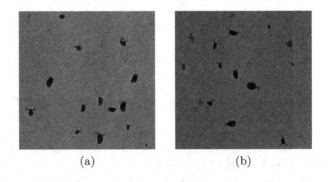

(a)   (b)

Fig. 3. Shadowgraph views of plankton.

noise or if sharp contours are caused by ringing and not by the object. Clearly specifying how such a sharp image is defined, if noise, ringing and non-ideal imaging conditions are considered is difficult.

In this paper we suggest a deep learning approach. Deep learning is a machine learning technique that uses deep networks of artificial neurons and has shown very good results in classification tasks [15]. Our aim is to create a deep learning classifier that is able to discriminate a sharp image from a blurred image.

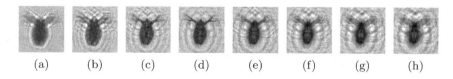

(a)   (b)   (c)   (d)   (e)   (f)   (g)   (h)

Fig. 4. Training images showing a restored region of interest with an increasing value of spherical correction. The input image is in (a), the sharpest image is in (d) (all images rotated 90°).

In order to create a training set, restorations with 60 increasing steps of defocus compensation are saved in a stack, similar to a focus stack. The plankton particles are segmented with Otsu's method [12] and each particle is enclosed with a bounding boxes. This bounding box defines a region of interest, which is isolated, scaled to the same size and saved for every restoration in the focal stack. This means we now have 60 images for each object and from these one or two must be categorized as sharp, while the rest is unsharp. An example is shown in Fig. 4. This selection of 'sharp' defines the discriminative power of the classifier.

With this technique 463 sharp images and a much larger number of unsharp images were obtained. To increase the size of the training data further, data augmentation was used and all sharp images were rotated or flipped, effectively multiplying the image count by four. In the next step, the set is balanced by only using the same amount of unsharp images as sharp images. These steps without data augmentation are repeated on separately captured images to isolate validation data.

For the neural network itself we require a network architecture, which must allow a good sharp/unsharp classification. Furthermore we want to evaluate, if increasing network complexity has benefits for this task. We want to see, if the network is the limiting factor and whether designing and tuning a network tailored to our task is a meaningful or useless undertaking.

For this evaluation we choose the topscoring Imagenet challenge [15] architectures of the year 2012 the 'Alexnet' [9], 2014 the 'Googlenet' [17] and 2015 the 'ResNet' [7]. Because of implementation details, we do not use Alexnet itself, but the Caffenet variant and for ResNet we use 32 layers.

To train these networks, we use stochastic gradient descent optimization with a starting learning rate of 0.01, which is reduced stepwise by a factor of 10 every 40 epochs. The network training graphs are shown in Fig. 5.

We see that all architectures achieve high validation accuracy results of over 95%. Because the sharp or unsharp differentiation for training and validation data is done subjectively by the author and includes corner cases, this number signifies the very high agreement between the neural network and the human author on image sharpness. Thus, the classifiers are very accurate. Some overfitting can be seen in the final iterations of the training graphs, visible by the fact that the validation loss is stable, while the training loss reaches almost zero. This is overcome by applying the early stopping strategy and using the model in iteration 50 as the final result.

Because the accuracy is the same, no gains can be expected from choosing a different network architecture. We arbitrarily choose Caffenet as the network architecture for the following evaluations.

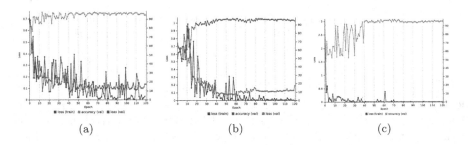

(a)   (b)   (c)

Fig. 5. Network training graphs. (a) Caffenet, (b) Googlenet (c), Resnet.

5   All-in-Focus Image

In this section the process of generating an all-in-focus image is described. The image is generated computationally and all plankton should appear sharp, even though it is located at different distances from the camera.

In the first step a blank image is prepared, which serves as the frame for refocused image parts which will be collected in the next steps. A virtual focal stack for different depths for the entire image is generated, by applying the WFC-algorithm with increasing spherical defocus compensation. For all bounding boxes of plankton in the refocusing stack, the image contents of the restoration with the highest sharpness classification rate is selected and copied into the prepared frame. The pixels in the prepared frame which remain blank are background pixels, hence we insert pixels from the original image.

The result all-in-focus image with the individual best-in-focus images selected using the trained deep classifier is shown in Fig. 6. Figure 3a shows the raw input image. The difference between both images illustrates the power and usefulness of all-in-focus images. Some restoration artifacts can be seen as white borders around some restored plankton objects. Nevertheless the plankton can now be precisely evaluated as it has clearly delimited edges and well resolved antennas. The effective depth of field of the entire shadowgraph system is extended from 2–3 cm to 20 cm, which is at present the size of our observation volume.

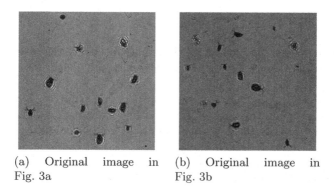

(a) Original image in Fig. 3a

(b) Original image in Fig. 3b

Fig. 6. Stitched all-in-focus images.

6 3D Reconstruction

This sharp image parameter value obtained by the classifier determines the distance of the plankton from the focus plane, allowing a three dimensional plankton rendering. Because defocus effects before and behind the focus plane are symmetric, there is an ambiguity. By setting the reference focus plane a few millimeters before the observation volume, this ambiguity is removed and we can assume that all objects are located behind the reference focus plane.

The defocus values of the sharpest instance in the restoration stack are converted to metric units of depth by observing the necessary wavefront deformation on a test target at the front of (small values) and behind the observation volume (large values). Finally a 3D rendering of the bounding boxes with its sharpest image at the correct distance can be made, see Fig. 7.

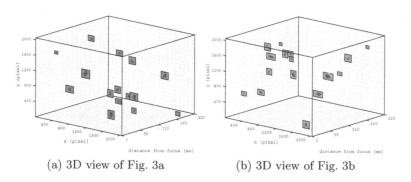

(a) 3D view of Fig. 3a

(b) 3D view of Fig. 3b

Fig. 7. 3D view of the observation volume using only the sharpest image for each plankton.

7   Conclusion

In this paper a novel technique for the sharp 3D reconstruction of volumes from a single non-holographic image is presented, which previously was only possible with holography.

Shadowgraph imaging has numerous applications and we have shown on images of marine plankton that it can benefit from application of the WFC-algorithm. It effectively increases the depth of field and improves the image quality in areas which are not in focus.

The deep classifier shows very good results and allows us to forgo the dense 3D volume generation and instead work with a sparse focal stack of only 60 layers. With the classifier we gain 3D information of the measurement volume from a single image with a single camera. This can be used for a 3D visualization of the acquisition volume. We see that a classifier trained with this technique is independent of the network architecture.

The all-in-focus images allows the evaluation of plankton objects in a large volume as if they were planar in a petri dish of a lab microscope. For our evaluation we used a 20 cm long observation volume, however we believe with the presented techniques this could be extended even further.

Overall, we believe that the single image 3D reconstruction enhanced shadowgraph with low coherence LED illumination is more robust and much cheaper than holography and therefore a good alternative. It has other benefits, such as a larger field of view due to lower resolution requirements, nevertheless a quantitative side-by-side comparison remains future work. Furthermore, our work will enhance the application of the shadowgraph in more areas of interest, for example in measuring the concentration of plastic particles in the ocean water column. In the future, we want to collaborate with marine scientists to support their research in this regard.

Acknowledgment. This work has partly been supported by the German Research Foundation (DFG) Cluster of Excellence FUTURE OCEAN under proposals CP1331 and CP1525 and by the Petersen-Foundation in Kiel under project 385.

References

1. Alvarez-Palacio, D., Garcia-Sucerquia, J.: Digital in-line holographic microscopy with partially coherent light: micrometer resolution. Revista mexicana de física **56**(6), 445–448 (2010)
2. Chengala, A., Hondzo, M., Sheng, J.: Microalga propels along vorticity direction in a shear flow. Phys. Rev. E **87**(5), 052704 (2013)
3. Cowen, R.K., Greer, A.T., Guigand, C.M., Hare, J.A., Richardson, D.E., Walsh, H.J.: Evaluation of the in situ ichthyoplankton imaging system (ISIIS): comparison with the traditional (bongo net) sampler. Fishery Bull. **111**(1), 1–12 (2013)
4. Cowen, R.K., Guigand, C.M.: In situ ichthyoplankton imaging system (ISIIS): system design and preliminary results. Limnol. Oceanogr. Methods **6**(2), 126–132 (2008)

5. Eigen, D., Puhrsch, C., Fergus, R.: Depth map prediction from a single image using a multi-scale deep network. In: Advances in Neural Information Processing Systems, pp. 2366–2374 (2014)
6. Harris, R., Wiebe, P., Lenz, J., Skjoldal, H.R., Huntley, M.: ICES Zooplankton Methodology Manual. Academic press, London (2000)
7. He, K., Zhang, X., Ren, S., Sun, J.: Deep residual learning for image recognition. In: IEEE Conference on Computer Vision and Pattern Recognition (CVPR), pp. 770–778 (2016)
8. Katz, J., Sheng, J.: Applications of holography in fluid mechanics and particle dynamics. Ann. Rev. Fluid Mech. **42**(1), 531–555 (2010)
9. Krizhevsky, A., Sutskever, I., Hinton, G.E.: ImageNet classification with deep convolutional neural networks. In: Advances in Neural Information Processing Systems, pp. 1097–1105 (2012)
10. Levin, A., Weiss, Y., Durand, F., Freeman, W.T.: Understanding and evaluating blind deconvolution algorithms. In: IEEE Conference on Computer Vision and Pattern Recognition, pp. 1964–1971 (2009)
11. Mazumdar, A.: Principles and techniques of schlieren imaging systems. Columbia University Computer Science Technical reports (2013)
12. Otsu, N.: A threshold selection method from gray-level histograms. IEEE Trans. Syst. Man Cybern. **9**(1), 62–66 (1979)
13. Pitois, S.G., Tilbury, J., Bouch, P., Close, H., Barnett, S., Culverhouse, P.F.: Comparison of a cost-effective integrated plankton sampling and imaging instrument with traditional systems for mesozooplankton sampling in the celtic sea. Front. Marine Sci. **5**, 5 (2018). https://doi.org/10.3389/fmars.2018.00005
14. Repetto, L., Piano, E., Pontiggia, C.: Lensless digital holographic microscope with light-emitting diode illumination. Opt. Lett. **29**(10), 1132 (2004)
15. Russakovsky, O., et al.: ImageNet large scale visual recognition challenge. Int. J.Comput. Vis. (IJCV) **115**(3), 211–252 (2015)
16. Settles, G.S.: Schlieren and Shadowgraph Techniques. Springer, Heidelberg (2001). https://doi.org/10.1007/978-3-642-56640-0
17. Szegedy, C., et al.: Going deeper with convolutions. In: IEEE Conference on Computer Vision and Pattern Recognition (CVPR), pp. 1–9 (2015)
18. Zelenka, C., Koch, R.: Improved wavefront correction for coherent image restoration. Opt. Express **25**(16), 18797 (2017). https://doi.org/10.1364/OE.25.018797

International Workshop on
Computational Forensics (IWCF 2018)

Message from the IWCF Chairs

With the advent of high-end technology, fraudulent efforts are on rise in many areas of our daily life, may it be fake paper documents, forgery in the digital domain or copyright infringement. In solving the related criminal cases use of pattern recognition (PR) principles is also gaining an important place because of their ability in successfully assisting the forensic experts to solve many of such cases.

The 7th IAPR International Workshop on Computational Forensics (IWCF) aimed at addressing the theoretical and practical issues related to this field, i.e. role of PR techniques for analyzing problems in forensics. Effort was to bring the people together who are working on these issues in different areas including document and speech processing, music analysis, digital security, forensic sciences, etc.

Like in the previous years, the workshop is a place for elaborate discussions of the academic and industrial works, documenting the advances in the related field and creating mutual collaboration on related areas. Interaction among practitioners and academic researchers received special attention in this workshop.

Each of the submission received for this workshop was reviewed at least three times. The program committee took into account the relevance of the papers to the workshop, the technical merit, the potential impact, and the originality and novelty. From these submissions, and taking into account the reviews, three papers were selected for presentation in the workshop.

The workshop also included two keynote presentations, respectively dedicated to academic and industrial point of view. The first one is given by Prof Chang-Tsun Li (University of Warwick, UK - Charles Sturt University, Australia) on Applications of Multimedia Forensics in Law Enforcement and the second one is given by Saddok Kebairi (Yooz company, France) on Document Fraud: Reality And Challenge For Companies.

Jean-Marc Ogier
Chang-Tsun Li
Nicolas Sidère

A Novel Method for Race Determination of Human Skulls

Casper Oakley[1], Li Bai[1], Iman Yi Liao[2(✉)], Olasimbo Arigbabu[2],
Nurliza Abdullah[3], and Mohamad Helmee Mohamad Noor[3]

[1] School of Computer Science, University of Nottingham, Nottingham NG8 1BB, UK
{psyco,bai.li}@nottingham.ac.uk

[2] School of Computer Science, University of Nottingham Malaysia Campus,
43500 Semenyih, Selangor, Malaysia
iman.liao@nottingham.edu.my, khyx5oaa@exmail.nottingham.edu.my

[3] Hospital Kuala Lumpur, 50586 Kuala Lumpur, Malaysia
azilrun@gmail.com, emeemd@yahoo.com.my

Abstract. Race determination of skulls of individuals is a continually growing subject in forensic anthropology. Traditionally, race determination has been conducted either entirely subjectively by qualified forensic anthropologists, or has been conducted through a semi-automated fashion through multivariate discriminant functions. This paper describes a novel method for completely automated race determination of CT scans of skulls, wherein skulls are preprocessed, reduced to a low dimensional model and segregated into one of two racial classes through a classifier. The classifier itself is chosen from a survey conducted against four different classification techniques. This method can both be used as a tool for completely automated race determination, or as decision support for forensic anthropologists. A total of 341 skulls with variance in race have been gathered by the University of Nottingham Malaysia Campus and used to train and test the method. The resultant accuracy of this method is 79%.

1 Introduction

Race determination of skulls is a field of growing interest in forensic anthropology. [1] suggests the importance of classifying race, and explains that four racial classes, Asian, Black, American Indian or White (along with an 'Unknown' class), are sufficient to describe anthropological features of our population, in regards to forensics. [2] suggests the importance of actual geographical location when discussing race in forensic anthropology, as opposed to a classification. Some equally state that racial classification is of little accuracy due to increases in inter-ancestral marriages [3].

Previous work on manual race determination has shown the importance of features on the skull for determining the race of an individual [4,5]. Furthermore, this work has shown the similarities and differences between determination of the race and sex of an individual from their skull. Race and sex both are described

© Springer Nature Switzerland AG 2019
Z. Zhang et al. (Eds.): ICPR 2018 Workshops, LNCS 11188, pp. 89–102, 2019.
https://doi.org/10.1007/978-3-030-05792-3_9

through combinations of different measurements, traditionally chartered manually using callipers. These measurements are then parsed to a multivariate discriminant function which classifies the skull [6]. A popular set of multivariate discriminant functions are available through software called "ForDisc" [7]. There also exist previous studies on the use of the rest of the skeleton for race and sex determination, including areas such as the fibia, the pelvis, and the general size of the body [8,9].

There exist three areas of focus in regards to determination of a skull: preprocessing of the raw data of the skull, transforming the skull into a low-dimensional space, and classifying the skull from its low-dimensional representation. Preprocessing of the skull consists of transforming the raw computed tomography (CT) data into a three-dimensional model, removing erroneous artefacts from the model, segmenting the ecto-cranial (exterior of the skull) from the endo-cranial (interior of the skull) and reducing the size of the skull. Methods for skull preprocessing have not been studied in depth, though [10] describes a novel method for endo-cranial and ecto-cranial feature segmentation through island detection and K-nearest-neighbours.

The task of transforming the features of a skull from a high-dimensional space to a low dimensional-space has been comprehensively studied. The problem itself is made up of two distinct parts: generating a correspondence between all entries in a dataset and reducing these correspondences into a low-dimensional space. In regards to the former, [11] describes the *iterative closest point* algorithm, in which points closest to each other are assumed to be corresponding points and transformations are iteratively found and applied to minimise distances between these points. [12] describes a similar method known as the *softassign procrustes algorithm*. There also exist some variations of the softassign procrustes and iterative closest point algorithms [13]. These methods themselves provide transformations to align two shapes, though they do not provide actual correspondences. The correspondences themselves can be produced by performing one iteration of iterative closest point between a single reference skull and every other skull, though this method relies strongly on the reference skull [14]. [14] also states that a second iteration of correspondence generation, where the reference skull is the mean skull from the previous iteration, reduces the importance of reference skull choice, though still is susceptible to high levels of variation. [15] explains that, if instead a binary tree of shapes with strong matchings is built, correspondences between landmarks can propagate back up the tree and produce a set of correspondences with less variance on the ordering of the shapes.

Extensive research has been conducted on dimensionality reduction. Traditionally, the task of dimensionality reduction is accomplished through feature projection methods such as principal component analysis [16], fisher linear discriminant (FLD) [17], non-negative matrix factorization (NMF) [18], and their variants, wherein a transformation is applied to the dataset such that the variance between data-points is minimised with respect to a set of new axes. These new axes are called principal components and are scored based on how much variance on the dataset they provide. When employing principal component analysis, an important aspect to consider is the quantity of principal components which are to not be removed. [19] describes a framework to select the most appropriate amount of principal components to be kept. There exist many other dimensionality reduction techniques [20], though principal component analysis has been deemed most appropriate for this application.

Highly similar to the problem of transforming the skull into a low-dimensional representation is the field of statistical shape modelling. Statistical shape models are shape representations of a set of some images or data. A statistical shape model itself is a model, generated by a dataset, which describes some object, along with its variations [21]. They have many applications in medical imaging including segmentation and classification [22–24].

Once a method has been produced to reduce the input data into a low-dimensional model, a technique is required to classify each input into the class of Caucasoid or Negroid. There already exist many classification techniques deriving from machine learning. [25] uses fisher discriminant analysis to classify the sexes of skulls from a statistical shape model, wherein linear fisher discriminant analysis is used to find a linear classifier by transforming the data into new axes such that the variance between classes is maximised. K-nearest neighbours is an approach to classification where all training data is stored and any data to be tested against it is classified as the average of its k nearest neighbours [26]. [27] describes a method for classification through support vector machines. [28] describes a method for classification using a bag of decision trees called random forests.

Unlike conventional forensic methods which rely on manual process of morphological assessment and morphometric analysis, we propose a novel automated assessment method for race determination from human skull based endo- and ecto-cranial segmentation and statistical shape modeling of skull.

The structure of the sections below is as follows. Section 2 describes the proposed approach for race determination which is composed of 4 main sub-stages: (1) pre-processing of 3D CT data to remove artefact, (2) separation of the ecto-cranial and endo-cranial layers, (3) alignment of the skulls to the same geometrical direction, correspondence generation and dimensionality reduction (4) classification. In Sect. 3, we present the experimental results and conclude our work in Sect. 4 of the paper.

2 Materials and Methods

2.1 Materials

This paper has been carried out with a dataset provided by the University of Nottingham Malaysia Campus. Within the dataset there are 341 CT scans of deceased individuals. The ages of the individuals are all greater than 17 and are distributed evenly across the racial classes. Of the individuals, there are 47 females and 294 males, evenly distributed across the racial classes. These have each been labelled according to their country of origin. These countries of origin have been replaced with the label that a forensic anthropologist would apply.

Table 1 shows a full table of the spread of the three classes. Due to an absence of data, the quantity of negroids was insufficient for accurate result gathering and thus were removed from this study.

Table 1. Frequency of each race

Racial class	Quantity
Mongoloid	242
Caucasoid	80
Negroid	19

2.2   Preprocessing

In order to generate a statistical shape model, first a dataset of meshes is generated. Figure 1 shows this process.

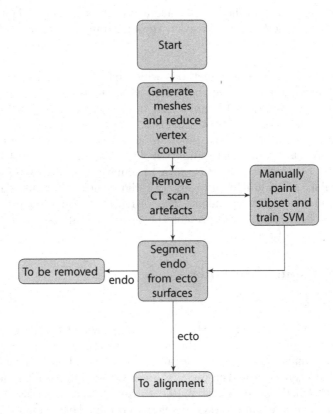

Fig. 1. Preprocessing procedure

Three-Dimensional Mesh Construction and Reduction. Each CT scan consists of a set of Digital Imaging and Communications in Medicine (DICOM) images, wherein each image represents a "slice" of the individual. These DICOM images are segmented by an internal MATLAB tool. Due to the particularly high resolution of a generated three-dimensional mesh (in the region of one million vertices), each mesh is reduced by 10% to a size of between 60,000 and 100,000 vertices, using a mesh decimation tool [29].

CT Scan Artefact Removal. CT scans inherently leave artefacts. These artefacts include small, barely noticable effects [30,31] which have already been removed from the dataset during CT generation. They also can leave large artefacts from the sides of the CT scanner. Along with this, they may fragment parts of their target, leaving some meshes with "floating islands". To remove these islands, an adjacency matrix is used to find and label each connected component in the mesh. All but the largest component is removed. Figure 2 gives an example of this.

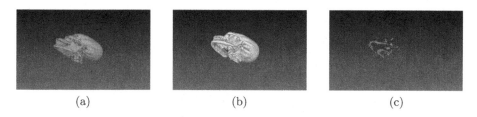

(a)   (b)   (c)

Fig. 2. (a) Skull without preprocessing. (b) Skull with preprocessing applied. (c) Components removed

Seperating the Ecto-Cranial and Endo-Cranial Surfaces. One important aspect of generating a statistical shape model with respect to skulls is that the accuracy of results partially correlates to the amount of vertices on each entry in the datasetheimann2009statistical. Thus, any methods which seek to reduce the amount of vertices is advantageous. As a result of the effects of CT scans on hollow objects, the inner layer of the skull, named the endo-cranial surface, is present with the outer layer of the skull, the ecto-cranial surface. An example endo-cranial and ecto-cranial surface can be seen in Fig. 3. As most racial features are defined through ecto-cranial features [32], a method for segmentation of the ecto-cranial and endo-cranial features would provide a statistical shape model which more accurately represents variances in skulls. A support vector machine to segment the endo-cranial and ecto-cranial features is proposed.

A support vector machine (SVM) is a linear classifier which optimises both classification rate as well as margin between points in training data. More formally, given a vector of weights, β, and a scalar, β_0, as bias, with a hyperplane:

$$f(x) = \beta_0 + \beta^T x$$

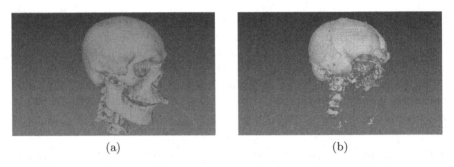

(a)   (b)

Fig. 3. (a) Ecto-cranial surface of a skull. (b) Corresponding endo-cranial surface

Where x is our training data, we wish to minimise the distance between each point in x and $f(x)$:

$$\min_{\beta,\beta_0} L(\beta) = 0.5 \cdot ||\beta||^2$$

$$\text{subject to } y_i(\beta^T x_i + \beta_0) \geq 1 \, \forall i$$

Support vector machines also can incorporate the kernel method, allowing any kernel to be applied to an SVM structure, essentially removing the linearity from it.

Table 2. SVM success rate

True positives	505257
False positives	24281
True negatives	171266
False negatives	23444
Sensitivity	0.956
Specificity	0.876

In order to produce a support vector machine which can segment endo-cranial and ecto-cranial features of the skull, training and testing data must be provided. A subset of 10 skulls were selected, where each were manually segmented. All endo-cranial points and all ecto-cranial points from all 10 skulls were put together and randomly sampled to produce training and testing datasets. In this new set of training and testing data, each vertex is assumed to be an independent data point. The SVM is trained with a radial basis function kernel. Table 2 shows the results from testing additional data against it. It is worth noting that the accuracy of the SVM is not especially important so long as it provides a good indicator of which vertices are endo-cranial features and which are ecto-cranial features, as the overall objective of ecto-cranial and endo-cranial segmentation is to reduce the complexity of the mesh of any skull. Thus, some points missing from the ecto-surface and some still existing in the endo-surface are not an issue.

At this point, faces are removed from any skulls, leaving a dense point cloud.

2.3 Alignment, Correspondence Generation and Dimensionality Reduction

In order for dimensionality reduction to be employed, firstly a correspondence must be produced between all shapes. Given two shapes, a correspondence between these shapes is a one-to-one mapping between each feature on one shape and each feature on the other. In order to produce a correspondence between two shapes, they must first be aligned with each other.

Alignment. Shape alignment is where, given one shape, another shape is transformed such that it is as similar as possible to the first shape. There are two broad categories for shape alignment; rigid and non-rigid, where a rigid alignment is exclusively a translation and a rotation applied to the target shape. A non-rigid alignment can involve deformation as well. We use a rigid alignment to align skulls. Formally, we find a translation matrix, t, and a rotation matrix, r, such that:

$$\min_{r,t} ||s_0 - (r \cdot s_1 + t)||$$

Where s_1 is some shape to be aligned to s_0. Alignment between each skull has been produced through a variant of the Iterative Closest Point (ICP) algorithm. In this variant, any two skulls are first aligned through PCA alignment to produce an approximation. Then, ICP further aligns the target shape to the base shape through an iterative expectation maximisation procedure until some error threshold has been reached. Additionally, if after some amount of iterations the error threshold has not been reached, then the target shape is assumed to be unaligned and is discarded from the dataset. The procedure is summarised in Fig. 4.

As stated earlier, it is vital to select the best base skull with which to align additional skulls to. In order to choose which skull is best suited to be the base skull, an exhaustive search has been applied, where each skull is used as the base skull and all other skulls are aligned to it. The base skull with the lowest average error (including any discarded targets) is selected as the base skull for alignment for the entire dataset. Once a correspondence has been generated between the base skull and each skull in the dataset, the alignment and correspondence process is applied once more, instead using the mean of all aligned skulls as the base skull.

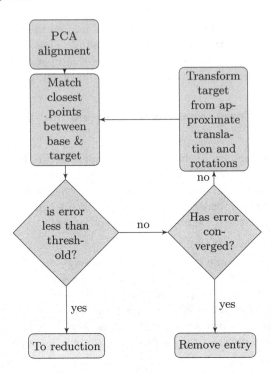

Fig. 4. Alignment procedure. Note, this is executed once with the base being the first skull in the dataset, once with the base being the mean of skulls

Correspondence Generation and Further Simplification. The most trivial correspondence to be generated is one such that each feature on a base shape is mapped to its representative closest feature on some target shape. In a mesh dense point correspondence, features are generally perceived to be individual points. Thus, a correspondence between the base skull and each other skull is produced with a mapping between the closest points in each mesh. This is essentially the same as the expectation step of ICP. This method is sufficient for skull matching, assuming that each skull is of a sufficient density. A 10% skull reduction rate in the preprocessing stage is sufficient for this method to generate good quality correspondences.

After alignment and correspondence, the back half of the skull is removed. It holds few features describing race, as seen in [33].

Dimensionality Reduction and Statistical Shape Generation. Given a set of correspondences between each skull in our dataset, we apply PCA to reduce the dimensionality to a set of principal components which maximise variance in our dataset. The dataset is represented by a vector, S, of size n:

$$S = (S_0, S_1, S_2...S_n)$$

where each skull S_i is a one-dimensional vector, such that each point in the mesh of S_i is three positions in S_i:

$$S_i = (S_{ix1}, S_{iy1}, S_{iz1}, S_{ix2}...S_{ixm}, S_{iym}, S_{izm})$$

A statistical shape model, $\mathbf{S}$ is the summation of the mean shape calculated from the dataset, as well as all principal components (eigenvectors) sorted by eigenvalue, θ, multiplied by some parameter input, b:

$$\mathbf{S} = \overline{S} + b_{0..c} \cdot \theta_{0..c}$$

$$\overline{S} = \frac{\sum_{i=1}^{n} S_i}{n}$$

Where c is a constant representing how many principal components to include. To find the ideal value of c, an exhaustive search is conducted. This model is in essence a normal distribution with mean $\overline{S}$ and variance θ, and expects shapes to be matched to it to follow a normal distribution.

The set of principal components, θ, is cross-producted to each dataset entry, S_i, to form a set of variances on the strongest c principal components. These are then used to form a classifier which is capable of determining race from these components.

2.4   Classification

Given a set of n reduced correspondences, each of c dimensions:

$$T = (S_{0,0..c} \cdot \theta_{0..c}, S_{1,0..c} \cdot \theta_{0..c}...S_{n,0..c} \cdot \theta_{0..c})$$

Along with a set of n labels:

$$Y = (y_0, y_1...yn)$$

A binary classifier f is to be built such that:

$$\min_{f} ||f(T_i) - Y_i||$$

whilst still fitting well to new reduced correspondences.

Different models for f have been tested. These include: fisher discriminant analysis, random forests, support vector machines and K-NN classifiers. Each classifier has been trained against a randomly sampled training and testing set, such that there are sufficient Caucasoid and Mongoloid entries in both the training and testing sets. They have each been trained against 50 different random permutations of training and testing data, and tested against a range of c, from $c = 3..150$. Results of these are discussed in Sect. 3.

New Shape Matching. The procedure for classifying a previously unseen skull is as follows:

1. Process the skull via the instructions in Fig. 1
2. Apply the statistical shape model to the skull to reduce it to a subset of components
3. Apply the classifier to the model's reduced representation.

3   Results

As mentioned in Sect. 2.1, the dataset provided by the University of Nottingham Malaysia Campus contains 242 Mongoloids and 80 Caucasoids. Each of these samples are above the age of 17. Each of the four binary classification techniques chosen to segregate Caucasoids from Mongoloids has been tested against random subsets of the original dataset. Due to the excess of Mongoloid data, the dataset itself is imbalanced. To combat this, measures have been taken to weigh the Caucasoid class so that it has the same relevance as the Mongoloid class.

Each classifier has been tested twice; Once to select the ideal count of principal components for the given classifier (c) and once to provide a measure of the accuracy of the classifier. For the first testing procedure, each classifier has been trained against a random sample of 50% of the dataset, and tested against the leftover 50%. For each test, The statistical shape model used has been generated exclusively against training data. This process has been repeated 20 times per value of c. We vary the value of c between 3 and 150. The classification accuracy is the measure used to compare classifiers against different values of c, where the classification accuracy is:

$$acc = \frac{TP + TN}{TP + TN + FP + FN}$$

Where TP is the amount of correctly classified 'positives', TN is the amount of correctly classified 'negatives', FP is the amount of incorrectly classified 'positives' and FN is the amount of incorrectly classified 'negatives'. Figure 5 shows the results for each classifier. Table 3 shows the optimal values of c for each classifier.

Given the optimal values of c, testing is conducted on each classifier. For each classifier, a 10 fold cross-validation [34] strategy takes place, wherein our dataset is divided into bins of 10% of n. For each bin, the classifier is trained

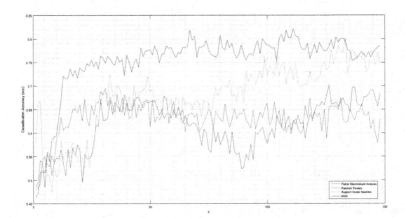

Fig. 5. A graph comparing classifiers to different counts of principal components

Table 3. Optimal values of c for each classifier

Classifier	Optimal c
Fisher discriminant analysis	126
Random forests	31
Support vector machines	133
kNN	111

Table 4. Results of applying 10 fold cross-validation strategy to each classifier

Classifier	Classification rate
Fisher discriminant analysis	0.8078
Random forests	0.8228
Support vector machines	0.7748
kNN	0.8018

against the other 90% of data and tested against the data inside the bin. The resultant classification accuracy rate is averaged across all bins. The result of 10 fold cross-validation testing can be found in Table 4. As with the previous method for finding optimal values of c, the statistical shape model used within each fold is built exclusively from training data.

Additionally, a leave-one-out strategy is applied to each classifier, similar to 10 fold cross-validation, but with each bin containing exactly one element. The results of applying this strategy can be found in Table 5. This table also includes specificity and sensitivity values, where specificity and sensitivity are calculated by:

$$Specificity = \frac{TN}{TN + FP}$$

$$Sensitivity = \frac{TP}{TP + FN}$$

These two measures provide more insight into the accuracy of the classifiers in relation to each class.

The results of the two above strategies show that the 'Random Forests' classifier has the strongest classification rate at a value of 0.8438. However, under closer scrutiny, it holds a specificity value of 0.5217 and a sensitivity value of 0.8955. SVMs on the other hand have a far higher specificity, with a specificity value of 0.6087 and sensitivity value of 0.8188, and a classification rate of 0.7898. Comparably, SVMs are capable of making predictions for both the Caucasoid class and the Mongoloid class, with prediction rates of 0.6087 and 0.8188 respectively.

Table 5. Results of applying the leave-one-out strategy to each classifier

Classifier	Classification rate	Specificity	Sensitivity
Fisher discriminant analysis	0.8018	0.3696	0.8711
Random forests	0.8438	0.5217	0.8955
Support vector machines	0.7898	0.6087	0.8188
kNN	0.6637	0.2474	0.8347

4   Conclusions

Race determination in forensic anthropology is intrinsically an area based on subjectivity. Forensic anthropologists will apply their knowledge of racial features onto the remains they have infront of themselves to determine a valid label it. This knowledge may be vastly different for different forensic anthropologists and is mostly based on tacit knowledge built from years of experience. Forensic anthropologists can instead use multivariate discriminant functions from software such as 'ForDisc' to provide an objective race determination. However, this requires high-precision calliper measurements which would only be able to be performed by an expert.

The method in this paper describes an alternative to race determination, which both does not rely on expert knowledge, and equally does not require high-precision measurements in order to produce an accurate result. The method uses real-life three dimensional data to produce a dense point cloud statistical shape model describing skulls. Additionally, classifiers have been compared to find the most suited binary classifier for PCA reduced point clouds describing skulls.

The final performance of the method is heavily dependent on training data. [21] states that in statistical shape modelling, you will most often find yourself with much less data than you would ideally want. Similarly, the method described in this paper potentially could reach a significantly higher classification rate given a larger dataset. This is believed to be the reason as to why all classifiers were able to predict Mongoloids easily, but struggled with Caucasoids, where fewer data entries had been provided.

The method itself has attained a classification rate of 79%. This rate is slightly less than best case accuracy claims by forensic anthropologists of 85% [35] and fairly competitive with the range of results (75.4% – 89.6%) reported in [36]. This method is not as accurate as forensic anthropologists, however it is still a powerful tool in decision support for forensic anthropologists. It can also be seen as a 'proof of concept' that there is potential for completely automated race classification in forensic anthropology.

Acknowledgments. The authors would like to thank the Hospital Kuala Lumpur for providing all data used. The research (NMRR-15-1761-2777) has received full ethics approval from the Ministry of Health, Malaysia.

References

1. Sauer, N.J.: Forensic anthropology and the concept of race: if races don't exist, why are forensic anthropologists so good at identifying them? Soc. Sci. Med. **34**(2), 107–111 (1992)
2. Cartmill, M.: The status of the race concept in physical anthropology. Am. Anthropol. **100**, 651–660 (1998)
3. National Institute of Health: Anthropological views. Accessed 06 Apr 2017
4. Johnson, D.R., O'higgins, P., Moore, W.J., McAndrew, T.J.: Determination of race and sex of the human skull by discriminant function analysis of linear and angular dimensions. Forensic Sci. Int. **41**(1–2), 41–53 (1989)
5. Snow, C.C., Hartman, S., Giles, E., Young, F.A.: Sex and race determination of crania by calipers and computer: a test of the Giles and Elliot discriminant functions in 52 forensic science cases. J. Forensic Sci. **24**(2), 448–460 (1979)
6. Konigsberg, L.W., Algee-Hewitt, B.F.B., Steadman, D.W.: Estimation and evidence in forensic anthropology: sex and race. Am. J. Phys. Anthropol. **139**(1), 77–90 (2009)
7. Ousley, S., Jantz, R.: Fordisc 3. Rechtsmedizin **23**(2), 97–99 (2013)
8. Dibennardo, R., Taylor, J.V.: Multiple discriminant function analysis of sex and race in the postcranial skeleton. Am. J. Phys. Anthropol. **61**(3), 305–314 (1983)
9. Işcan, M.Y.: Forensic anthropology of sex and body size. Forensic Sci. Int. **147**, 107–112 (2004)
10. Jantz, R.L., Mahfouz, M., Shirley, N.R., Fatah, E.A.: Improving sex estimation from crania using 3-dimensional CT scans. Department of Justice (2013)
11. Besl, P.J., McKay, N.D.: Method for registration of 3-D shapes. In: Robotics-DL Tentative, pp. 586–606. International Society for Optics and Photonics (1992)
12. Rangarajan, A., Chui, H., Bookstein, F.L.: The softassign procrustes matching algorithm. In: Duncan, J., Gindi, G. (eds.) IPMI 1997. LNCS, vol. 1230, pp. 29–42. Springer, Heidelberg (1997). https://doi.org/10.1007/3-540-63046-5_3
13. Rusinkiewicz, S., Levoy, M.: Efficient variants of the ICP algorithm. In: 2001 Proceedings of Third International Conference on 3-D Digital Imaging and Modeling, pp. 145–152. IEEE (2001)
14. Vos, F.M., et al.: A statistical shape model without using landmarks. In: 2004 Proceedings of the 17th International Conference on Pattern Recognition, ICPR 2004, vol. 3, pp. 714–717. IEEE (2004)
15. Brett, A.D., Taylor, C.J.: A method of automated landmark generation for automated 3D PDM construction. Image Vis. Comput. **18**(9), 739–748 (2000)
16. Jolliffe, I.: Principal Component Analysis. Wiley, Hoboken (2002)
17. Fisher, R.A.: The use of multiple measurements in taxonomic problems. Ann. Eugen. **7**(2), 179–188 (1936)
18. Lee, D.D., Seung, H.S.: Learning the parts of objects by non-negative matrix factorization. Nature **401**(6755), 788 (1999)
19. Peres-Neto, P.R., Jackson, D.A., Somers, K.M.: How many principal components? Stopping rules for determining the number of non-trivial axes revisited. Comput. Stat. Data Anal. **49**(4), 974–997 (2005)
20. Fodor, I.K.: A survey of dimension reduction techniques. Cent. Appl. Sci. Comput. Lawrence Livermore Natl. Lab. **9**, 1–18 (2002)
21. Heimann, T., Meinzer, H.-P.: Statistical shape models for 3D medical image segmentation: a review. Med. Image Anal. **13**(4), 543–563 (2009)

22. Barratt, D.C., et al.: Instantiation and registration of statistical shape models of the femur and pelvis using 3D ultrasound imaging. Med. Image Anal. **12**(3), 358–374 (2008)

23. Fleute, M., Lavallée, S.: Building a complete surface model from sparse data using statistical shape models: application to computer assisted knee surgery. In: Wells, W.M., Colchester, A., Delp, S. (eds.) MICCAI 1998. LNCS, vol. 1496, pp. 879–887. Springer, Heidelberg (1998). https://doi.org/10.1007/BFb0056276

24. Frangi, A.F., Rueckert, D., Schnabel, J.A., Niessen, W.J.: Automatic construction of multiple-object three-dimensional statistical shape models: application to cardiac modeling. IEEE Trans. Med. Imaging **21**(9), 1151–1166 (2002)

25. Luo, L., et al.: Automatic sex determination of skulls based on a statistical shape model. Comput. Math. Methods Med. **2013** (2013)

26. Cover, T., Hart, P.: Nearest neighbor pattern classification. IEEE Trans. Inf. Theory **13**(1), 21–27 (1967)

27. Suykens, J.A.K., Vandewalle, J.: Least squares support vector machine classifiers. Neural Process. Lett. **9**(3), 293–300 (1999)

28. Liaw, A., Wiener, M.: Classification and regression by randomforest. R news **2**(3), 18–22 (2002)

29. Kobbelt, L., Campagna, S., Seidel, H.-P.: A general framework for mesh decimation. In: Graphics Interface, vol. 98, pp. 43–50 (1998)

30. Sijbers, J., Postnov, A.: Reduction of ring artefacts in high resolution micro-CT reconstructions. Phys. Med. Biol. **49**(14), N247 (2004)

31. Glover, G.H., Pelc, N.J.: An algorithm for the reduction of metal clip artifacts in CT reconstructions. Med. Phys. **8**(6), 799–807 (1981)

32. Ilayperuma, I.: Evaluation of cephalic indices: a clue for racial and sex diversity. Int. J. Morphol. **29**, 112–117 (2011)

33. Hu, Y., et al.: A hierarchical dense deformable model for 3D face reconstruction from skull. Multimed. Tools Appl. **64**(2), 345–364 (2013)

34. Kohavi, R., et al.: A study of cross-validation and bootstrap for accuracy estimation and model selection. In: IJCAI, Stanford, CA, vol. 14, pp. 1137–1145 (1995)

35. Cranial features and race. http://johnhawks.net/explainer/laboratory/race-cranium/. Accessed 04 Apr 2017

36. Spradley, M.K., Hefner, J.T., Anderson, B.: Ancestry assessment using random forest modeling. J. Forensic Sci. **59**(3), 583–589 (2014)

Anchored Kernel Hashing for Cancelable Template Protection for Cross-Spectral Periocular Data

Kiran B. Raja[1,2(✉)], R. Raghavendra[2], and Christoph Busch[2]

[1] University of South-Eastern Norway (USN), Kongsberg, Norway
kiran.raja@usn.no
[2] Norwegian Biometrics Laboratory, NTNU - Gjøvik, Gjøvik, Norway
{kiran.raja,raghavendra.ramachandra,christoph.busch}@ntnu.no

Abstract. Periocular characteristics is gaining prominence in biometric systems and surveillance systems that operate either in NIR spectrum or visible spectrum. While the ocular information can be well utilized, there exists a challenge to compare images from different spectra such as Near-Infra-Red (NIR) versus Visible spectrum (VIS). In addition, the ocular biometric templates from both NIR and VIS domain need to be protected after the extraction of features to avoid the leakage or linkability of biometric data. In this work, we explore a new approach based on anchored kernel hashing to obtain a cancelable biometric template that is both discriminative for recognition purposes while preserving privacy. The key benefit is that the proposed approach not only works for both NIR and the Visible spectrum, it can also be used with good accuracy for cross-spectral protected template comparison. Through the set of experiments using a cross-spectral periocular database, we demonstrate the performance with $EER = 1.39\%$ and $EER = 1.61\%$ for NIR and VIS protected templates respectively. We further present a set of cross-spectral template comparison by comparing the protected templates from one spectrum to another spectra to demonstrate the applicability of the proposed approach.

Keywords: Template protection
Cross-spectral periocular recognition · Hashing

1 Introduction

Many of the current day biometric systems are based on the physiological characteristics due to ease of capturing data such as face data in unobtrusive manner. The recent works have investigated the use of periocular region and indicated it's use as a supplementary information [1,6–8,10,13,16,22]. The works have focused on visible spectrum (VIS) periocular recognition, and Near-Infra-Red (NIR) spectrum periocular recognition. A limited number of the recent works have evaluated the cross-spectrum periocular recognition (NIR to Visible spectrum (VIS)) [1,8,22].

© Springer Nature Switzerland AG 2019
Z. Zhang et al. (Eds.): ICPR 2018 Workshops, LNCS 11188, pp. 103–116, 2019.
https://doi.org/10.1007/978-3-030-05792-3_10

The variability of the data from NIR and VIS domain introduces a challenge in cross-spectral data verification and this is acknowledged by many existing works, for instance in [1,8,22]. An added challenge is to provide a template protection mechanism that can be employed in both the domains. Our key motivation remains that the template protection mechanisms should preserve the privacy of biometric data adhering to recent guidelines enforced by European Union (EU) General Data Protection Regulation (GDPR) 2016/679 [2] which does not discriminate the data from NIR or VIS.

According to guidelines of ISO-24745 [3] and GDPR 2016/679 [2], irrespective of the spectrum employed for biometric system, biometric data must be *protected* in a template format such that the biometric characteristic as source shall be remain usable even under the compromise of the entire database. The template protection schemes must also minimize the risks of inverting the templates to biometric raw images adhering to the principles of *irreversibility*. Under the extreme scenarios, the template of same biometric characterisitc from the same spectrum or from different spectrum of any compromised database should be rendered unusable to access other services using exactly the same biometric characteristic. Therefore, it is necessary to make biometric reference data *unlinkable* irrespective of spectrum employed for the same biometric characteristics. While these properties of *irreversibility* and *unlinkability* are accounted for, a biometric system should not compromise in the identification or verification performance, even under the challenging conditions of highly varying data due to cross-spectrum comparison (NIR versus VIS). An inherent need therefore is to preserve the *privacy* of the subject while operating with pre-determined performance of biometric system without any *template protection* mechanisms. Summarizing, the challenge therefore is to protect the data not only in one particular domain (NIR or VIS), but also to maintain the sensitiveness and privacy of biometric data across domains while providing optimal biometric recognition performance.

Motivated by such arguments provided above, in this work, we investigate the template protection scheme that can be adapted across spectrum and provide good recognition performance. To the best of our knowledge, there are no reported works that have provided the template protection schemes for biometric data captured across spectrum. Further, we limit our work to explore the problem in a *closed set biometric system* where the enrolment data of all users in database is known. *The apriori assumption thus remains our primary argument to employ data-dependent hashing to derive protected template.* It has to be noted that there exist a number of data-dependent and data-independent schemes in the earlier works that have been explored for a single spectrum template protection in earlier works. The template protection mechanisms can be classified under (1) biometric cryptosystems [23] and, (2) cancelable biometrics based systems [5,14,14,15,17–20].

In this work, we present a new approach for biometric template protection that is *designed for closed set biometric system (i.e., known subjects and enrolment dataset) but independent of spectrum (VIS - NIR).* The approach is based on deriving the protected templates using the data-dependent hashing approach while introducing the cancelability through the use of randomly chosen anchor points. The key feature relies on employability of anchor points for hashing from one particular spectrum (for e.g., VIS spectrum) to data captured in other spectrum. The hashing approach is further supplemented through the kernalization to maximize the separability of hashed templates for two different subjects (inter-subject) while minimizing the distance of hashed templates stemming from same subject (intra-subject). Given the *apriori* known enrolment set (i.e., closed set), we adopt supervised hashing approach to optimize the biometric performance while maintaining the properties of ideal template protection. Further, to validate the applicability of the proposed approach, we present set of results on a recent large scale cross-spectral periocular dataset - Cross-eyed database which consists of periocular images corresponding to 120 subjects (240 unique periocular instances) captured in both NIR and VIS spectrum.

Our contributions from this work can thus be listed as below:

1. Presents a novel approach of cancelable biometric template protection using anchored points and kernalized hashing that can be employed across different spectrum such as NIR and VIS.
2. Demonstrates the use of anchor point based hashing as a mode of achieving cancelability for template protection. The approach is demonstrated to work for both NIR and VIS spectrum template protection.
3. Presents an experimental evaluation of new template protection approach on a large scale closed-set cross-spectral periocular database. To the best of our knowledge, this is the first work attempting at cross-spectral template protection. The obtained results exemplify the performance of the template protection scheme which achieves the performance comparable to unprotected biometric system.

In the remainder of this article, Sect. 2 describes the proposed biometric template protection system and Sect. 3 presents the experiments including a brief discussion of the database in Sect. 3.1. Section 4 presents the concluding remarks and lists potential future work.

2   Proposed Biometric Template Protection

The proposed framework consists of extracting the features from the given periocular image followed by protected template creation as shown in Fig. 1. Binarized Statistical Image Features (BSIF) are extracted from each periocular image using a set of filters which serve as unprotected features. These biometric features from the enrolment database is used to learn the hash projection function using anchored kernels. Through the randomly chosen anchor points, the proposed approach obtains the cancelable biometric template for a given biometric image. In the similar manner, the learned hash function is used to transform the biometric features emerging from the probe attempts to obtain the cancelable protected templates. The protected templates are further used in biometric pipeline for verification where they are compared using simple Hamming distance to obtain the comparison score. The obtained comparison score for a particular probe attempt determines the acceptance or rejection of the attempt by the system. Each of the individual step in the proposed framework is provided in the section below.

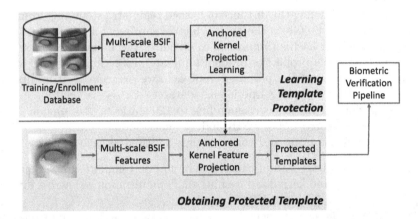

Fig. 1. Schematic of the proposed template protection scheme in closed-set biometric verification pipeline.

2.1   Multi-scale Fused BSIF Features

Given the biometric image (periocular image), the first step is to extract the features. We employ multi-scale fused feature representation which consists of the texture features extracted using Binarized Statistical Image Features (BSIF) owing to high performance reported earlier on this database [22]. The textural features are extracted using a set of filters that provide holistic, multi-feature and multi-level feature representation. Following the earlier works [8, 22], we employ BSIF filters of size 9×9, 11×11, 13×13, 15×15, 17×17 with a bit size of 11 leading to 2048 levels of the histogram features. The features are represented as f_1, f_2, f_3, f_4 and f_5 corresponding to 5 different filters respectively. In order to reduce the difference between the features of images of same person and increase the difference between images of different persons, we employ feature fusion leading to a total number of 10240 features for each image. The equivalent representation of the fused features is given by $f = \{f_1|f_2|f_3|f_4|f_5\}$ where $|$ operator represents the fusion of the individual histogram features obtained from different filters.

2.2   Anchored Kernel Hash Function

Given the features f of an image in an enrolment database of l subjects, to obtain the unique templates, we need to derive r hash functions resulting in r

bit representation. Thus, the objective is to learn r hash functions $\{h_k\}_{k=1}^r$ for r hash bits given $\mathbf{X}_l$. If $\mathbf{X}_l$ is l labelled samples $\{x_1, x_2, \ldots x_l\}$, the similarity label matrix can be represented by $\mathbf{S}_{ij} = 1$ for $i = j$ and $\mathbf{S}_{ij} = -1$ for $i \neq j$ where i and j are biometric samples. The goal in obtaining the unique hash functions can therefore be interpreted as learning hash function H such that:

$$\begin{aligned} \mathbf{S}_{ij} &= 1, D_H(x_i, x_j) = 0 \\ \mathbf{S}_{ij} &= -1, D_H(x_i, x_j) \neq 0 \end{aligned} \tag{1}$$

Where $D_H(x_i, x_j)$ is the Hamming distance between hash of two templates $H(x_i)$ and $H(x_j)$, assuming the binary representation of the biometric templates. The practical implication for a system operating on r binary bits is that when $\mathbf{S}_{ij} = -1$, the Hamming distance $D_H(x_i, x_j) \rightarrow r$ as theoretically there can be r differing bits. The generalized conclusion of this observation leads to the fact that the distance between two dissimilar hash of r bits is r [11]. The goal of learning hash representation is therefore to minimize the distance between two hash functions ($= 0$ in ideal case) and maximize the distance between the dissimilar biometric templates ($= r$ for r bit hash representation). One method to achieve such a goal can be through kernalized representation as suggested by [11] which helps in maximizing the Hamming distance between two dissimilar hash and minimizing Hamming distance between two similar hash through employing the inner product as described in earlier work [11]. We therefore adopt the approach of kernalized representation in this work. The Hamming distance between two templates can further be represented as inner product given by $\odot$:

$$H(x_i) \odot H(x_j) = H(x_i)H^T(x_j) \tag{2}$$

where $H(x_i)$ and $H(x_j)$ are hash of two templates.

For a hash representation of r bits, the problem of obtaining best hash codes in a similarity space S can be given as an optimization problem as given by Eq. 3[1].

$$\underset{H_l \in -1, 1^{l \times r}}{\text{minimize}} \; Q = \left\| \frac{H(x_i)H^T(x_j)}{r} - S \right\|_F^2 \tag{3}$$

where $\|.\|_F^2$ represents the Frobenius norm. For a r bit hash code of sample $[h_1(x), h_2(x) \ldots h_r(x)] \in \{1, -1\}^{l \times r}$ for l subjects. The matrix representation of kernalized hashes can be given as:

$$\begin{bmatrix} h_1(x_1) \; h_2(x_1), \; \ldots \; h_r(x_1) \\ h_1(x_2) \; h_2(x_2), \; \ldots \; h_r(x_1) \\ \ldots \\ h_1(x_l) \; h_2(x_l), \; \ldots \; h_r(x_l) \end{bmatrix} \tag{4}$$

---

[1] For the sake of simplicity, the detailed derivations of the problem is not presented here. The reader if further referred to [11] and [9] for details.

The representation in Eq. 4 can be rewritten as 5 using a set of anchors [11]:

$$h_k(x) = sgn \sum_{j=1}^{m} (k(x_j, x)a_{jk}) \tag{5}$$

$$= sgn(\mathbf{k}^T(x)a_k)$$

where m is the number of anchors chosen from the dataset and $k(x)$ is a kernel function. Considering the Eqs. 3 and 5, the optimization can be written as:

$$\min_{H_l \in -1,1^{l \times r}} Q = ||sgn(K_l A)(sgn(K_l A))^T - rS||_F^2 \tag{6}$$

$$\approx -2sgn(K_l a_k)(sgn(K_l a_k))^T R_{k-1}$$

The solution of the Eq. 6 is provided through Spectral Relaxation and Sigmoid Smoothing as proposed in [11]. As it can be noted from the Eq. 5, the use of anchor points provide a basis for the *Anchored Kernel Hashing* [12] which forms the basis for our template extraction framework.

2.3   Cancelability Through Random Anchors

In order to satisfy the cancelability property, we choose the anchor points corresponding to a specific application where randomized anchors are used for kernel representation as given by Eq. 7. The anchor points for m points are chosen according to a specific application or database, for example specific application s_1 or specific application s_2, generally represented by $\mathfrak{s}$. Thus, the anchor points a is replaced by $a^{\mathfrak{s}}$.

$$h_k(x) = sgn \sum_{j_s=1}^{m} (k(x_j, x)a_{jk}^{\mathfrak{s}}) \tag{7}$$

In practicality, choosing these anchor points can be a challenge to make the templates cancelable and therefore, in this work we propose to choose the anchor points based on a subset of samples corresponding to randomly chosen users which reduces the chances of guessability. The underlying argument for the low chances of guessability is that there can be a number of combinations to select the subset of users x in larger sample set X (also, enrolment set). The set of hash function is finally used to transform the unprotected biometric features x to hashed representation x^h simply by employing the following transformation: $x^h = x * H^T$.

2.4   Protected Template Comparison in Same Spectrum

Given a protected biometric reference template corresponding to $_{nir}x_r^h$ and the biometric probe template $_{nir}x_p^h$ in NIR domain, the Hamming distance between the two biometric templates is computed through measuring the number of differing bits as compared to total number of bits. The obtained Hamming distance $D(_{nir}x_r^h, _{nir}x_p^h)$ is considered as the biometric comparison score.

In the similar manner, given a protected biometric reference template corresponding to $_{vis}x_r^h$ and the biometric probe template $_{vis}x_p^h$ in VIS domain, the Hamming distance between the two biometric templates is computed through Hamming distance $D(_{vis}x_r^h,_{vis}x_p^h)$ is considered as the biometric comparison score.

2.5   Protected Template Comparison in Cross-Spectrum

In alignment with the motivation of this article, we intend to perform the cross-spectral template comparison in protected domain. Thus, given a protected biometric reference template corresponding to $_{vis}x_r^h$ from visible domain and the biometric probe template $_{nir}x_p^h$ in NIR domain, the Hamming distance between the two biometric templates is computed through Hamming measure $D(_{vis}x_r^h,_{nir}x_p^h)$ is considered as the biometric comparison score.

Table 1. Details of the cross-spectrum periocular image database

Camera (Spectrum)	Subjects Subjects	Unique eye Instances	Samples per Instance	Total images
NIR - camera	120	240	8	1920
Visible camera	120	240	8	1920

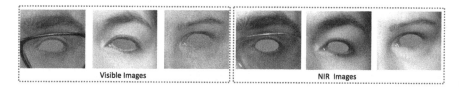

Visible Images   NIR Images

Fig. 2. Sample images from Cross-Eyed periocular subset. Note that the iris and sclera portions of images are masked by the providers of database.

3   Experiments and Results

This section presents the database, evaluation protocols and the obtained results using the proposed approach. The proposed approach is also compared against the performance of unprotected template comparison.

3.1   Cross-Spectral Periocular Database

This section presents the details of the database employed in this work for the purpose of evaluating the proposed biometric template protection method. *Reading Cross-Spectral Periocular Dataset (Cross-Eyed)* [21][2], was used to benchmark the proposed approach with template protection and the same cross-spectral biometric verification system without template protection. The dataset

---

[2] Available by request at www.crosseyed.eu.

consists of periocular images captured in both VIS and NIR domain with a custom developed dual spectrum imaging sensor. The unique property of the images in this dataset is that they are captured at the same time through mirror splitting of the images resulting in minimal changes in pairs of NIR-VIS images. The database consists of 120 subjects in total from various nationalities and ethnicities. For each of the 120 subjects, 8 images are captured from eyes in VIS and NIR spectra and the complete distribution of the images are given in the Table 1. A set of sample images from the database are presented in Fig. 2.

3.2   Database Division

In order to evaluate the proposed approach, we divide the database in three parts constituting *development, testing set-1* and *testing set-2* with disjoint subjects and images. The distribution of the database subset is provided in the Table 2. We employ the *development set* consisting of 10 subjects (20 unique periocular instances, a total of 320 samples) to derive the optimal parameters for the hashing approach, number of anchor point and to tune the parameters of the kernalization. The *testing set-1* corresponds to dataset of 20 subjects which is used to validate the parameters obtained for the proposed approach. Finally, the performance of the proposed approach is reported using the *testing set-2* which consists of images from the rest of the 90 subjects who are not present within the development set or testing set-1.

Table 2. Division of the database for the experimental validation. The development database is employed for choosing the parameters of the hashing approach, number of anchor point and to tune the parameters of the kernalization.

Description	Development* (Parameter Selection)	Testing Set-1 (Parameter Validation)	Testing Set-2 (Performance Evaluation)
Number of Subjects (NIR)	10	20	90
Number of Subjects (VIS)	10	20	90
Number of Unique Ocular Images			
VIS	20	40	180
NIR	20	40	180
Number of samples per eye instance	8	8	8
Total images (NIR)	160	320	1440
Total images (VIS)	160	320	1440

3.3   Performance Metrics

As the focus of the current work is to measure the performance of the proposed approach to protect the biometric templates and to provide robust performance, we present the results in two different terms. To denote the robustness in terms of dealing with symmetrical errors of False Accepts and False Rejects, we present the Detection Error Trade-off (DET) which presents the False Accept

Rate (FAR) against False Reject Rate (FRR). In order to complement the DET, we also present the Equal Error Rate (EER). The performance is also provided in terms of Genuine Match Rate (GMR) versus False Match Rate (FMR) which is derived on the basis of False Match Rate (FMR) and the False Non-Match Rate (FNMR)[4]. Higher values of GMR at a specified FMR indicate superior recognition accuracy at verification. The GMR is defined using False Non Match Rate (FNMR) (%) at a given False Match Rate (FMR) and is given by:

$$GMR = 1 - FNMR$$

3.4   Experimental Settings

This section presents the specific details of the settings employed in this work for the evaluation. All the periocular images are resized to a common size of 128×128 pixels for the sake of computational complexity. Further, to derive the unprotected and also protected templates, we employ BSIF histograms extracted using 9×9, 11×11, 13×13, 15×15, 17×17 with a bit size of 11 leading to 2048 levels of the histograms. In order to derive the optimal setting for kernels, anchors and hashing, we employ the specific parameter as follows: number of anchor points equal to 100 ($\approx> (number-of-subjects)/2$), kernel - exponential kernel based on the Hamming distance.

3.5   Experiments and Results

In this section, we present the experiments conducted in two specific parts which correspond to unprotected biometric template verification and protected biometric template verification. Further, for the case of protected template verification, we present three cases of protected template verification corresponding to NIR spectrum alone, VIS spectrum alone, NIR versus VIS templates. All the experiments correspond to closed-set verification where the enrolment samples are available prior hand to derive the hash projection and protected templates for enrolment set. We specifically follow three protocols for three separate cases: (1) NIR data alone (2) VIS data alone (3) NIR versus VIS data. In each of these cases, we employ first 4 images for enrolment set and rest of the 4 images for probe set.

Unprotected Biometric Verification Performance. Considering the biometric system has no template protection mechanism in-place, we employ the BSIF histograms and χ^2 distance to obtain the performance of unprotected templates [8]. The results from the obtained experimental evaluation on *testing set-2* is presented in the Table 3 for VIS templates and Table 4 for NIR templates.[3]

---

[3] It has to be noted that the performance reported here cannot be directly compared with performance reported earlier due to changes in number of images in enrolment and probe set. A slight change in the performance can be observed as compared to earlier reported results.

Table 3. Verification - VIS images

Schemes	Verification accuracy	
	EER	GMR @ FMR = 0.01%
Unprotected	2.05	96.63
Protected	**1.61**	**93.33**

Table 4. Verification - NIR images

Schemes	Verification accuracy	
	EER	GMR @ FMR = 0.01%
Unprotected	2.51	96.89
Protected	**1.39**	**93.09**

As seen from the results, it can be noted that the EER obtained for NIR and VIS image unprotected comparison results in EER equalling to 2.51% and 2.05% respectively. We also present the unprotected biometric performance when NIR data is enrolled and VIS data is probed in Table 5. As it can be noted, the challenging nature of cross-spectral data verification can be seen from EER equalling to 10.18%.

Table 5. Verification performance of cross-spectrum (NIR v/s VIS) image comparison for various algorithms

Schemes	Verification accuracy	
	EER	GMR @ FMR = 0.01%
Unprotected	**10.18**	**17.80**
Protected	13.32	11.07

Cross-Spectral Protected Template Comparison. Further, Table 5 presents the results of protected templates when NIR templates are compared against VIS in protected domain.

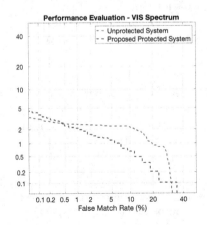

Fig. 3. VIS templates

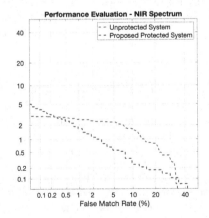

Fig. 4. NIR templates

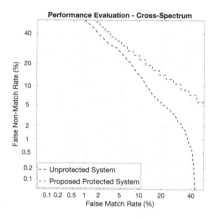

Fig. 5. NIR versus VIS

Protected Biometric Verification Performance. This section presents the results and analysis with the proposed template protection scheme. Along the lines of unprotected template comparison, we present the results for NIR template verification alone, VIS template verification alone and NIR versus VIS template verification. The results of the protected templates using the proposed approach is presented in Table 4 for NIR spectrum and in Table 3 for VIS spectrum which correspond to an EER of 1.61% and 1.39% indicating the applicability of the proposed approach. The obtained results are highly comparable to templates without any protection. One can note a slight performance improvement in protected template performance and this is mainly due to optimized hash representation for the closed set of enrolment templates. The DET curves for the experimental evaluation can be seen in Figs. 4 and 3.

Similarly, we also validate the proposed approach for protected template comparison for cross-spectral template protection as indicated in Table 5 and correspondingly DET presented in Fig. 5. It can be noted that the protected template comparison from NIR against VIS data results in a degraded performance. This is in-line with the unprotected data comparison from NIR to VIS data which is already a challenging task. We provide the arguments for performance in the section below.

3.6   Discussion

The set of observations from the experimental results are listed herewith:

- It can be observed from the obtained results, the proposed approach of template protection is agnostic of the spectrum, i.e., can be used for NIR or VIS spectrum. The template protection scheme performs with better accuracy that is comparable to unprotected templates when both enrolment and probe data emerge from the same spectrum in the closed-set. This can be attributed to optimized hash representation for closed-set enrolment data.

- However, the challenge of verifying the templates from NIR against VIS can be evidently seen with the drop in performance, both in protected and unprotected domain. The performance degradation is seen in both the cases with a very high EER.
- Although the EER is reasonably high (10.18%, 13.32% for unprotected and protected template comparison respectively), the GMR in the cross-spectral comparison of both unprotected and protected data are very low indicating the need for robust methods and further investigations.

Potential future works can investigate on joint template learning using both NIR and VIS images so that common features across both domain are identified. Another direction is to adapt the approach from closed-set biometric system to open-set biometric system. This implies investigating data-independent template protection mechanisms that can be used in both spectrum and cross-spectrum biometric systems.

4   Conclusion

Template protection in biometric applications are important to preserve the privacy and sensitiveness of the biometric data. The challenge in cross-spectral applications is that they provide different kind of data and thus, a common template protection algorithm may not work for optimally for both NIR and VIS spectrum. Further, it is necessary to obtain good biometric performance even when the templates are compared from different spectrum. In this work, we have presented a new template protection technique based on anchored kernel hashing which works for data from both VIS and NIR spectrum. The proposed approach being highly cancelable, provides privacy protection for biometric templates. The detailed set of experiments on the large scale cross-spectral biometric dataset has demonstrated promising results for template protection for both NIR and VIS spectrum. The obtained protected templates using the proposed approach have provided a performance of EER lesser than 2% for both VIS and NIR spectrum data indicating the applicability of anchored kernel hashing. The limited applicability is also demonstrated for cross-spectral protected template verification which reflected the need for further investigations.

Future works in this direction include in evaluating the strengths of proposed privacy preserving template protection schemes by incorporating new security and privacy analysis. Another future work can be in the direction of open-set biometric data where the enrolment images are not available while learning the hashing space. The scalability of proposed approach can be evaluated for handling the changes due to open-set data or unconstrained data for template protection, especially in cross-spectral imaging scenario.

Acknowledgement. This work is partially carried out under the funding of the Research Council of Norway (Grant No. IKTPLUSS 248030/O70).

References

1. Alonso-Fernandez, F., Mikaelyan, A., Bigun, J.: Comparison and fusion of multiple iris and periocular matchers using near-infrared and visible images. In: 2015 International Workshop on Biometrics and Forensics (IWBF), pp. 1–6. IEEE (2015)
2. European Council: Regulation of the european parliament and of the council on the protection of individuals with regard to the processing of personal data and on the free movement of such data (general data protection regulation), April 2016
3. ISO/IEC JTC1 SC27 Security Techniques: ISO/IEC 24745:2011. information technology - security techniques - biometric information protection (2011)
4. ISO/IEC TC JTC1 SC37 Biometrics: ISO/IEC 19795–1:2006. Information Technology–Biometric Performance Testing and Reporting–Part 1: Principles and Framework. International Organization for Standardization and International Electrotechnical Committee, March 2006
5. Jin, A.T.B., Ling, D.N.C., Goh, A.: Biohashing: two factor authentication featuring fingerprint data and tokenised random number. Pattern Recogn. **37**(11), 2245–2255 (2004)
6. Raja, K.B., Raghavendra, R., Busch, C.: Binarized statistical features for improved iris and periocular recognition in visible spectrum. In: Proceedings of IWBF, pp. 1–6 (2014)
7. Raja, K.B., Raghavendra, R., Busch, C.: Collaborative representation of deep sparse filtered feature for robust verification of smartphone periocular images. In: 23rd IEEE International Conference on Image Processing, ICIP 2016, pp. 1–5, October 2016
8. Raja, K.B., Raghavendra, R., Busch, C.: Cross-spectrum periocular authentication for nir and visible images using bank of statistical filters. In: 2016 IEEE International Conference on Imaging Systems and Techniques (IST), pp. 227–231. IEEE (2016)
9. Raja, K.B., Raghavendra, R., Busch, C.: Towards protected and cancelable multispectral face templates using feature fusion and kernalized hashing. In: International Conference on Information Fusion (IFIP-FUSION), pp. 1–8. IEEE (2018)
10. Raja, K.B., Raghavendra, R., Stokkenes, M., Busch, C.: Smartphone authentication system using periocular biometrics. In: 2014 International Conference on Biometrics Special Interest Group, pp. 27–38. IEEE (2014)
11. Liu, W., Wang, J., Ji, R., Jiang, Y.G., Chang, S.F.: Supervised hashing with kernels. In: 2012 IEEE Conference on Computer Vision and Pattern Recognition (CVPR), pp. 2074–2081. IEEE (2012)
12. Liu, W., Wang, J., Kumar, S., Chang, S.F.: Hashing with graphs. In: Proceedings of the 28th International Conference on Machine Learning (ICML 2011), pp. 1–8. Citeseer (2011)
13. Park, U., Ross, A., Jain, A.K.: Periocular biometrics in the visible spectrum: a feasibility study. In: 3rd IEEE International Conference on Biometrics: Theory, Applications, and Systems, BTAS 2009, pp. 1–6 (2009)
14. Patel, V.M., Ratha, N.K., Chellappa, R.: Cancelable biometrics: a review. IEEE Sig. Process. Mag. **32**(5), 54–65 (2015)
15. Pillai, J.K., Patel, V.M., Chellappa, R., Ratha, N.K.: Secure and robust iris recognition using random projections and sparse representations. IEEE Trans. Pattern Anal. Mach. Intell. **33**(9), 1877–1893 (2011)
16. Raghavendra, R., Raja, K.B., Yang, B., Busch, C.: Combining iris and periocular recognition using light field camera. In: 2nd IAPR Asian Conference on Pattern Recognition, ACPR 2013. IEEE (2013)

17. Ratha, N.K., Chikkerur, S., Connell, J.H., Bolle, R.M.: Generating cancelable fingerprint templates. IEEE Trans. Pattern Anal. Mach. Intell. **29**(4), 561–572 (2007)
18. Ratha, N.K., Connell, J.H., Bolle, R.M.: Enhancing security and privacy in biometrics-based authentication systems. IBM Syst. J. **40**(3), 614–634 (2001)
19. Rathgeb, C., Breitinger, F., Busch, C.: Alignment-free cancelable iris biometric templates based on adaptive bloom filters. In: Proceedings of 2013 International Conference on Biometrics, ICB 2013 (2013). https://doi.org/10.1109/ICB.2013.6612976
20. Rathgeb, C., Gomez-Barrero, M., Busch, C., Galbally, J., Fierrez, J.: Towards cancelable multi-biometrics based on bloom filters: a case study on feature level fusion of face and iris. In: 2015 IWBF, pp. 1–6, March 2015. https://doi.org/10.1109/IWBF.2015.7110225
21. Sequeira, A.F., Chen, L., Wild, P., Radu, P., Ferryman, J.: Cross-Eyed: Reading Cross-Spectrum Iris/Periocular Dataset (2016). www.crosseyed.eu
22. Sequeira, A., et al.: Cross-eyed-cross-spectral iris/periocular recognition database and competition. In: 2016 International Conference of the Biometrics Special Interest Group (BIOSIG), pp. 1–5. IEEE (2016)
23. Uludag, U., Pankanti, S., Prabhakar, S., Jain, A.K.: Biometric cryptosystems: issues and challenges. Proc. IEEE **92**(6), 948–960 (2004)

Categorization of Document Image Tampering Techniques and How to Identify Them

Francisco Cruz[1(✉)], Nicolas Sidère[1], Mickaël Coustaty[1],
Vincent Poulain d'Andecy[1,2], and Jean-Marc Ogier[1]

[1] L3i Laboratoire, Université de La Rochelle, La Rochelle, France
{francisco.cruz,nicolas.sidere,mickael.coustaty,
vincent.poulaindAndecy,jean-marc.ogier}@univ-lr.fr
[2] Yooz, Aimargues, France
vincent.poulaindAndecy@yooz.fr

Abstract. We present in a descriptive way the first results of our study of the problem of document image tampering detection. We aim at helping the community by establishing certain guidelines in what refers to the categorization and targeting of this problem. We propose a categorization of the main types of forgeries performed by a direct manipulation of the document image. That applies to most of the cases we observed in real world forged documents according to our sources from external private companies. In addition, we describe a set of visual clues result of these tampering operations that can be addressed when developing automatic methods for its detection.

Keywords: Forensics · Document security · Document analysis

1 Introduction

Detection of tampered images has been an active topic within the forensics community way earlier than the surge of digital images. The surge of new acquisition devices and image processing techniques has been a double-edged sword for the progress on this field. While there have been important achievements on tampering detection in the last decades, now the forgers also have way more resources to conduct more realistic forgeries.

In this paper we address the particular case of document image tampering. While this problem shares most of the theory developed for images in general, documents have many particularities that can be used in our favor to develop algorithms devised for this problem [1].

Document image tampering is a relevant problem in terms of negative economic impact for governmental offices and private companies. Not only companies related with banks or insurance are targets of this practice, but also medium and small companies have reported some of these activities in the last years with

© Springer Nature Switzerland AG 2019
Z. Zhang et al. (Eds.): ICPR 2018 Workshops, LNCS 11188, pp. 117–124, 2019.
https://doi.org/10.1007/978-3-030-05792-3_11

a large economic impact. The current easiness for editing an image has fostered the tampering of documents such as payslips, invoices, contracts or identification cards, although any other may be target of this practice. The heterogeneity in types of documents is one of the main problems when facing this task, and often it is required to develop ad-hoc methods for each case and it is difficult to provide generic solutions.

The development of automatic tools for document forgery detection has been focused on both the incorporation of security mechanisms and the detection of tampered areas. Security mechanisms comprises watermarks, hashing signatures, or physical elements as we can find on paper money, among others. Detection of tampered zones of a document image has been mainly tackled by computer vision and machine learning techniques. In this paper we focus on the latest type.

We focus on the problem of detecting tampered regions from heterogeneous documents. The main contribution of this paper is to provide an initial categorization of the particularities of this task and to highlight a set of visual clues that are present in general in tampered document images. We aim at providing a better understanding to the document forgery field that fosters the research on this topic by establishing certain guidelines in what refers to the categorization and targeting of this problem.

The rest of the paper is organized as follows. In Sect. 2 we describe the different categories we identified on types of forgeries. Then, in Sect. 3 we describe the set of visual clues present as a result of some of these tampering operations. Finally, in Sect. 4 we draw the main conclusions of this work.

2   Categorization of Document Forgeries

The term document forgery gives a lot of space to define which situations we are facing. In this paper we deal specifically with digital document images, either digitized from a paper version or native digital documents. Next we describe the different sources of information we used in our analysis. Then, we describe the proposed categorization.

2.1   Data Sources

To justify the following categorization, we first describe the set of resources used to conduct our analysis. First, we collected valuable insights and opinions from private companies with access to real examples of document manipulations used to defraud other entities. Second, we have at our disposal several datasets result of several collaborative activities between volunteers, personal from our team and our partners, in order to generate realistic cases of tampered documents according to the guidelines provided by them. In particular, we have a set of 200 administrative documents that have been tampered. The full set of documents contains invoices of multiple providers, contracts, shopping receipts, letters, and bank receipts. Each document in the dataset contains at least one forgery. In total, the dataset contains 481 forgery instances. Last, we had access to other collections of documents from previous works in our research group used to develop security systems to ensure the integrity of documents [2]. From these works we have collections of thousands of documents subjected to multiple print&scan operations, image processing modifications such as blur and noise adding in multiple sizes and fonts.

After the analysis of all this data we were able to identify several categories of forgeries that comprise most of the common forgery cases found in real-case scenarios. We believe this categorization may help the community by providing a better definition of the problem and casuistic. Next we describe them in detail.

2.2   Types of Document Manipulation

We present a categorization of the most common document image manipulations according to the process used to perform them. After analyzing our sources of forged documents and validating our conclusions with external companies, we concluded that the following categorization comprises most of the observed cases. We propose the following four categories:

- Imitation (IMI)
- Intra document Copy-Paste (CPI)
- Inter document Copy-Paste (CPO)
- Information removal (CUT).

Next we describe each of them. Note that we focus on the operations performed directly on the document content once this has been created. Another well identified case of document forgery not tackled in this categorization is the named document re-engineering. There, the document is build from zero according to a predefined template or imitating all the elements from the target document layout. Since this method is not a manipulation of a document itself, but a creation of a new document, we decided not to include it in the following categorization. However is it important to highlight it and take it into account for a complete definition of this task.

Imitation
We refer to the first type of document manipulation as *imitation*. In this case the forger aims to imitate the intrinsic properties of the content of the document with emphasis on the font characteristics such as name, size, serif, color, *etc*. Thus, the forger identifies the most similar font in views to replace an existent part of the content or to add new information. Note that this modification can be done either at the physical version of the document (before the digitization process by sticking the new content into the document paper), or at the digital one (by introducing new content using a text or image editor). We show an example of this kind of forgery at Fig. 1 (left).

PAGNY SUR MEUSE
PAGNY SUR MAR

Fig. 1. Two examples of tampering operations. Left image shows and *imitation* operation where the word 'MAR' has been introduced. Right image shows a *copy-paste* operation where the digit '4' has been pasted at the end of the date.

Intra Document Copy-Paste

This type of tampering operation is the well-known *copy-paste* scenario where the forger copies a region from the target document and paste it on other area in order to modify the original information or to add a new one. In this case, the source of the copy and the target is the same document. Thus, the final document image will contain a region that exactly matches another part of it. We consider it is important to differentiate between the source of the copy, since in order to develop methods to identify these manipulations one could benefit from the particularities of this operation [3]. We show an example of this kind of forgery at Fig. 1 (right).

Inter Document Copy-Paste

The second case of *copy-paste* operation diverge with respect to the previous one in what regards to the source of the copy. Now the source and target documents are different, which adds extra difficulty since we do not have any reference to search for as the source document is unknown. Similarly to the previous case, the objective of this manipulation is to modify the content of the target document or to add new information. This kind of forgery will result similar than the one displayed in Fig. 1 (right).

Information Removal

This type of tampering operation aims at removing the content from a region of the document. This process can be done by using both a *copy-paste* operation where the source is, for example, a region from the background, or a crop operation where a part of the image is subtracted. These operations are usually combined with some post-processing techniques in order to fill the 'hole' leave by the crop.

3   Visual Clues

By analyzing our dataset, and according to the proposed categorization, it is possible to establish some guidelines in views to develop methods either to detect forgeries in a general way or to focus on a precise case of tampering. This is possible since each of the previous categories of forgeries introduces a set of image inconsistencies that can often be perceived by the human eye. In this section we describe the set of visual clues produced by the alteration of the image. Some of these artifacts can be more or less visible to the human eye as we will show, but they can always be exploited by automatic systems for its detection.

Considering that an original and genuine document should have a homogeneous pattern according to its layout, all visual inconsistencies should be considered as possible relevant clues. The list of clues we describe here comes from a study we conducted on the set of documents described in the previous section. Note that the results of this study are open to new categories, since are very dependent of the type of document and the tools used. However, from our experience and from the opinions from our partners, we consider it provides an adequate representation of the problem and establish preliminary guidelines for the community. We categorize them in two main categories:

- Inconsistencies on the morphology of characters.
- Inconsistencies on document texture.

In the next subsections we will describe each of them, as well as illustrate some of the most common types according to examples extracted from our database.

Fig. 2. Two examples of visual clues. Left image shows an example of alignment discrepancy where the number '1' has been pasted in an incorrect position. Right image shows a size discrepancy at the central number '4'.

3.1   Morphology

Morphology alterations are one of the most clear indicators when looking for manipulations [4–7]. We consider in this category discrepancies in alignment, size, skew and shape of text components. For clarity purposes we display captions at word level, but note that the same effect can be produced at character and text line level.

Alignment
An alignment discrepancy is produced when the forged character is located outside the word range defined by its base-line and top-line. The same concept can be applied at line level for forged words. We can also include in this category miss-alignments produced at the horizontal inter-character space and interline

space, however these scenarios are usually more difficult to identify correctly since they may be part of the document layout. In that case, to avoid false positives it is required to perform a high-level analysis of the document (layout segmentation, semantic analysis, etc.). We show an example of character miss-alignment in Fig. 2 (left).

Size

Size discrepancy refers to a divergence in size between a forged text entity and its surrounding ones. This can be observed at word level when a character or set of characters stand out in size with respect to the rest, and at text line level, if a word or set of words do not share the same size features. Again, one has to be careful to not mislead this discrepancy with a layout detail. The incorporation in this scenario of neighboring information has been a useful strategy to deal with this issue. We show an example of size discrepancy in Fig. 2 (right).

Skew

Skew discrepancies are observed when the orientation of a text entity do not match the orientation of the text entity where it belong. This can occur at character level within a word, a word within a text line, or a text line within a paragraph. An analysis of the surrounding elements is also required to validate this feature. We show an example in Fig. 3 (left).

Fig. 3. Two examples of visual clues. Left image shows a skew discrepancy in the number '7'. Right image shows a shape inconsistency where number '9' has been copied and cropped out the number '0'.

Shape

We refer as shape discrepancy to the case where a character has a different shape compared to another equal symbol. Assuming two characters with the same font type, they have to have the same shape. A discrepancy in this context can be a good indicator of manipulation. Usually this effect is produced when a region is pasted near another character, and the background area crops a part of it. We show an example in Fig. 3 (right).

3.2 Texture

Texture descriptors have been widely use in the forensics literature to identify manipulations in natural images [8]. The same applies to the case of document images [9], however, do to the nature of the content from a document image, we can highlight some particular features which are very useful to identify possible forgeries. In the following, we describe color divergences, blur and noise, and inconsistencies in the background.

Color Divergence

Color divergences at word and text line level are relevant indicators of a possible manipulation. This is usually produced when the forger performs an *imitation* or a *copy-paste* operation from a region with different color or gray level intensity. In order to detect this discrepancy it is required to perform a comparison with neighboring areas as well as basic layout analysis in order to avoid comparing different semantic regions than may differ in color (titles, table and form fields, etc.). We show an example in Fig. 4 (left).

Blur and Noise

Blur and noise discrepancies can be also produced after an *imitation* or *copy-paste* operation. Similarly to the previous case, an uniform blur is expected within regions of the document. Significant changes in the blur gradient or the apparition of noise around a character or word may be an indication of a tampered area. We show an example in Fig. 4 (center).

Fig. 4. Examples of color (left), blur (center), and background (right) inconsistencies.

Background Incoherence

Every operation from our forgery categorization is susceptible to leave some traces at background level. This traces can be present at both frequency and spatial domains, thus, by analyzing incoherences at background texture or color one can be able to identify suspicious areas. We show an example in Fig. 4 (right).

4   Conclusion

In this paper we presented the initial results of our study of the problem of document image tampering detection. These results may help to the community by establishing certain guidelines in what refers to the categorization and targeting of this problem.

We presented a categorization of the types of forgeries usually performed on document images. We focused on the type of tampering result of a direct modification of the document image content. From our collaboration with third parties from private companies, and the experience of previous works on document security, we proposed four categories of forgeries that apply to most of the cases we observed in real world manipulations of this type.

In addition we described some of the most frequent visual clues that can be addressed when developing automatic methods for the detection of these forgeries. We presented two main groups of visual clues, regarding morphology and texture features.

Acknowledgments. This project has been granted by the Region Nouvelle Aquitaine and European Union supporting the project "Securdoc: développement d'un prototype de détection de fraude de document numérique" framed at the "programme opérationnel FEDER/FSE 2014–2020" (grant number P2016-BAFE-186).

References

1. van Beusekom, J., Stahl, A., Shafait, F.: Lessons learned from automatic forgery detection in over 100,000 invoices. In: Garain, U., Shafait, F. (eds.) IWCF 2012/2014. LNCS, vol. 8915, pp. 130–142. Springer, Cham (2015). https://doi.org/10.1007/978-3-319-20125-2_12
2. Tkachenko, I., Gomez-Krmer, P.: Robustness of character recognition techniques to double print-and-scan process. In: 14th IAPR International Conference on Document Analysis and Recognition, ICDAR, vol. 09, pp. 27–32, November 2017
3. Prabhu, A.S., Shah, Z., Shah, M.: Robust detection of copy move forgeries for scanned documents using multiple methods. Int. J. Comput. Sci. Issues **9**, 436 (2012)
4. Malik, M.I., et al.: Proceedings of the 2nd ICDAR International Workshop on Automated Forensic Handwriting Analysis, AFHA 2013, Washington DC, USA, 22–23 August 2013, vol. 1022 (2013)
5. Bertrand, R., Gomez-Krämer, P., Terrades, O.R., Franco, P., Ogier, J.-M.: A system based on intrinsic features for fraudulent document detection. In: 12th International Conference on Document Analysis and Recognition, Washington, DC, United States, vol. 12, pp. 106–110 (2013)
6. van Beusekom, J., Shafait, F., Breuel, T.M.: Document signature using intrinsic features for counterfeit detection. In: Srihari, S.N., Franke, K. (eds.) IWCF 2008. LNCS, vol. 5158, pp. 47–57. Springer, Heidelberg (2008). https://doi.org/10.1007/978-3-540-85303-9_5
7. van Beusekom, J., Shafait, F., Breuel, T.M.: Text-line examination for document forgery detection. Int. J. Doc. Anal. Recogn. (IJDAR) **16**(2), 189–207 (2013)
8. Sencar, H.T., Memon, N.: Overview of state-of-the-art in digital image forensics, pp. 325–347
9. Cruz, F., Sidre, N., Coustaty, M., Poulain D'Andecy, V., Ogier, J.M.: Local binary patterns for document forgery detection. In 14th IAPR International Conference on Document Analysis and Recognition, ICDAR, pp. 1223–1228, November 2017

Multimedia Information Processing for Personality and Social Networks Analysis Workshop (MIPPSNA 2018)

Preface

Progress in the autonomous analysis of human behavior from multimodal information has lead to very effective methods able to deal with problems like action, gesture, activity recognition, pose estimation, opinion mining, user tailored retrieval, etc. However, it is only recently that the community has been starting to look into related problems associated with more complex behaviors, including personality analysis, deception detection, among others. We organized the *Multimedia Information Processing for Personality and Social Networks Analysis Workshop and Contest* Collocated with the *24th International Conference on Pattern Recognition (ICPR2018)*. On the one hand, the workshop aimed to compile the latest efforts on automatic analysis of unconscious human behavior in the context of social media. On the other hand, associated to the workshop we organized an academic contest running two tasks in the same direction. We organized an information fusion task in the context of multimodal image retrieval in social media. Also, we ran another task in which we aim to infer personality traits from written essays, including textual and handwritten information. This volume compiles five submissions reporting high quality research on Multimedia Information Processing for Personality and Social Networks Analysis. Three submissions are associated to the organized contest and two other papers cover general aspects of human behavior analysis. We are grateful with authors, reviewers and the overall ICPR organizing team for giving us the opportunity to organize this event.

July 2018

Hugo Jair Escalante
Bogdan Ionescu
Esaú Villatoro
Gabriela Ramírez
Sergio Escalera
Martha Larson
Henning Müller
Isabelle Guyon

Overview of the Multimedia Information Processing for Personality & Social Networks Analysis Contest

Gabriela Ramírez[1], Esaú Villatoro[1(✉)], Bogdan Ionescu[2],
Hugo Jair Escalante[3,4], Sergio Escalera[4,7], Martha Larson[5,6], Henning Müller[7],
and Isabelle Guyon[4,8]

[1] Universidad Autónoma Metropolitana Unidad Cuajimalpa (UAM-C),
Mexico City, Mexico
{gramirez,evillatoro}@correo.cua.uam.mx
[2] Multimedia Lab, University Politehnica of Bucharest, Bucharest, Romania
bionescu@imag.pub.ro
[3] Instituto Nacional de Astrofísica, Óptica y Electrónica, Cholula, Mexico
hugojair@inaoep.mx
[4] ChaLearn, Berkeley, California, USA
sergio.escalera.guerrero@gmail.com
[5] MIR Lab, Delft University of Technology, Delft, Netherlands
m.a.larson@tudelft.nl
[6] University of Applied Sciences Western Switzerland (HES-SO), Sierre, Switzerland
[7] Computer Vision Center (UAB), University of Barcelona, Barcelona, Spain
henning.mueller@hevs.ch
[8] Université Paris-Saclay, Paris, France
isabelle@clopinet.com

Abstract. Progress in the autonomous analysis of human behavior from multimodal information has lead to very effective methods able to deal with problems like action/gesture/activity recognition, pose estimation, opinion mining, user tailored retrieval, etc. However, it is only recently that the community has been starting to look into related problems associated with more complex behavior, including personality analysis, deception detection, among others. We organized an academic contest co-located with ICPR2018 running two tasks in this direction. On the one hand, we organized an information fusion task in the context of multimodal image retrieval in social media. On the other hand, we ran another task in which we aim to infer personality traits from written essays, including textual and handwritten information. This paper describes both tasks, detailing for each of them the associated problem, data sets, evaluation metrics and protocol, as well as an analysis of the performance of simple baselines.

Keywords: Information fusion · Personality analysis
Social networks · Handwritten recognition
Multimedia information processing

© Springer Nature Switzerland AG 2019
Z. Zhang et al. (Eds.): ICPR 2018 Workshops, LNCS 11188, pp. 127–139, 2019.
https://doi.org/10.1007/978-3-030-05792-3_12

1   Introduction

Computer Vision and Multimedia information processing are fruitful research fields that have focused on several tasks, among them the analysis of human behavior. Although great advances have been obtained in the so-called Looking at People field (see e.g., [2,8]), it has only been recently that attention from this area is targeting problems that have to do with more complex and subconscious behavior. For instance, personality and social behavior are only starting to be explored from computer vision and multimedia information processing perspectives [1]. This is the case due to a lack of data and benchmarks to evaluate such tasks.

Nevertheless, the availability of massive amounts of multimodal information together with the dominance of social networks as a fundamental channel where users interact have attracted the interest of the community in this direction of research. It should be noted that tools for effectively analyzing this behavior can have a major impact into everyone's life, with applications in health (e.g., support for mental disorders), security (e.g., forensics, preventive applications), human computer/machine/robot interaction (e.g., affective/interactive interfaces) and even entertainment (e.g., user-tailored systems).

We organize an academic contest collocated with the 2018 ICPR International Conference on Pattern Recognition[1], comprising two tracks on the analysis of non-obvious human behavior from multimodal and social media data. On one hand we focus on information fusion for social image retrieval and diversification (DivFusion Task) using multimodal information obtained from social networks. This is a follow up of past challenges on diversification organized as part of the MediaEval Benchmarking Initiative for Multimedia Evaluation[2]. On the other hand, we organize the first competition on recognizing personality from digitized written documents (HWxPI Task). A new data set is released comprising in addition to images the transcripts of documents. With this track we aim to set the basis for research on inferring personality from user handwriting (including taking into account errors and the type of writing). Both tracks are at the frontier of research on Looking At People and multimedia information processing.

In this paper we describe the proposed tasks, the associated data sets and evaluation protocol in detail. Results obtained by baseline methods are reported and future work directions motivated by the contest are discussed.

The remainder of the paper is organized as follows. Section 2 describes the DivFusion task. Section 3 describes the HWxPI task. Section 4 outlines preliminary conclusions and future work directions.

---

[1] http://www.icpr2018.org/.
[2] http://www.multimediaeval.org/.

2   DivFusion Task

2.1   Overview

Diversification of image search results is now a hot research problem in multimedia. Search engines such as Google Image Search are fostering techniques that allow for providing the user with a diverse representation of search results, rather than providing redundant information, e.g., the same perspective of a monument or location. The DivFusion task builds on the MediaEval Retrieving Diverse Social Images Tasks that were addressing specifically the diversification of image search results in the context of social media. Figure 1 illustrates a diversification example from MediaEval 2015.

(a) Common retrieval results

(b) Results after diversification

Fig. 1. Example of retrieval and diversification results for query "Pingxi Sky Lantern Festival" (to 14 results): (a) Flickr initial retrieval results; (b) diversification achieved with the approach from TUW [11] (best approach from MediaEval 2015).

Participants receive a list of image search queries with up to 300 photos retrieved from Flickr and ranked with Flickr's default "relevance" algorithm[3]. The data are accompanied by various metadata and content descriptors. Each query comes also with a variety of diversification system outputs (participant runs from previous years), ranging from clustering techniques, greedy approaches, re-ranking, optimization and multi-system methods to human-machine-based or human-in-the-loop (i.e., hybrid) approaches. They are to

---

[3] https://www.flickr.com/services/api/.

employ fusion strategies to refine the retrieval results to improve the diversification performance of the existing systems even more.

The challenge reuses the publicly available data sets issued from the 2013–2016 MediaEval Retrieving Diverse Social Images tasks [4–7], together with the participant runs. The data consist of hundreds of Flickr image query results (>600 queries, both single- and multi- topic) and include: images (up to 300 results images per query), social metadata (e.g., description, number of comments, tags, etc.), descriptors for visual, text, social information (e.g., user tagging credibility), as well as deep learning features, expert annotations for image relevance and diversification (i.e., clustering of images according to the similarity of their content). An example is presented in Fig. 1. The data are accompanied by 180 participant runs that correspond to the output of various image search retrieval diversification techniques (each run contains the diversification of each query from a data set). These allow to experiment with different fusion strategies.

2.2 Data Set

The data consist of a set of 672 queries and 240 diversification system outputs and is structured as following, according to the development—validation—testing procedure:

- *devset* (development data): contains two data sets, i.e., devset1 (with 346 queries and 39 system outputs) and devset2 (with 60 queries and 56 system outputs);
- *validset* (validation data): contains 139 queries with 60 system outputs;
- *testset* (testing data): contains two data sets, i.e., seenIR data (with 63 queries and 56 system outputs, it contains the same diversification system outputs as in the devset2 data) and unseenIR data (with 64 queries and 29 system outputs, it contains unseen, novel diversification system outputs).

Overall the provided data consist of the following (which varies slightly depending on the data set, as explained below): *images Flickr*—the images retrieved from Flickr for each query; *images Wikipedia*—representative images from Wikipedia for each query; *metadata*—various metadata for each image; *content descriptors*—various types of content descriptors (text-visual-social) computed on the data; *ground truth* — relevance and diversity annotations for the images; *diversification system outputs*—outputs of various diversifications systems. For more information, see the challenge web page[4].

Development Data Set. *Devset1* contains single-topic, location related queries. For each location, the following information is provided: location name—is the name of the location and represents its unique identifier; location name query id—each location name has a unique query id code to be used for preparing the official runs; GPS coordinates—latitude and longitude in degrees; link to

---

[4] http://chalearnlap.cvc.uab.es/challenge/27/track/28/description/.

the Wikipedia web page of the location; a representative photo retrieved from Wikipedia in jpeg format; a set of photos retrieved from Flickr in jpeg format (up to 150 photos per location); an xml file containing metadata from Flickr for all the retrieved photos; visual and textual descriptors; ground truth for both relevance and diversity. *Devset2* contains single-topic, location related queries. For each location, the following information is provided: location name—is the name of the location and represents its unique identifier; location name query id—each location name has a unique query id code to be used for preparing the official; GPS coordinates—latitude and longitude in degrees; link to the Wikipedia web page of the location; up to 5 representative photos retrieved from Wikipedia in jpeg format; a set of photos retrieved from Flickr in jpeg format (up to 300 photos per location); an xml file containing metadata from Flickr for all the retrieved photos; visual, text and credibility descriptors; ground truth for both relevance and diversity.

Validation Data Set. Contains both single- and multi-topic queries related to locations and events. For each query, the following information is provided: query text formulation—is the actual query formulation used on Flickr to retrieve all the data; query title—is the unique query text identifier, this is basically the query text formulation from which spaces and special characters were removed; query id—each location name has a unique query id code to be used for preparing the official runs; GPS coordinates—latitude and longitude in degrees (only for one-topic location queries); link to the Wikipedia web page of the query (when available); up to 5 representative photos retrieved from Wikipedia in jpeg format (only for one-topic location queries); a set of photos retrieved from Flickr in jpeg format (up to 300 photos per query); an xml file containing metadata from Flickr for all the retrieved photos; visual, text and credibility descriptors; ground truth for both relevance and diversity.

Test Data Set. *SeenIR* data contains single-topic, location related queries. It contains the same diversification system outputs as in the *devset2* data. For each location, the provided information is the same as for *devset2*. No ground truth is provided for this data. *UnseenIR* data contains multi-topic event related and general purpose queries. It contains unseen, novel diversification system outputs. For each query, the following information is provided: query text formulation—is the actual query formulation used on Flickr to retrieve all the data; query title— is the unique query text identifier, this is basically the query text formulation from which spaces and special characters were removed; query id—each query has a unique query id code to be used for preparing the official runs; a set of photos retrieved from Flickr in jpeg format (up to 300 photos per query); an xml file containing metadata from Flickr for all the retrieved photos; visual, text and credibility descriptors. No ground truth is provided for this data.

Ground Truth. The ground truth data consists of relevance ground truth and diversity ground truth. Ground truth was generated by a small group of expert annotators with advanced knowledge of the query characteristics. For more information on ground truth statistics, see the recommended bibliography on the source data sets [4–7].

Relevance ground truth was annotated using a dedicated tool that provided the annotators with one photo at a time. A reference photo of the query could be also displayed during the process. Annotators were asked to classify the photos as being relevant (score 1), non-relevant (score 0) or with a "do not know" answer (score -1). A definition of relevance was available to the annotators in the interface during the entire process. The annotation process was not time restricted. Annotators were recommended to consult any additional information about the characteristics of the location (e.g., from the Internet) in case they were unsure about the annotation. Ground truth was collected from several annotators and final ground truth was determined after a majority voting scheme.

Diversity ground truth was also annotated with a dedicated tool. The diversity is annotated only for the photos that were judged as relevant in the previous step. For each query, annotators were provided with a thumbnail list of all the relevant photos. The first step required annotators to get familiar with the photos by analysing them for about 5 min. Next, annotators were required to re-group the photos into similar visual appearance clusters. Full size versions of the photos were available by clicking on the photos. A definition of diversity was available to the annotators in the interface during the entire process. For each of the clusters, annotators provided some keyword tags reflecting their judgments in choosing these particular clusters. Similar to the relevance annotation, the diversity annotation process was not time restricted. In this particular case, ground truth was collected from several annotators that annotated distinct parts of the data set.

2.3 Evaluation

Performance is assessed for both diversity and relevance. We compute Cluster Recall at X (CR@X)—a measure that assesses how many different clusters from the ground truth are represented among the top X results (only relevant images are considered), Precision at X (P@X)—measures the number of relevant photos among the top X results and F1-measure at X (F1@X)—the harmonic mean of the previous two. Various cut off points are to be considered, e.g., X = 5, 10, 20, 30, 40, 50. Official ranking metrics is the CR@20. This metric simulates the content of a single page of a typical web image search engine and reflects user behavior, i.e., inspecting the first page of results in priority. Metrics are to be computed individually on each test data set, i.e., seenIR data and unseenIR data. Final ranking is based on overall mean values for CR@20, followed by P@20 and then F1@20.

2.4 Baseline

To serve as reference, each of the provided data sets is accompanied by a baseline system consisting of the Flickr initial retrieval results obtained with text queries. These are obtained with the Flickr's default relevance retrieval system. The testset baseline is also provided. It achieves the following performance: average metrics—CR = 0.3514, P = 0.6801, and F1 = 0.4410; metrics on SeenIR data— CR = 0.3419, P = 0.8071, F1 = 0.4699; metrics on UnseenIR data—CR = 0.3609, P = 0.5531, F1 = 0.4122.

2.5   Discussion

15 teams registered to the task but none of them managed to finish the competition by the deadline. One reason for this is the large and very rich data. Therefore, it is difficult to maneuver in the time alloted by the competition. Even though no system results were analysed, the provided evaluation data and tasks remain open and anyone interested in benchmarking fusion techniques can take advantage of this framework.

3   HWxPI Task

3.1   Overview

According to Pennebaker, language is a good indicator of our personality, since through language one can express its way of thinking and feeling [9]. The personality can be determined by stable patterns of behavior surfaced in any particular situation. In other words, the personality is defined by the characteristics that do not change, and that are independent of the situation in which a person is [12]. Consequently, an automatic method can be use for extracting these patters in any production of a subject. In this fashion, using more views of the same subject can lead to identify complementary aspects of her or his personality.

In this task we aim to provide a standardized multimodal corpus for the personality identification problem. Particularly, the HWxPI task consists of estimating the personality traits of users from their handwritten texts and the corresponding transcripts. The traits correspond to the big five personality model used in psychology: extroversion, agreeableness, conscientiousness, emotional stability, and openness to experience.

The challenge comprises two phases: development and evaluation. For the first phase, the participants were encouraged to develop systems using a set of development pairs of handwritten essays (including image and text) from 418 subjects. Each subject has an associated class 1 and 0, corresponding to the presence of a strong or a weak presence of a specific personality trait. Thus, participants had to develop five binary classifiers to predict the pole of each trait.

For the final evaluation phase, an independent set of 293 unlabeled samples were provided to the participants. The provided predictions used the models trained on the development data.

The complete schedule of our challenge was managed through Codalab[5]. Particularly, the first phase started February 20th and during the following three

---

[5] https://competitions.codalab.org/competitions/18362.

and a half month participants could follow their performance on the validation set. A total of 9 participants submitted predictions for the validation set. The final phase started on June 13th and same as in the previous phase, participant were able to see the results of their approach, this time, on the test set. For this phase, only two participants submitted predictions.

3.2   Data Set

The corpus used in this task consists of handwritten Spanish essays from Mexican undergraduate students. A subset of this corpus and the gathering methodology is described in [10]. The textual modality is a transcription of the essays marked with seven tags of some handwritten phenomena: <D:description> (drawing), <IN> (insertion of a letter into a word), <MD> (modification of a word, that is a correction of a word), <DL> (elimination of a word), <NS> (when two words were written together; e.g., "Iam" instead of "I am") and, SB (syllabification). The image modality was captured by scanner without edition of any type to the jpg file.

Each pair of text plus image is labeled with the personality of its authors. Accordingly, the big five model of personality was used with traits: extroversion, agreeableness, conscientiousness, emotional stability, and openness to experience. Using the TIPI questionnaire [3] with answers of each subject, we could determine the class for each trait. The instrument provided a series of norms to decide the direction of each trait among four classes: high, medium high, medium low and low. For the HWxPI task, we binarize the classes to 1 for subjects with high and medium high and 0 for low and medium low traits.

Table 1. Participants in the corpus divided by gender and average age per partition (train-validation-test).

Partition	Female	Male	Total
Train	209	209	418
Validation	125	293	293
Test	59	66	125

Table 2. Number of subjects by class per trait.

Trait	Train		Validation		Test	
	High	Low	High	Low	High	Low
Openness	239	179	71	54	192	101
Consciousness	171	247	61	64	137	156
Extroversion	212	206	168	125	68	57
Agreeableness	177	241	61	64	142	151
Emot. Stability	186	232	73	52	148	145

The total number of instances in the corpus is 836, divided into three subsets: training, validation and test. The participants were given the training subset with the corresponding solution, the validation set was also available for tuning if necessary, while the test partition was used for the evaluation. The distribution of users (also referred to as subjects) per partition is shown in Table 1. And the information about the users per trait is shown in Table 2.

Finally, an example of a pair of image and text is given in Table 3. The image we provide has the complete letter sheet with considerable blank spaces.

Table 3. Example of handwritten essay in Spanish, its manual transcription with added tags and its corresponding English translation

| Manual transcription | Una vez sali <FO:salí> con un amigo no muy cercano, fuimos a comer y en la comida el chico se comportaba de forma extraña algo como <DL> desagradable <DL> <DL> con un <MD> aire de superioridad <MD> algo muy desagradable tanto para <DL> mi <FO:mí> como para las personas que estaban en nuestro alrededor pero ya despues <FO:después> cuando se dio cuenta de <DL> su comportamiento cambio <FO:cambió> la forma de como <FO:cómo> se portaba y fue muy humilde. |
| English translation | Once I went out with a friend not so close to me, we went to eat and while eating the guy was acting a little weird kind of rude as he was superior to me, it was rude for me as for the people around us but after he realized his behavior he changed the way he was acting and he was humble. |

3.3 Evaluation

We used Area under the ROC curve (AUC metric) to measure the performance of classification methods.

3.4 Baseline and Preliminaries Results

Since we have two modalities we use two baselines: one for text only and one for images only. For the first baseline (B_text) we preprocessed the transcriptions removing symbols and numbers. We keep the tags without the correction (for FO tag) without the description of the drawing (for the D tag). Then, we represented the text using character tri-grams with the TF weighting and an SVM classification.

For the second baseline (B_image) we relied on visual information only. We extracted histograms of oriented gradient (HoG) from the handwritten images and used them as input to the classification model. Nine bins and a cell size of 32×32 pixels was considered. SVM was used for classification.

Participant Teams. During the development phase of our challenge we evaluated the methods of two participants over the validation set. The results per trait are shown in Fig. 2. We can see that while the overall performance of the text baseline (B_text) is better than the participants, for some traits the participants performed better, particularly for agreeableness (*agr* in the figure) and openness (*ope* in the figure).

The first team called P_JR used the scanned image (visual information only) of the hand-written essay divided into patches and a convolutional neural network (CNN) as the classifier. From the 418 images in color in the train set, they obtained 216 patches of each scan in gray scale and then binarized them resulting in approximately 90,000 images. The CNN consists of five convolutional layers to extract features of the patches and 3 fully connected layers to perform the classification.

The second team called P_EC used the transcriptions (text) by using a Bag of Words (BoW) and LIWC features for each subject representation. Then they concatenate these vectors with features extracted from the essay images (i.e., slant, size, space, etc.). The image features were extracted at character level, for the character segmentation task they trained a region proposal network over the EMNIST and Chars74k (handwritten) data sets. The features mentioned above were extracted using the character bounding box and the extreme points of the character contour.

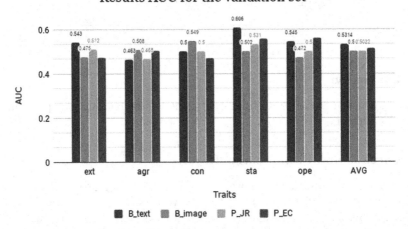

Fig. 2. AUC performance for baselines (B_text and B_image) and participants (P_JR and P_EC) in the development phase of the challenge.

For the final phase, results can be seen in Fig. 3. Similar to the development, the average performance for the text baselines is slightly better than the results of the participants.

Results AUC for the test set

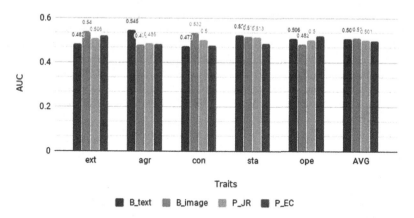

Fig. 3. AUC performance for baselines (B_text and B_image) and participants (P_JR and P_EC) in the final phase of the challenge.

3.5 Discussion

Identifying a subject's personality given a small sample of handwritten text (transcriptions and/or images) is a very difficult task. We can see from the results of this challenge that relying only on the images can be useful to identify traits such as conscientiousness (*con*). Using only text from the transcriptions of each essay can help to identify emotional stability (*sta*) in both subsets as well.

As the results show, both participants have slightly lower performances than our baselines. However, the team called P_EC has a consistently better performance on openness. This team used a combination of both modalities (text and visual information). More experiments need to be done to determine the pertinence of use of both modalities for other traits.

4 Discussion

The two challenges describes in this paper make two large and interesting data sets available to the scientific community. Despite the limited participation the resources can clearly be useful in future research and with a longer time available to experiment this can lead to much more interesting results than in the short time available for the competition. Both resources will remain accessible for research and should help in the multimodal analysis of data about people, in this cases the need for diversity in the retrieval of images from social networks and on the detection of personality traits from handwritten texts.

Acknowledgements. Gabriela Ramirez and Esaú Villatoro would like to thank the UAM-C for the facilities provided in this project. Their research was partially supported by CONACYT-Mexico under project grant 258588 and under the Thematic Networks program (Language Technologies Thematic Network, project 281795). Bogdan Ionescu's work was supported by the Romanian Ministry of Innovation and Research, UEFISCDI, project SPIA-VA, agreement 2SOL/2017, grant PN-III-P2-2.1-SOL-2016-02-0002. We would like also to acknowledge the contribution of the task co-organizers: Andrei Jitaru and Liviu Daniel Stefan, University Politehnica of Bucharest, Romania. Hugo Jair Escalante was supported by INAOE. Sergio Escalera's work has been partially supported by the Spanish project TIN2016-74946-P (MINECO/FEDER, UE) and CERCA Programme / Generalitat de Catalunya.

References

1. Escalera, S., Baró, X., Guyon, I., Escalante, H.J.: Guest editorial: apparent personality analysis. IEEE Trans. Affect. Comput. **9**(3), 299–302 (2018). https://doi. org/10.1109/TAFFC.2018.2864230
2. Escalera, S., Gonzàlez, J., Escalante, H.J., Baró, X., Guyon, I.: Looking at people special issue. Int. J. Comput. Vis. **126**(2–4), 141–143 (2018). https://doi.org/10. 1007/s11263-017-1058-y
3. Gosling, S.D., Rentfrow Jr., P.J., Swann, W.B.: A very brief measure of the big-five personality domains. J. Res. Pers. **37**(6), 504–528 (2003). https://doi.org/10. 1016/S0092-6566(03)00046-1. http://www.sciencedirect.com/science/article/pii/ S0092656603000461
4. Ionescu, B., Gînscă, A.L., Zaharieva, M., Boteanu, B.A., Lupu, M., Müller, H.: Retrieving diverse social images at MediaEval 2016: challenge, dataset and evaluation. In: MediaEval 2016 Workshop (2016)
5. Ionescu, B., Gînscă, A.L., Boteanu, B., Lupu, M., Popescu, A., Müller, H.: Div150multi: a social image retrieval result diversification dataset with multi-topic queries. In: International Conference on Multimedia Systems, pp. 46:1–46:6 (2016)
6. Ionescu, B., Popescu, A., Lupu, M., Gînscă, A.L., Boteanu, B., Müller, H.: Div150cred: a social image retrieval result diversification with user tagging credibility dataset. In: ACM Multimedia Systems Conference, pp. 207–212 (2015)
7. Ionescu, B., Radu, A.L., Menéndez, M., Müller, H., Popescu, A., Loni, B.: Div400: a social image retrieval result diversification dataset. In: ACM Multimedia Systems Conference, pp. 29–34 (2014)
8. Moeslund, T.B., Hilton, A., Krüger, V., Sigal, L. (eds.): Visual Analysis of Humans - Looking at People. Springer, Heidelberg (2011). https://doi.org/10.1007/978-0-85729-997-0
9. Pennebaker, J.W.: The Secret Life of Pronouns: What Our Words Say About Us, 1st edn. Bloomsbury Press, New York (2011)
10. Ramírez-de-la-Rosa, G., Villatoro-Tello, E., Jiménez-Salazar, H.: TxPIu: a resource for personality identication of undergraduates. J. Intell. Fuzzy Syst. **34**(5), 2991–3001 (2018).https://doi.org/10.3233/JIFS-169484, https://content.iospress.com/ articles/journal-of-intelligent-and-fuzzy-systems/ifs169484

11. Sabetghadam, S., Palotti, J., Rekabsaz, N., Lupu, M., Hanbury, A.: TUW @ MediaEval 2015 retrieving diverse social images task. In: MediaEval 2015 Workshop (2015)
12. Vinciarelli, A., Mohammadi, G.: A survey of personality computing. IEEE Trans. Affect. Comput. **5**, 273–291 (2014)

Handwritten Texts for Personality Identification Using Convolutional Neural Networks

José E. Valdez-Rodríguez, Hiram Calvo[✉], and Edgardo M. Felipe-Riverón

Centro de Investigación en Computación, Instituto Politécnico Nacional,
J.D. Bátiz e/ M.O. de Mendizábal, 07738 Ciudad de México, Mexico
jvaldezr1000@alumno.ipn.mx, {hcalvo,edgardo}@cic.ipn.mx

Abstract. The task consists in estimating the personality traits of users from their handwritten texts. To classify them, we use the scanned image of the subject hand-written essay divided in patches and we propose in this work an architecture based on a Convolutional Neural Network (CNN) as classifier. The original dataset consists of 418 images in color, from which we obtained 216 patches of each image in grayscale and then we binarized them resulting in approximately 90,000 images. The CNN consists of five convolutional layers to extract features of the patches and three fully connected layers to perform the classification.

Keywords: Personality traits · CNN · Image processing Handwritten text

1 Introduction

In this paper we tackle the problem of automatic personality identification based on handwritten texts from students [13]. Handwriting is a kind of behavioral biometrics. A writer can be recognized by capturing his or her specific characteristics of handwriting habits. The tasks consists of estimating the personality traits of users from their handwritten texts. Each subject has an associated class 1 and 0, corresponding to the presence of a high pole or a low pole of a specific personality trait. The traits correspond to the Big Five personality model used in psychology: Extraversion, Agreeableness, Conscientiousness, Emotional stability, and Openness to experience [14]. The five-factor model of personality is a hierarchical organization of personality traits using both natural language adjectives and theoretically based personality questionnaires that supports the comprehensiveness of the model and its applicability across observers and culture [11], but in this case we will use their handwritten essays as their personality descriptor. As the classification is based on images, we choose to use a Convolutional Neural Network (CNN) as classifier because CNNs are well suited to

---

We thank Instituto Politécnico Nacional (SIP, COFAA, EDI and BEIFI), and CONACyT for their support for this research.

Z. Zhang et al. (Eds.): ICPR 2018 Workshops, LNCS 11188, pp. 140–145, 2019.
https://doi.org/10.1007/978-3-030-05792-3_13

deal with images as their input and they are capable to recognize handwritten characters according to [8]. In this paper we propose a CNN model that works with patches of the original image; this CNN consists of five convolutional layers to extract features of the patches and three fully connected layers to perform the classification and will be described in the next sections.

2   Previous Work

In this work we present a solution for a new task named HWxPI: Handwritten texts for Personality Identification, so there is not much work directly related to this task. A similar approach is made by [3], they use a multilayer perceptron as the classifier and they use only the handwritten letter 't' of each author. Another similar work is made by [12], they use handwritten essays and divided them; first, sentence by sentence and then, letter by letter, and use a Support Vector Machine (SVM) [6] to classify the personality traits. Both methods mentioned before use a different personality traits model. The baseline method for this task consists of extracting Histogram of Oriented Gradients [4] features from the images and a SVM as classifier. Previous work on recognizing authors of a given handwritten text has been made [15] obtaining a high accuracy. They use a CNN to find the author of a handwritten essay. Another approach was made by LeCun et al. [8], they use handwritten numbers from 0 to 9 and classify them using a CNN. In this work we propose a CNN capable of classifying the personality of the author from their handwritten essays. From this previous work, we take their established models and modify them to be used in this task. In the next sections we will give a deep description of our proposal.

3   Proposed Method

In this section we present our CNN model and the preprocessing of the images. We have decided to name it as Writerpatch. The dataset of this work was provided by the 2018 ICPR Multimedia Information Processing for Personality and Social Networks Analysis Challenge named HWxPI: Handwritten texts for Personality Identification [13]. This dataset consists of handwritten Spanish essays from undergraduate Mexican students. An example of these images can be seen in Fig. 1. The resolution of these images is variable, so we decided to normalize each one to 2000×2600 pixels.

As the number of the images is small we needed to expand the dataset, this expansion was made by cropping the images in patches of 200×200 pixels each and shifting 50 pixels to the right and 20 down, to finally obtain 216 patches per each image. We selected that number based on the amount of text authors have, as some authors have more text than others. A preprocessing method was needed, first we converted the color images to grayscale, those methods were based on [5]. An example of these patches is shown in Fig. 2. We obtained a total of 90,288 images to train our model.

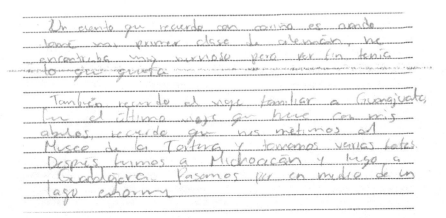

Fig. 1. Sample of the HWxPI dataset.

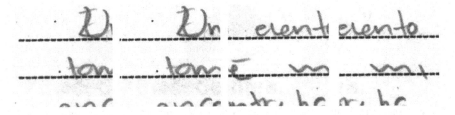

Fig. 2. Sample of patches of Fig. 1.

3.1   CNN Model

The CNN model we used to classify the resulting patches in personality traits was based on the original AlexNet [7] which is a model that can classify different types of images; and Half DeepWriter [15] which was used to classify handwritten texts of different authors. Our CNN model consists of five convolutional layers with ReLU [2] as activation function to extract features of the images such as line forms of character strokes of each author; then we used two fully connected layers with tangential hyperbolic function [2] as activation function to perform the classification and finally an output layer that consists of two neurons. Once we get the classification for every patch, we join the patches of the original image and vote the results of the patches to get the classification of one original image. The total number of classes are five but we built a separate model one class as classes are not mutually exclusive, and at the end we append results to provide the final composite classification. A representation of one layer of our CNN-based model can be seen in Fig. 3: In this representation we include layer names, kernel sizes, number of kernels and the strides of the layer.

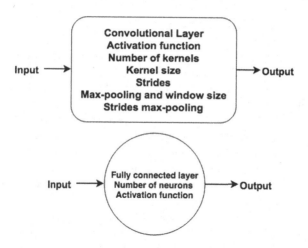

Fig. 3. Single layer representation of a convolutional layer and a fully connected layer.

As loss function we use the categorical cross entropy function [8] given by Eq. 1.

$$H_{y'}(y) := -\sum_i (y_i' \log(y_i) + (1 - y_i') \log(1 - y_i)) \tag{1}$$

As mentioned before, our CNN is based on different CNN models; to create our model we modified the kernel sizes, activation functions and number of kernels used in each layer. Our proposed CNN model is depicted in Fig. 4.

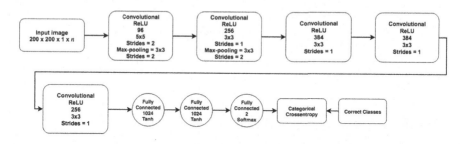

Fig. 4. Writerpatch CNN model.

We trained our model from scratch using the dataset mentioned before using the Backpropagation (BP) method [10] and Stochastic Gradient Descent (SGD) [9] with learning rate equal to 0.001. We used 100 iterations and a batch size of 50. From the full dataset of patches we used 80% for training, 10% for validation and 10% for testing. The input image has a size of 200×200 pixels and $n = 50$ (batch size).

4   Experiments and Results

In this section we describe the results of our model; we implemented our model with the Python toolbox, *Tensorflow* [1] which can be trained on a GPU for swift performance. We trained our models on two GPU NVIDIA GTX 1080; it took a day for training and less than a second for testing a single image. To evaluate our method we use the metrics provided by the authors of the contest mentioned in Sect. 3. Results are shown in Table 1. For this task, systems were ranked by the area under the curve (AUC) measure. We report both the validation set and the final evaluation sets results with our method; larger numbers indicate better performance, except for regression metrics, which are error-based, and thus, smaller is better.

As for the validation sets, other participants using images exclusively, as we did, reported lower AUC results (below 0.5023). Other systems achieved better results (up to AUC = 0.5314) using text transcriptions (not image based).

Regarding the final evaluation set, we could not compare our results with other participants because the competition organizers kept results private.

Table 1. Evaluation of our method.

	Baseline (validation set)	Our method (validation set)	Our method (final evaluation)
AUC	0.5014	**0.5023**	0.5009
F1 (multiclass)	**0.2629**	0.1931	0.2025
F1 (multilabel)	**0.4994**	0.2916	0.2738
BAC (multiclass)	**0.2091**	0.1888	0.2011
BAC (multilabel)	0.5014	**0.5023**	0.5009
PAC (multiclass)	0.0136	**0.0136**	0.0135
PAC (multilabel)	0.5028	**0.5028**	0.5063
Regression ABS	−0.0004	**−0.0876**	−0.1384
Regression R2	−1.0008	**−1.1753**	−1.2769

5   Conclusions and Future Work

We have presented a CNN model capable of predicting the personality of an author given his or her manuscript as an image. We obtained better performance by developing independent classifiers with this model for each class. Because the amount of data for this kind of models must be large, expanding the small dataset into approximately 90,000 images rendered the classification possible in most of the cases. We found that processing the images in patches instead of the complete image yielded better results. Although achieved AUC values are far from a good performance classifier, several approaches for tackling this task indicate that automatically obtaining personal traits from handwritten images is a difficult work, at least for this dataset. Particularly, different sizes of provided images, and the varying amount of written text between different individuals added further complication.

As a future work we plan to experiment with different handwritten corpora, in order to find better kernel sizes, different loss and activation functions to further validate and improve our proposed model.

References

1. Abadi, M., et al.: TensorFlow: large-scale machine learning on heterogeneous systems (2015). Software available from tensorflow.org
2. Arora, R., Basu, A., Mianjy, P., Mukherjee, A.: Understanding deep neural networks with rectified linear units. arXiv preprint arXiv:1611.01491 (2016)
3. Champa, H., AnandaKumar, K.: Artificial neural network for human behavior prediction through handwriting analysis. Int. J. Comput. Appl. 0975–8887 Volume (2010)
4. Dalal, N., Triggs, B.: Histograms of oriented gradients for human detection. In: IEEE Computer Society Conference on Computer Vision and Pattern Recognition, CVPR 2005, vol. 1, pp. 886–893. IEEE (2005)
5. Gonzalez, R.C., Woods, R.E., Eddins, S.L., et al.: Digital Image Processing Using MATLAB, vol. 624. Pearson-Prentice-Hall, Upper Saddle River (2004)
6. Hearst, M.A., Dumais, S.T., Osuna, E., Platt, J., Scholkopf, B.: Support vector machines. IEEE Intell. Syst. Appl. **13**(4), 18–28 (1998)
7. Krizhevsky, A., Sutskever, I., Hinton, G.E.: ImageNet classification with deep convolutional neural networks. In: Advances in Neural Information Processing Systems, pp. 1097–1105 (2012)
8. LeCun, Y., et al.: Handwritten digit recognition with a back-propagation network. In: Advances in Neural Information Processing Systems, pp. 396–404 (1990)
9. LeCun, Y., Bottou, L., Bengio, Y., Haffner, P.: Gradient-based learning applied to document recognition. Proc. IEEE **86**(11), 2278–2324 (1998)
10. LeCun, Y.A., Bottou, L., Orr, G.B., Müller, K.-R.: Efficient BackProp. In: Montavon, G., Orr, G.B., Müller, K.-R. (eds.) Neural Networks: Tricks of the Trade. LNCS, vol. 7700, pp. 9–48. Springer, Heidelberg (2012). https://doi.org/10.1007/978-3-642-35289-8_3
11. McCrae, R.R., John, O.P.: An introduction to the five-factor model and its applications. J. Pers. **60**(2), 175–215 (1992)
12. Prasad, S., Singh, V.K., Sapre, A.: Handwriting analysis based on segmentation method for prediction of human personality using support vector machine. Int. J. Comput. Appl. **8**(12), 25–29 (2010)
13. Ramírez-de-la Rosa, G., et al.: Overview of the multimedia information processing for personality & social networks analysis contest. In: ICPR Workshop Proceedings (2018)
14. Tupes, E.C., Christal, R.E.: Recurrent personality factors based on trait ratings. J. Pers. **60**(2), 225–251 (1992)
15. Xing, L., Qiao, Y.: DeepWriter: a multi-stream deep CNN for text-independent writer identification. CoRR, abs/1606.06472 (2016)

Recognition of Apparent Personality Traits from Text and Handwritten Images

Ernesto Pérez Costa[(✉)], Luis Villaseñor-Pienda, Eduardo Morales,
and Hugo Jair Escalante

Computer Science Department,
Instituto Nacional de Astrofísica, Óptica y Electrónica,
72840 Puebla, Mexico
epcosta114@gmail.com

Abstract. Personality has been considered as one of the most difficult human attributes to understand. It is very important as it can be used to define the uniqueness of a person, and it has a direct impact into several aspects of everyone's life. This paper describes our participation in the HWxPI challenge @ ICPR 2018, an academic competition focusing on the development of methods for estimation of apparent personality from handwritten and textual information. The proposed solution combined information extracted from both text and images. From the textual modality, words, and other linguistic features were considered; whereas handwritten information was represented with shape features extracted from segmented characters. Although the task was extremely hard, we show that the considered features indeed convey useful information that can be used to estimate apparent personality.

Keywords: Apparent personality estimation · Big Five Model
Text mining · Handwritten analysis

1 Introduction

Personality is one of the most intricate human attributes, and it is known to describe the uniqueness of a person. Personality is one of the fundamental aspects, by which we can understand behavioral patterns. In fact, it has been a long-term goal for psychologists to understand human personality and its impact on human behavior [5].

The importance of personality is such that there is a growing interest on the development of methodologies, tools and computational resources for analyzing the *apparent* personality of subjects, see e.g., [3,4]. Although it is clear that automated tools will never replace qualified experts for the analysis of personality. Automated techniques will represent a support tool that can simplify the task to specialists. Is in this context that the *Handwritten texts for Personality Identification (HWxPI) @ICPR2018* is proposed [8]. The HWxPI competition aims

© Springer Nature Switzerland AG 2019
Z. Zhang et al. (Eds.): ICPR 2018 Workshops, LNCS 11188, pp. 146–152, 2019.
https://doi.org/10.1007/978-3-030-05792-3_14

at developing methods for inferring the apparent personality traits (in binarized variables) of subjects starting from handwritten and textual information.

This paper describes our participation in the HWxPI competition. For the challenge we devised a solution that combines information derived from both text and images depicting handwritten imagery. A standard bag of words and linguistic features derived from psycholinguistic studies were used to characterize text. Shape information extracted from handwritten processed images was also considered. We report experimental results analyzing the performance of different combination of features. Although the proposed task was extremely complicated, our results are encouraging and evidence that the considered features indeed convey discriminative information.

The remainder of this paper is organized as follow. Section 2 describes the dataset adopted for the HWxPI challenge. Section 3 presents the proposed methodology. Section 4 reports experimental results. Finally, Sect. 5 outlines conclusions from this work.

2   Dataset

The corpus used in this task consists of handwritten Spanish essays from undergraduate Mexican students (see [8] for details). For each essay two files are available: a manual transcript of the text and a scan image of the original sheet where the subject hand-wrote the essay, see Fig. 1.

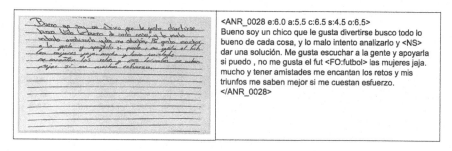

Fig. 1. Handwritten texts for Personality Identification dataset example

The texts of manual transcriptions have tags to mark some handwritten phenomena namely: FO (the previous word is misspelled), D (there is a drawing here; e.g. an emoji, a signature, etc.), <IN> (insertion of words into the text), <MD> (modification of a word, that is a correction of a word; e.g. when the subject forgot to write a letter and modified the word), <DL> (elimination of a word), <NS> (when two words were written together; e.g. Iam instead of I am) and, SB (syllabification). Each essay is labeled with five classes corresponding to five personality trait in the Big Five Model of Personality. The traits are Extraversion, Agreeableness, Conscientiousness, Emotional stability (Neuroticism), and

Openness to experience. The classes for each trait are 1 and 0 corresponding to the high pole and low pole of each trait, respectively. To assign each label in the dataset they use an instrument named TIPI (Ten Item Personality Inventory), this instrument includes a specific set of norms for each trait. Figure 2 shows the number of essays associated to training, validation and test phases.

Set	Number of Essays
Training	418
Validation	125
Test	293

Fig. 2. Data distribution

Figure 3 shows the distribution of samples per trait (left) and the number of traits with high presence across samples (right). It can be seen that the data set is more or less balanced (left plot) among the classes. Also, it can be seen that most samples show high levels on 1–3 traits (right plot). This data distribution could have an impact into the performance of evaluated models. Further details in the data set can be find in [8].

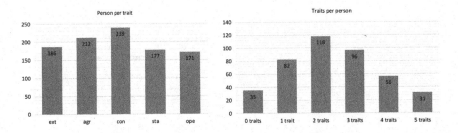

Fig. 3. Data distribution

3   Methodology

This section describes the proposed method for approaching the task associated to the HWxPI challenge. As previously mentioned our approach consisted of combining features extracted from both available modalities. Accordingly, we describe in this section the considered representations for each modality, together with the classification model adopted.

3.1   Text Analysis

An hypothesis of this work is that by analyzing textual information from essays it is possible to accurately recognize personality traits. Accordingly, we analyzed standard features directly derived from text. Specifically, we first extracted the bag of words representation of essays by considering a *tf-idf* weighting scheme. Prior to indexing documents they were tokenized and stemming was applied.

In addition to a standard bag of words, we relied on psycholinguistic features. Specifically, we considered features extracted by relying on the Linguistic Inquiry and Word Count (LIWC) resource[1]. LIWC is a resource that, given a text, analyzes the proportion of words reflecting different emotions, thinking styles, concerns and other psycholinguistic aspects that can be inferred from texts. The considered features include both syntactic (e.g.,ratio of pronouns) and semantic information (e.g., positive emotion words), which were validated by expert judges. The motivation for using these features is a study that previously found significant correlations between these features and each of the Big Five personality traits [7]. For the experiments we used all of LIWC features.

3.2   Handwriting Analysis

Handwriting Analysis, also known as Graphology is a scientific method of identifying, evaluating and understanding personality through the strokes and patterns revealed by handwriting. It is known that handwriting conveys information that is correlated with true personality including emotional outlay, fears, honesty, defenses and many other individual traits. Because of this, we also analyzed information derived form the handwriting images available with the corpus.

Specifically, we extracted shape features from the available images as follows. In each available image, characters were segmented, for this task a Faster R-CNN [9] model was trained over the EMNIST [1] and Chars74k [2] datasets. Faster R-CNN needs the image and the bounding boxes for the different regions of interest. As long as we are interested in handwritten characters we extracted the bounding boxes of each image from both of EMNIST and Chars74k datasets. Then we calculate some shape features using each character bounding box. The shape features mentioned were obtained on binary image utilizing OpenCV3. Initially color images were converted to gray scale images and then into binary images. Then image bounding boxes were extracted by using the trained CNN, see Figs. 4 and 5 and then we obtained the character contour for each segmented bounding box.

The shape features were obtained as follows:

- Height: distance from the baseline to the top most point.
- Width: distance from the left most point to the right most point.
- Slant: calculated from the character contour extreme points, this feature is illustrated in Fig. 6.

---

[1] https://liwc.wpengine.com/how-it-works/.

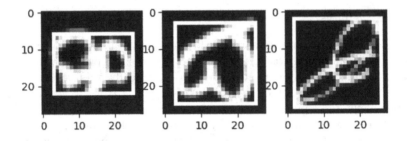

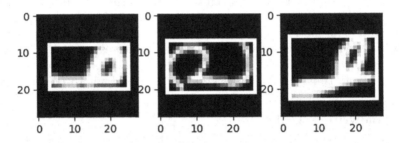

Fig. 4. Examples of segmentation results using trained Faster R-CNN.

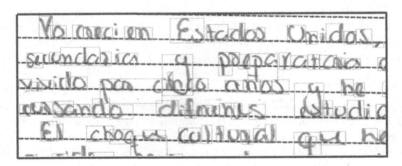

Fig. 5. Segmentation results on the transcript image.

- Space: distance between the x_0 and x_1 point coordinates of the words bounding boxes.
- Pen Pressure: gray level mean of the letter.

3.3   Classification and Feature Combination

For classification we relied on a series of support vector machine (SVM) classifiers. Each SVM was trained to recognize the low-high presence of each of the 5 considered traits.

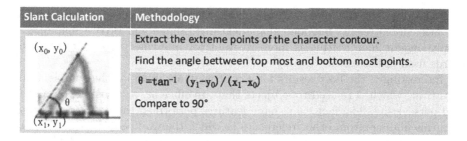

Fig. 6. Slant estimation

Below we report results obtained when combining the different feature spaces available. In doing so, we relied in the feature union functionality of scikit learn [6] toolkit. This feature allows us to combine feature spaces assigning weights to each representation regardless of thee number of features available. This is particularly helpful given that the bag of words representation has a much more higher dimensionality than the other two feature spaces.

4   Experimental Results

This section reports experimental results obtained with the proposed methodology. The different configurations were evaluated with a k-fold cross validation scheme. Specifically, $k = 10$ was set. In accordance with the challenge, we used the area under the ROC curve (AUC) as evaluation measure. Table 1 shows the results obtained for different combination of feature spaces (in all cases the same classifier was used). We report the per-trait classification performance together with the one *vs* rest classification performance.

Table 1. Results of cross validation study on training essays.

Features	Extraversion	Agreeableness	Conscientiousness	Neuroticism	Openness	One vs Rest
LIWC	0.51 (±0.03)	0.49 (±0.02)	0.47 (±0.01)	0.45 (±0.03)	0.54 (±0.04)	0.49 (±0.01)
BoW	0.52 (±0.01)	0.50 (±0.02)	0.49 (±0.01)	0.53 (±0.01)	0.50 (±0.01)	0.51 (±0.00)
Shape	0.50 (±0.03)	0.50 (±0.02)	0.57 (±0.03)	0.45 (±0.03)	0.53 (±0.03)	0.52 (±0.02)
LIWC+BoW	0.43 (±0.01)	0.47 (±0.02)	0.49 (±0.02)	0.48 (±0.02)	0.50 (±0.03)	0.47 (±0.02)
LIWC+Shape	0.53 (±0.02)	0.47 (±0.02)	0.48 (±0.03)	0.44 (±0.03)	0.53 (±0.04)	0.49 (±0.02)
BoW+Shape	0.50 (±0.03)	0.50 (±0.02)	0.56 (±0.03)	0.48 (±0.02)	0.52 (±0.03)	0.52 (±0.01)
BoW+LIWC+Shape	0.43 (±0.02)	0.47 (±0.02)	0.48 (±0.02)	0.48 (±0.02)	0.49 (±0.02)	0.47 (±0.02)

From this figure it can be seen that the approached problem is extremely complex, as most configurations obtained performance around values of 0.5 of AUC. Hence, the data set proved to be extremely complex. Please note that this is not a particularity of our method but of all methods evaluated in the competition, see [8].

Regarding the different feature spaces, there is not a clear trend, however the best global results included shape features (Shape and BoW+Shape). This result suggest handwriting is more relevant for inferring personality than the words used in the essay.

Interestingly, the best results for a trait were obtained for the conscientiousness trait, which is related to subjects that are efficient, responsible, organized, and persevering. The fact that shape features performed the best for this trait, confirms findings from other references in which the way people writes is correlated with this trait. Similarly, the openness trait was also recognized with good accuracy. The most difficult trait to recognize was the emotional stability one, most methods obtained performance lower to 0.5.

In order to participate in the challenge, we submitted the best run Bow+Shape for the final phase. However, we obtained an AUC of 0.49. After release of the labels for the test data we will perform a detailed analysis of the results in order to draw conclusions.

5   Conclusions

We described our participation in the HWxPI challenge, whose focus was on estimating the presence of personality traits from written essays. We proposed a solution that combined information from different modalities and succeeded at obtaining satisfactory results. As future work we would like to examine additional text features such as polarity, gender, Part Of Speech (POS) tags to obtain a feature vector that represents the information more precisely.

References

1. Cohen, G., Afshar, S., Tapson, J., van Schaik, A.: EMNIST: an extension of MNIST to handwritten letters. arXiv preprint arXiv:1702.05373 (2017)
2. De Campos, T., Bodla, R.B., Varma, M.: The chars74k dataset (2009)
3. Escalante, H.J., et al.: Explaining first impressions: modeling, recognizing, and explaining apparent personality from videos. CoRR, abs/1802.00745 (2018)
4. Jacques, C.S., et al.: First impressions: a survey on computer vision-based apparent personality trait analysis. CoRR, abs/1804.08046 (2018)
5. Matthews, G., Deary, J., Whiteman, C.: Personality Traits. Cambridge University Press, Cambridge (2009)
6. Pedregosa, F., et al.: Scikit-learn: Machine learning in Python. J. Mach. Learn. Res. **12**, 2825–2830 (2011)
7. Pennebaker, J.W., King, L.A.: Linguistic styles: language use as an individual difference. J. Pers. Soc. Psychol. **77**(6), 1296–1312 (1999)
8. Ramirez, G., et al.: Overview of the multimedia information processing for personality & social networks analysis contest. In: Proceedings of the MIPPSNA Workshop (2018)
9. Ren, S., He, K., Girshick, R., Sun, J.: Faster R-CNN: towards real-time object detection with region proposal networks. IEEE Trans. Pattern Anal. Mach. Intell. **6**, 1137–1149 (2017)

Multimodal Database of Emotional Speech, Video and Gestures

Tomasz Sapiński[1], Dorota Kamińska[1(✉)], Adam Pelikant[1], Cagri Ozcinar[2], Egils Avots[3], and Gholamreza Anbarjafari[3]

[1] Inst of Mechatronics and Info Sys, Lodz University of Technology, Łódź, Poland
{tomasz.sapinski,dorota.kaminska,adam.pelikant}@p.lodz.pl
[2] Computer Science and Statistics, Trinity College Dublin, Dublin 2, Ireland
[3] iCV Research Lab, Institute of Technology, University of Tartu, Tartu, Estonia
{ea,shb}@icv.tuit.ut.ee

Abstract. People express emotions through different modalities. Integration of verbal and non-verbal communication channels creates a system in which the message is easier to understand. Expanding the focus to several expression forms can facilitate research on emotion recognition as well as human-machine interaction. In this article, the authors present a Polish emotional database composed of three modalities: facial expressions, body movement and gestures, and speech. The corpora contains recordings registered in studio conditions, acted out by 16 professional actors (8 male and 8 female). The data is labeled with six basic emotions categories, according to Ekman's emotion categories. To check the quality of performance, all recordings are evaluated by experts and volunteers. The database is available to academic community and might be useful in the study on audio-visual emotion recognition.

Keywords: Multimodal database · Emotions · Speech · Video Gestures

1 Introduction

Emotions are evoked by different mechanisms such as events, objects, other people or phenomena that lead to various consequences manifesting in our body. Automatic affect recognition methods utilize various input types i.e., facial expressions [13,14,21,33,36], speech [18,25], gestures and body language [20,27] and physical signals such as electroencephalography (EEG) [16], electromyography (EMG) [17], electrodermal activity [11] etc. Although it has been investigated for many years, it is still an active research area because of growing interest in application exploiting avatars animation, neuromarketing and sociable robots [12]. Most research focuses on facial expressions and speech. About 95% of the literature dedicated to this topic concentrates on mimics as a source for emotion analysis [9]. Because speech is one of the most accessible forms of the

© Springer Nature Switzerland AG 2019
Z. Zhang et al. (Eds.): ICPR 2018 Workshops, LNCS 11188, pp. 153–163, 2019.
https://doi.org/10.1007/978-3-030-05792-3_15

above mentioned signals, it is the second most commonly used source for automatic recognition. Considerably less research utilizes body gestures and posture. However, recent development of motion capture technologies and it's increasing reliability led to a significant increase in literature on automatic recognition of expressive movements.

Gestures have to be recognised as the most significant way to communicate non-verbally. They are understood as movement of extremities, head, other parts of the body and facial expressions, which communicate the whole spectrum of feelings and emotions. It has been reported that gestures are strongly culture-dependent [6,19]. However, due to exposure to mass-media, there is a tendency of globalization of some gestures especially in younger generations [26]. For this very reason, gestures might be a perfect supplement for emotion recognition methods that do not require specified sensors and may be examined from a distance.

Automatic affect recognition is a pattern recognition problem. Therefore, standard pattern recognition methodology, which involves database creation, feature extraction and classification, is usually applied. The first part of this methodology is the crucial one. During the selection of samples for an emotional database one has to consider a set which would guarantee minimization of individual features, such as age and gender, as well as provide a wide range of correctly labelled complex emotional states. What is more, one should also focus on choosing the right source of affect: mimics, body language and speech seem to be the most appropriate due to lack of requirement of direct body contact with any specialized equipment during sample acquisition.

As it is presented in Sect. 2 just several publicly accessible multimodal databases exists, which contain simultaneously recorded modalities such as face mimic, movements of full body and speech. Thus, there is clearly a space and a necessity to create such emotional databases.

In this article, the authors describe an emotional database consisting of audio, video and point cloud data representing human body movements. The paper adopts the following outline. Section 2 presents a brief review of other relevant multimodal emotional corpora. Sections 3 and 4 describe the process of creating the database and the process of recording. Section 5 presents the process of emotional recordings evaluation. Finally, Sect. 6 gives the conclusions.

2   Related Works

3D scanned and even thermal databases of different emotions have been constructed [4,24]. The most well known 3D datasets are the BU-3DFE [35], BU-4DFE [34], Bosphorus [32] and BP4D [37]. BU-3DFE and BU-4DFE both contain posed datasets with six expressions, the latter having higher resolution. The Bosphorus tries to address the issue of having a wider selection of facial expressions and BP4D is the only one among the four using induced expressions instead of posed ones. A sample of models from a 3D database can be seen in Fig. 1.

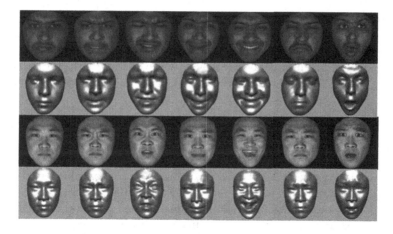

Fig. 1. 3D facial expression samples from the BU-3DFE database [35].

With RGB-D databases, however, it is important to note that the data is unique to each sensor with outputs having varying density and error, so algorithms trained on databases like the IIIT-D RGB-D [10], VAP RGB-D [15] and KinectFaceDB [23] would be very susceptible to hardware changes. For comparison with the 3D databases, an RGB-D sample has been provided in Fig. 2. One of the newer databases, the iCV SASE [22] database, is RGB-D dataset solely dedicated to head pose with free facial expressions.

Even though depth based databases are relatively new compared to other types and there are very few of them, they still manage to cover a wide range of different emotions. With the release of commercial use depth cameras like the Microsoft Kinect [23], they will only continue to get more popular in the future.

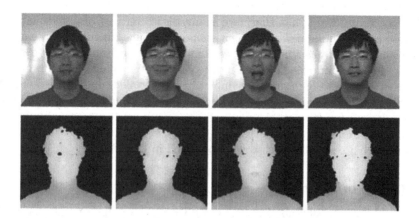

Fig. 2. RGB-D facial expression samples from the KinectFaceDB database [23].

A comprehensive survey in [24] showed that some wider multimodal databases such as the database created by Psaltis et al. [29] and emoFBVP database [30] includes face, body gesture and voice signals. Such databases are attracting lots of attentions of researchers, however there is still a big demand for having bigger and more comprehensive multimodal databases.

3 Main Assumptions

3.1 Acted vs Natural Emotions

Emotional databases can be divided into three categories, taking into account their source: spontaneous, invoked and acted or simulated emotions.

The spontaneous or "natural" samples are obtained by recording in an undisturbed environment, usually people are unaware of the process or it is not their main focus. TV programs such as talk shows, reality shows or various types of live coverage are good examples of this type of acquisition. However, the quality of such material might be questionable due to factors such as background noise, artifacts, overlapping voice. These components may obscure the exact nature of recorded emotions. Such recordings do not provide position and movements of the whole body of the subject as well as cloud representing human body movements. Moreover collections of samples must be evaluated by human decision makers to determine the gathered emotional states.

Another method of sample acquisition is recording an emotional reaction provoked by staged situations or aids such as videos, images or computer simulations. Although this method is favoured by psychologists, it's main disadvantage is lack of results repeatability, as reaction to the same stimuli might differ from person to person and is highly dependant on the recorded individual. Moreover, provoking full-blown emotions might be ethically problematic.

Third source are acted out emotional samples. Subjects can be both actors as well as unqualified volunteers. This type of material is usually composed of high quality recordings, with clear undisturbed emotion expression.

We are fully aware that there are many disadvantages of acted emotional database. For example in [5] the scientists pointed out that full-blown emotions expressions rarely appear in the real world and acted out samples may be exaggerated. However, in order to obtain three different modalities simultaneously and gather clean and high quality samples in a controlled, undisturbed environment the decision was made to create a set of acted out emotions. This approach provides crucial fundamentals for creating a corpus with a reasonable number of recorded samples, diversity of gender and age of the actors (see Table 1) and the same verbal content, which was emphasized in [2].

3.2 Choice of Emotions

Research in the field of emotion recognition varies based upon number and type of recognized states. The most influential models and relevant for affective computing applications can be classified into three main categories:

Table 1. Table presents age and sex of actors participating in the project

No.	1	2	3	4	5	6	7	8	9	10	11	12	13	14	15	16
Sex	m	f	m	f	m	m	f	m	f	f	m	m	f	m	f	f
Age	43	47	58	46	56	39	37	30	31	27	25	29	27	46	64	36

- categorical concepts such as *anger* or *fear* [7],
- dimensional such as *activation, pleasure* and *dominance* [31],
- componential, which arrange emotions in a hierarchical manner, may contains more complex representations like in Plutchik's weel of emotions [28].

Analyzing state-of-the-art affect recognition research one can observe how broad spectrum of emotion has been used in various types of research. However, most authors focus on sets containing six basic emotions (according to Ekman's model). It is caused by the fact that facial expressions of emotion are similar across many cultures. This might hold in the case of postures and gestures as well [3]. Thus, we decided to follow the commonly used approach and categorized samples in the corpus into fear, surprise, anger,sadness, happiness, disgust. What is more, this approach provides us the possibility to compare future results with previous studies of the same research group [1,8], which is currently impossible because of inconsistent representation in other available databases.

4   Acquisition Process

The recordings were performed in the rehearsal room of *Teatr Nowy im. Kazimierza Dejmka w Łodzi*. Each recorded person is a professional actor from the aforementioned theater. A total of 16 people were recorded - 8 male and 8 female, aged from 25 to 64. Each person was recorded separately.

Before the recording all actors were presented with a short scenario describing the sequence of emotions they had to present in order: neutral state, sadness, surprise, fear, disgust, anger, happiness. In addition they were asked to utter a short sentence in Polish, same for all emotional states *Każdy z nas odczuwa emocje na swój sposób* (English translation: *Each of us perceives emotions in a different manner*). All emotions were acted out 5 times. The total number of gathered samples amounted to 560, 80 for each emotional state.

The recordings took place in a quiet, well lit environment. The video was captured against a green background (as visible in Fig. 3). A medium shot was used in order to keep the actors face in the frame and compensate for any movement during the emotion expression. In case of Kinect recordings the full body was in frame, including the legs (as visible in Fig. 4).

The samples consist of simultaneous audio, video, cloud point and skeletal data feeds. They were performed using a video camera (Sony PMW-EX1), dictaphone (Roland R-26) and a Kinect 2 device. The data was gathered in form of wav audio files (44,1 kHz, 16bit, stereo), mp4 videos (1920 × 1080, MPEG-4) with redundant audio track, and xef files containing the 3d data.

Figure 3 shows frames from the video recordings of different emotional expressions presented by the actors. In Fig. 4 one can see the body poses captured during emotion expression. Figure 5 presents an example of emotional speech audio recordings.

Fig. 3. Screen-shots of facial expression of six basic emotions fear, surprise, anger, sadness, happiness, disgust.

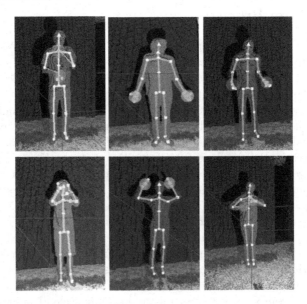

Fig. 4. Examples of actors poses in six basic emotions fear, surprise, anger, sadness, happiness, disgust.

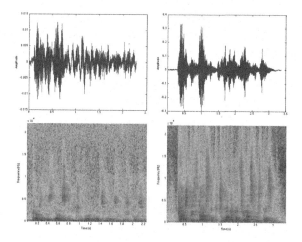

Fig. 5. Oscillogram and spectrogram for two different emotional states acted out by the same person. Left: neutral, right: anger.

5 Data Evaluation

To ensure the quality of the samples a perception test was carried out with 12 subjects (6 male and 6 female). They were presented with the three modalities separately. They were allowed to watch or listen to each sample only once and then determine the presented emotional state. Each volunteer had to assess one sample of each emotion presenting by every actor - in total 96 samples. The results are presented in Fig. 6.

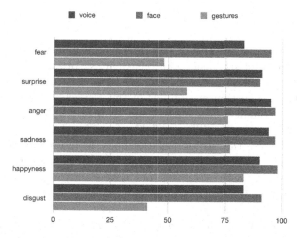

Fig. 6. Mean recognition rates in % for all three modalities presented and evaluated separately.

Analyzing the chart one can observe that the highest recognition rate occurred for facial emotion expressions. Comparable, however slightly lower results were obtained in case of speech. Using gestures offered the lowest recognition rate, however it can serve as a significant, supporting information when recognition is based on all three modalities. The results obtained for three modalities simultaneously are presented in Fig. 7.

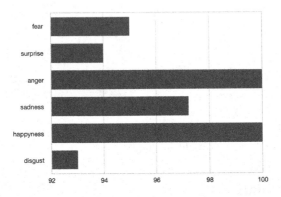

Fig. 7. Mean recognition rates in % for all three modalities presented and evaluated simultaneously.

One can notice that presenting three modalities simultaneously provides an increase in recognition performance. For all emotional states the obtained results are above 90%. In case of anger and happiness the recognition was 100% correct.

6   Conclusion

This paper presents the process of creation a multimodal emotional database consisting recordings of six basic emotions (fear, surprise, anger, sadness, happiness, disgust) as well as natural state, performed by 16 professional actors. It contains a large collection of samples in three synchronized modalities (560 samples for each modality: face, speech and gestures) which makes this corpus interesting for researchers in different fields, from psychology to affective computing. What is more, the position of the body includes the legs, while most database focus only on hands, arms and head. Due to the size of data (especially recordings from Kinect), the corpus is not accessible via a website, however it can be made available for research upon request.

Acknowledgement. The authors would like to thank Michał Wasażnik (psychologist), who participated in experimental protocol creation. This work is supported Estonian Research Council Grant (PUT638), the Scientific and Technological Research Council of Turkey (TÜBİTAK) (Proje 1001 - 116E097), Estonian-Polish Joint Research Project, the Estonian Centre of Excellence in IT (EXCITE) funded by the European

Regional Development Fund. We gratefully acknowledge the support of NVIDIA Corporation with the donation of the Titan XP GPU used for this research.

References

1. Baltrušaitis, T., et al.: Real-time inference of mental states from facial expressions and upper body gestures. In: 2011 IEEE International Conference on Automatic Face & Gesture Recognition and Workshops (FG 2011), pp. 909–914. IEEE (2011)
2. Burkhardt, F., Paeschke, A., Rolfes, M., Sendlmeier, W.F., Weiss, B.: A database of German emotional speech. In: Ninth European Conference on Speech Communication and Technology (2005)
3. Camras, L.A., Oster, H., Campos, J.J., Miyake, K., Bradshaw, D.: Japanese and american infants' responses to arm restraint. Dev. Psychol. **28**(4), 578 (1992)
4. Daneshmand, M., et al.: 3D scanning: a comprehensive survey. arXiv preprint arXiv:1801.08863 (2018)
5. Douglas-Cowie, E., Cowie, R., Schröder, M.: A new emotion database: considerations, sources and scope. In: ISCA Tutorial and Research Workshop (ITRW) on Speech and Emotion (2000)
6. Efron, D.: Gesture and environment (1941)
7. Ekman, P.: Universal and cultural differences in facial expression of emotion. Nebr. Sym. Motiv. **19**, 207–283 (1971)
8. Gavrilescu, M.: Recognizing emotions from videos by studying facial expressions, body postures and hand gestures. In: 2015 23rd Telecommunications Forum Telfor (TELFOR), pp. 720–723. IEEE (2015)
9. Gelder, B.D.: Why bodies? Twelve reasons for including bodily expressions in affective neuroscience. Philos. Trans. R. Soc. B: Biol. Sci. **364**(364), 3475–3484 (2009)
10. Goswami, G., Vatsa, M., Singh, R.: RGB-D face recognition with texture and attribute features. IEEE Trans. Inf. Forensics Secur. **9**(10), 1629–1640 (2014)
11. Greco, A., Valenza, G., Citi, L., Scilingo, E.P.: Arousal and valence recognition of affective sounds based on electrodermal activity. IEEE Sens. J. **17**(3), 716–725 (2017)
12. Gupta, R., Khomami Abadi, M., Cárdenes Cabré, J.A., Morreale, F., Falk, T.H., Sebe, N.: A quality adaptive multimodal affect recognition system for user-centric multimedia indexing. In: Proceedings of the 2016 ACM on International Conference on Multimedia Retrieval, pp. 317–320. ACM (2016)
13. Haamer, R.E., et al.: Changes in facial expression as biometric: a database and benchmarks of identification. In: 2018 13th IEEE International Conference on Automatic Face & Gesture Recognition (FG 2018), pp. 621–628. IEEE (2018)
14. Haque, M.A., et al.: Deep multimodal pain recognition: a database and comparison of spatio-temporal visual modalities. In: 2018 13th IEEE International Conference on Automatic Face & Gesture Recognition (FG 2018), pp. 250–257. IEEE (2018)
15. Hg, R., Jasek, P., Rofidal, C., Nasrollahi, K., Moeslund, T.B., Tranchet, G.: An RGB-D database using microsoft's kinect for windows for face detection. In: 2012 Eighth International Conference on Signal Image Technology and Internet Based Systems (SITIS), pp. 42–46. IEEE (2012)
16. Jenke, R., Peer, A., Buss, M.: Feature extraction and selection for emotion recognition from EEG. IEEE Trans. Affect. Comput. **5**(3), 327–339 (2014)

17. Jerritta, S., Murugappan, M., Wan, K., Yaacob, S.: Emotion recognition from facial EMG signals using higher order statistics and principal component analysis. J. Chin. Inst. Eng. **37**(3), 385–394 (2014)
18. Kamińska, D., Sapiński, T., Anbarjafari, G.: Efficiency of chosen speech descriptors in relation to emotion recognition. EURASIP J. Audio Speech Music Process. **2017**(1), 3 (2017)
19. Kendon, A.: The study of gesture: some remarks on its history. In: Deely, J.N., Lenhart, M.D. (eds.) Semiotics 1981, pp. 153–164. Springer, Heidelberg (1983). https://doi.org/10.1007/978-1-4615-9328-7_15
20. Kiforenko, L., Kraft, D.: Emotion recognition through body language using RGB-D sensor. Vision Theory and Applications Computer Vision Theory and Applications, pp. 398–405. SCITEPRESS Digital Library (2016) In: 11th International Conference on Computer Vision Theory and Applications Computer Vision Theory and Applications, pp. 398–405. SCITEPRESS Digital Library (2016)
21. Lopes, A.T., de Aguiar, E., De Souza, A.F., Oliveira-Santos, T.: Facial expression recognition with convolutional neural networks: coping with few data and the training sample order. Pattern Recognit. **61**, 610–628 (2017)
22. Lüsi, I., Escarela, S., Anbarjafari, G.: SASE: RGB-depth database for human head pose estimation. In: Hua, G., Jégou, H. (eds.) ECCV 2016. LNCS, vol. 9915, pp. 325–336. Springer, Cham (2016). https://doi.org/10.1007/978-3-319-49409-8_26
23. Min, R., Kose, N., Dugelay, J.L.: KinectFaceDB: a kinect database for face recognition. IEEE Trans. Syst. Man Cybern. Syst. **44**(11), 1534–1548 (2014)
24. Noroozi, F., Corneanu, C.A., Kamińska, D., Sapiński, T., Escalera, S., Anbarjafari, G.: Survey on emotional body gesture recognition. arXiv preprint arXiv:1801.07481 (2018)
25. Noroozi, F., Sapiński, T., Kamińska, D., Anbarjafari, G.: Vocal-based emotion recognition using random forests and decision tree. Int. J. Speech Technol. **20**(2), 239–246 (2017)
26. Pease, B., Pease, A.: The Definitive Book of Body Language. Bantam, New York City (2004)
27. Pławiak, P., Sośnicki, T., Niedźwiecki, M., Tabor, Z., Rzecki, K.: Hand body language gesture recognition based on signals from specialized glove and machine learning algorithms. IEEE Trans. Ind. Inform. **12**(3), 1104–1113 (2016)
28. Plutchik, R.: The nature of emotions human emotions have deep evolutionary roots, a fact that may explain their complexity and provide tools for clinical practice. Am. Sci. **89**(4), 344–350 (2001)
29. Psaltis, A., et al.: Multimodal affective state recognition in serious games applications. In: 2016 IEEE International Conference on Imaging Systems and Techniques (IST), pp. 435–439. IEEE (2016)
30. Ranganathan, H., Chakraborty, S., Panchanathan, S.: Multimodal emotion recognition using deep learning architectures. In: 2016 IEEE Winter Conference on Applications of Computer Vision (WACV), pp. 1–9. IEEE (2016)
31. Russell, J., Mehrabian, A.: Evidence for a three-factor theory of emotions. J. Res. Pers. **11**, 273–294 (1977)
32. Savran, A., Alyüz, N., Dibeklioğlu, H., Çeliktutan, O., Gökberk, B., Sankur, B., Akarun, L.: Bosphorus database for 3D face analysis. In: Schouten, B., Juul, N.C., Drygajlo, A., Tistarelli, M. (eds.) BioID 2008. LNCS, vol. 5372, pp. 47–56. Springer, Heidelberg (2008). https://doi.org/10.1007/978-3-540-89991-4_6

33. Wan, J., et al.: Results and analysis of ChaLearn lap multi-modal isolated and continuous gesture recognition, and real versus fake expressed emotions challenges. In: ChaLearn LAP, Action, Gesture, and Emotion Recognition Workshop and Competitions: Large Scale Multimodal Gesture Recognition and Real versus Fake expressed emotions, ICCV, vol. 4 (2017)
34. Yin, L., Chen, X., Sun, Y., Worm, T., Reale, M.: A high-resolution 3D dynamic facial expression database. In: 8th IEEE International Conference on Automatic Face and Gesture Recognition, FG 2008, pp. 1–6. IEEE (2008)
35. Yin, L., Wei, X., Sun, Y., Wang, J., Rosato, M.J.: A 3D facial expression database for facial behavior research. In: 7th International Conference on Automatic face and gesture recognition, FGR 2006, pp. 211–216. IEEE (2006)
36. Zhang, K., Huang, Y., Du, Y., Wang, L.: Facial expression recognition based on deep evolutional spatial-temporal networks. IEEE Trans. Image Process. **26**(9), 4193–4203 (2017)
37. Zhang, X., et al.: BP4D-spontaneous: a high-resolution spontaneous 3D dynamic facial expression database. Image Vis. Comput. **32**(10), 692–706 (2014)

From Text to Speech: A Multimodal Cross-Domain Approach for Deception Detection

Rodrigo Rill-García[1(✉)], Luis Villaseñor-Pineda[1], Verónica Reyes-Meza[2], and Hugo Jair Escalante[1]

[1] Instituto Nacional de Astrofísica, Óptica y Electrónica, Santa María Tonanzintla, 72840 Puebla, Mexico
{rodrigo.rill,villasen,hugojair}@inaoep.mx
[2] Centro Tlaxcala de Biología de la Conducta, Universidad Autónoma de Tlaxcala, Tlaxcala, Mexico
veronica.reyesm@uatx.mx

Abstract. Deception detection -identifying when someone is trying to cause someone else to believe something that is not true- is a hard task for humans. The task is even harder for automatic approaches, that must deal with additional problems like the lack of enough labeled data. In this context, transfer learning in the form of cross-domain classification is a task that aims to leverage labeled data from certain domains for which labeled data is available to others for which data is scarce. This paper presents a study on the suitability of linguistic features for cross-domain deception detection on multimodal data. Specifically, we aim to learn models for deception detection across different domains of written texts (one modality) and apply the new knowledge to unrelated topics transcribed from spoken statements (another modality). Experimental results reveal that by using LIWC and POS n-grams we reach a in-modality accuracy of 69.42%, as well as an AUC ROC of 0.7153. When doing transfer learning, we achieve an accuracy of 63.64% and get an AUC ROC of 0.6351.

Keywords: Linguistic analysis · Cross-domain classification
Multimodal data analysis · Deception detection

1 Introduction

Even the apparently best decision, given certain data, can be unreliable if the data was inaccurate or, even worse, wrong. Of course uncertainty is inherent to data, but what does it happen when the given information was purposely inaccurate/wrong? According to the Oxford dictionary, deception is the action of deceiving someone, that is, "deliberately cause (someone) to believe something that is not true, especially for personal gain". While decisions made by deceptive information can be benign in our daily lives, there are cases where the outcomes

© Springer Nature Switzerland AG 2019
Z. Zhang et al. (Eds.): ICPR 2018 Workshops, LNCS 11188, pp. 164–177, 2019.
https://doi.org/10.1007/978-3-030-05792-3_16

can involve important consequences. That is why deception detection has been a topic of interest.

Based on previous research [1–4], there is a well-known assumption that a difference exists in the way liars communicate in contrast with truth tellers, and that such difference(s) can be pointed out with the help of machine learning. However, when it comes to text processing it is also well-known that different representations of text work differently on distinct domains. Additionally, a generally accepted hypothesis is that deception highly relies on context and motivation. Even further, the way people express themselves is different when it comes to writing or speaking.

With the previous considerations, particularly the last one, this paper presents a study on the capability of different representations to learn to detect deception in a given domain and using such model to predict deceptive behavior in another one. By domain, we refer to a set of topics and a modality (understood as a source of information); therefore, our study involves a cross-topic multimodal transfer.

What is the motivation for transferring knowledge? Deception detection is a hard task for humans, so getting labeled data on this topic is a drawback independently from the domain. Given this, it is desirable to build systems able to work on as different domains as possible with the collected data so far. Furthermore, there is another major drawback: the data used for research is mostly reduced to willingly cooperation (subjects are asked to help on their own will). Recalling the Oxford's definition, deceiving applies particularly when the deceiver looks for personal gain.

Under these both scopes, the present study considered both an artificial dataset dealing with 3 different topics (written modality), and a real-life court dataset (transcribed modality). Different type of features are evaluated with different classifiers, under the hypothesis that stylistic analysis is useful for detecting liars no matter if they are writing or speaking (cross-modality), or what they are talking about (cross-topic).

Among the tested classifiers, Random Forest (RF) seems to be the most useful for both in-domain and cross-domain classification. Regarding the considered features, Linguistic Inquiry and Word Count (LIWC) often shows the best performance; and in the most cases when LIWC doesn't achieve the best results, a concatenation of LIWC features with the Bag-of-Terms (BoT) representation of Part of Speech (POS) tags gives the boost to fulfill the LIWC's weaknesses. With the given results, our study suggests that features able to extract style are, indeed, useful for transferring across multiple topics and modalities.

2   Related Work

When it comes to deception detection in text, we can divide research in two trends: analyzing handwritten/typed text, and analyzing text obtained from speech transcriptions. Furthermore, we can make another distinction between two approaches: analyzing in-domain and cross-domain. Of particular interest to this paper are the works studying at least transcriptions (handwritten/typed text is desirable too) and preferably multiple topics.

A reference work is that presented by Newman *et al.* [3]. They report 5 study cases on 3 domains/topics and from 3 sources (video, typing and handwriting) using LIWC; they used cross-domain analysis to draw conclusions on representative features for both truths and lies. By combining all the 5 studies, they reach a 61% accuracy.

Pérez-Rosas and Mihalcea [1] introduce a dataset of 3 typed topics from 4 different ethnic groups to experiment on cross-cultural deception detection. They achieved 60–70% accuracies for classifiers trained on different cultures by using psycholinguistic features (LIWC) across topics; they point out that psycholinguistic classes for words work as a bridge across languages.

Pérez-Rosas *et al.* [4] present a novel dataset, composed of videos collected from public court trials, for deception detection in real-life trial data. Although they use a multimodal approach, they show results for pure-text analysis of the video transcriptions; by using Decision Trees (DT) with Unigrams, they achieve a 60.33% accuracy. This is of particular interest since court trials are not reduced to specific topics, and people in there are indeed trying to achieve a personal benefit. Therefore, this dataset is a better approach for real-life deception detection on topic free contexts.

A new multimodal analysis on a dataset constructed over the same topics used by Newman *et al.* is used by Abouelenien *et al.* [5]. In this case, the database is composed entirely from videos; therefore, the text analysis is performed on transcriptions. They use LIWC along with Unigrams in DT for classification, achieving a high variance in accuracy for the 3 different topics separately. By training on 2 different topics and testing in the third one, they achieve results in the range of 45.0–51.72% accuracy. One year later, they constructed a new balanced dataset under similar conditions for gender-based deception detection [6]. Their experiments are performed for both female and male subjects jointly and separately, using different linguistic features on DT. Over different topics and genders there is not a clear tendency on which features are better, but apparently it is easier to detect deception in women.

Wu *et al.* [7] revisit the court database presented by Pérez-Rosas *et al.* for a more extensive multimodal analysis. In this case, the text analysis is performed by using Global Vectors for Word Representation (Glove) over different classifiers. The best result for only-transcripts presented in their paper is an AUC of 0.6625 using a Naive Bayes (NB) classifier.

When analyzing these works, even if there is a cross-domain analysis to some extent, there is no a particular interest for transferring knowledge across modalities. Unlike them, multimodal transfer is a fundamental part of our study (particularly from the written modality to the transcribed one).

3   Datasets

As aforementioned, this study focused on transferring learning between two data sets containing information in different modalities (see Table 1). The first one,

"Multilingual Deception Datasets" [1], is composed of written labeled texts on 3 topics by people from 4 different cultural backgrounds. The topics covered are Abortion, Best Friend and Death Penalty; for each topic, participants were asked to write a short essay about their real opinions, followed by a deceptive essay. Although 4 different cultural sets were collected, in this work only the one collected from American English was used (as by now we are not interested in deception across cultures). This subset is composed of 600 different essays, 100 truthful and 100 deceptive for each of the three topics.

The second dataset, "Real-life Trial Deception Detection Dataset", is formed by public real-life trial videos available in the web, as well as statements made by exonerees and some by defendants on TV episodes. Labeling is done by using the verdict (guilty, non-guilty and exonerated). Within this dataset, three types of data are provided: the clip itself, a manual annotation on gestures, and the transcripts of the statements. For this work purposes, only the transcriptions are used, resulting in 121 texts: 60 truthful and 61 deceptive.

Table 1. Summary of the used datasets.

Dataset	Deceptive texts/ truthful texts	Topics	Modality
Multilingual deception datasets	300/300	Abortion (A), Best friend (B), Death penalty (D)	Typed text
Real-life trial deception detection dataset	61/60	Court statements (C)	Transcribed text

4 Multimodal Cross-Domain Analysis

The goal of this paper is to analyze the cross-domain capabilities of a number of linguistic features, where a domain is composed by a set of topics and a modality. We are particularly interested in text obtained directly by writing or as result of transcribing speech (see Fig. 1). Under these two assumptions, we are not interested on *what* is told but *how*; we call this *style*.

Figure 1 depicts a general diagram of the adopted cross-domain transfer strategy; from the diagram, one should notice that the topics from both modalities are not expected to be the same at any moment. Because the goal of our study is to analyze the performance of features, we adopted a trivial cross-domain solution: the same features are used for representing samples in both source and target domains; more specifically, a classification model is trained on source domain data and tested on target data.

Using the work of Sapkota *et al.* [8] as reference, we propose a BoT of character n-grams (including punctuation) as a baseline representation; this is because

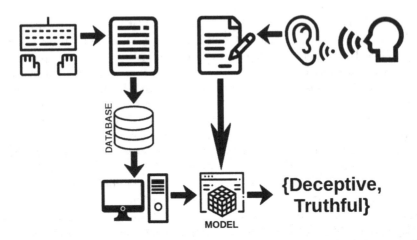

Fig. 1. Graphical representation of multimodal transfer from written text to transcribed text. Our study focuses in the features used by the computer to create the model.

the information captured by these features have shown successful results for single domain and cross-domain Authorship Attribution. Therefore, a supposition is made that these features are good for identifying style. Additionally to that representation, we propose some additional features as well as combinations thereof intended to be vocabulary-independent (i.e. the resulting vector doesn't allow to recover original words from the corpus). The rest of this section describes the full text pre-processing and the different features considered in the study.

4.1 Preprocessing

First, all the samples were separated into different text files. Then, each individual file was automatically cleaned to delete repeated consecutive blank spaces (e.g. *An   example → An example*) and repeated consecutive punctuations (e.g. *Awesome!!!! → Awesome!*), as well as to provide proper spaces when punctuation is used (e.g. *A, B and C. → A, B and C.*).

In the case of the court dataset, an additional manual cleaning was done to delete annotator comments (like *person laughs*); when the comment stated that the speech was inaudible/incomprehensible, it was substituted by a question mark (?). Fillers such as *uh, ahm, ahh*, etc. were substituted by ellipsis (...); numbers were not normalized to a single expression.

4.2 Feature Extraction

This section describes the features subject of our study.

Character N-Grams. Each individual text file was analyzed using the Natural Language Toolkit (NLTK) from Python. For each file, both character 3-grams and 4-grams were found and stored into two new separate files.

LIWC. Inspired by some articles presented in the related work section [1,3,5, 6], we represent each text from both datasets through its LIWC vector using the LIWC2007_English131104 dictionary. However, unlike previous work, we use the full list of LIWC attributes (getting thus 64 different features); although selecting certain categories seems reasonable according to previous studies, our purpose here was to use as much information as possible to transfer learning from one source domain into the target one. Therefore, we take a greedy approach where it is better to get useless information rather than potentially losing useful information. For this specific features, punctuation was ignored.

POS Tagging. As we are interested in style, it sounds reasonable to analyze what kind of words are being used instead of the words themselves. To do this, we code each file into its POS tags by using the Stanford POS Tagger [9] (v3.9.1). The result is again stored in a new text file for each text.

POS N-Grams. As with LIWC, we took inspiration from previous work [1,4–6] and decided to use a POS-based n-grams representation. We experimented with POS 1-grams and 3-grams. As with character n-grams, each text file was analyzed with NLTK.

Bags of Terms. Once character 3/4-grams and POS 1/3-grams were obtained, each of those features were represented separately in a BoT model, where each different n-gram counted as a different term. However, these bags were acquired for 15 different study cases; therefore, 15 training and 15 test bags were gotten for each of the 4 different features. For this task, we used the Scikit-learn library from Python; note that the test bags were constructed using the vocabulary obtained from its respective training bag.

Mixed Features. Additionally to the aforementioned features, LIWC vectors were concatenated with POS BoTs to create two new representations. This two particular types of representation were chosen to be fused because, unlike character n-grams, they are independent of the specific vocabulary of the corpus.

Summarizing, 7 different feature vectors were acquired for each set:

- Bag of Character 3-grams (C3G)
- Bag of Character 4-grams (C4G)
- LIWC vector (LIWC)
- Bag of POS tags 1-grams (POS1)
- Bag of POS tags 3-grams (POS3)
- LIWC vector + Bag of POS tags 1-grams (LIWC + POS1)
- LIWC vector + Bag of POS tags 3-grams (LIWC + POS3).

4.3 Classification

The classes associated to the approached classification problem were: "True" if the statement/sample was truthful and "False" if it was deceptive. For the 15 study cases (look at Table 2), a total of 210 datasets were arranged: 15 study cases * 7 representations per study case * 2 sets per representation (1 for training and 1 for testing). From the 15 cases, seven are cross-domain ones: three of them are just cross-topic ones, while the other four are also cross-modality ones (see Table 3). Even if our particular interest is to transfer from text to speech (transcript), two cases of transfer from speech to text are studied for comparison and further analysis on multimodal transfer.

5 Experiments and Results

As above mentioned, 15 different study cases were analyzed. Whenever the target data is the same as the source data, the validation is performed by a 10-fold cross-validation; this is used to appreciate the loss when transferring into a new domain. One should note that for same-domain experiments, the representation for both training and test documents was obtained by analyzing the whole corpus. This means that the corresponding performance is optimistic, in the sense that test samples were represented using information from the test partition. This makes these results to be even harder to beat by cross-domain problems.

On the other hand, when the target data is from a different domain, its instances are classified using the model created from the source domain. Each of the study cases was tested with four different classifiers: NB, SVM, DT and RF[1]. The performance of each model was evaluated with many metrics, but for analysis just accuracy and AUC ROC for the "False" class are taken into account[2].

Table 4 shows the best results we got in accuracy when validating within the training set (that is, in-domain). When an equivalent experiment was done in the paper that first presented the given dataset, it is shown for comparison. Out of 4, our study outperforms in 3 experiments; interestingly, the one left uses the same features and classifier as us. This is probably caused by the version of the LIWC dictionary used or the program created to extract the vectors given the dictionary.

Table 5 shows the study cases when cross-topic validation was done. Again, our results are compared to the ones reported by the original article; out of 3 studies, we surpass the baseline only in one. In our case, we show some loss due to transfer in 2 of 3 cases, slightly improving the in-topic baseline in the third case. Pérez-Rosas and Mihalcea [1], instead, improve relevantly their in-topic baseline in 2 of 3 cases, while weakening about the same magnitude in the third one.

By analyzing Tables 4 and 5, we can notice that Death Penalty achieves the lowest results both in-domain and as target domain. The particular interest of our study relies in transferring learning from different written domains at the same time into a different spoken domain; however, when one of those written domains individually performs worse than the others, the final transfer could be

---

[1] They were all implemented on Weka using the default values.

[2] Tables containing all the results gotten from each classifier can be found in Appendix A, but DT are not included since they were constantly outperformed by the other classifiers.

Table 2. Study cases. A: abortion, B: best friend, D: death penalty, C: court, (V): transcribed from video, (W): originally written. All topics preceding (x) were acquired from the source described by x.

Training data	Test data
A(W)	-
AB(W)	-
ABD(W)	-
ABD(W)	C(V)
AB(W)	C(V)
AB(W)	D(W)
AD(W)	-
AD(W)	B(W)
B(W)	-
BD(W)	-
BD(W)	A(W)
C(V)	-
C(V)	AB(W)
C(V)	ABD(W)
D(W)	-

Table 3. The four different cross-modality study cases.

Training data	Test data
ABD(W)	C(V)
AB(W)	C(V)
C(V)	ABD(W)
C(V)	AB(W)

affected in a negative way. To gain insight on this, cross-modality analysis was performed both by using the three written topics (Abortion, Best Friend and Death Penalty) and by excluding Death Penalty (Abortion and Best Friend). Additionally, transfer is done too from spoken modality to written modality for the sake of accumulating evidence on the bidirectionality of the proposed representations.

Table 6 presents the results for accuracy when the model is trained with the source modality and validated with the target modality. From Table 4, we retrieve also our best results when the target domain was the source domain and the best ones gotten from the paper where the dataset was originally introduced, if available. When transferring from written text to transcripts, the result improves by using more topics for training. When transferring in the opposite direction, the result actually decreases by adding an additional topic.

Table 4. Best accuracies when validating in-domain. Whenever two results are compared, the best one is in **bold**.

Experiment	Result	Features	Classifier	Original article	Features
A(W)	72.50	LIWC	SVM	**73.03**[1]	LIWC (All)
AB(W)	72.50	LIWC + POS1	RF	-	-
ABD(W)	70.50	LIWC + POS1	RF	-	-
AD(W)	71.25	LIWC	RF	-	-
B(W)	**77.50**	C4G	SVM	75.98 [1]	LIWC (Linguistic)
BD(W)	68.75	C4G, LIWC	SVM, RF	-	-
C(V)	**69.42**	C4G	SVM	60.33 [4]	UNIGRAMS
D(W)	**64.00**	C4G	RF	60.36 [1]	LIWC (Linguistic)

Table 5. Best accuracies by doing cross-topic validation. Whenever two results are compared, the best one is in **bold**.

Experiment	Result	Features	Classifier	Original article	Features
AB(W)→D(W)	64.50	LIWC + POS1	RF	**77.23**[1]	UNIGRAMS
AD(W)→B(W)	**65.50**	POS1	RF	60.78 [1]	UNIGRAMS
BD(W)→A(W)	68.00	LIWC, C3G	RF	**80.36**[1]	UNIGRAMS

Overall, the loss observed is lesser when transferring from text to transcript, probably because of the amount of data used for training (written samples are in the range of 400–600 instances, while there are only 121 transcripts). Additionally, we can observe that by training with the 3 topics of written texts our result is better than the in-source result reported for the court in the original paper.

Table 6. Best accuracies by doing cross-modality validation. In-domain results were trained and validated with the target domain. When compared, the best in-domain result is <u>underlined</u>. When comparing the result of transfer with the baseline, the best result is in **bold**.

Experiment	Result	Features	Classifier	Baseline in-domain	Our best in-domain
ABD(W)→C(V)	**63.64**	POS1	RF	60.33 [4]	<u>69.42</u>
AB(W)→C(V)	**60.33**	LIWC	RF	**60.33** [4]	<u>69.42</u>
C(V)→AB(W)	60.00	LIWC	SVM	-	72.5
C(V)→ABD(W)	57.67	LIWC	NB	-	70.5

Tables 7, 8 and 9 present similar results to the ones of Tables 4, 5 and 6, but using AUC ROC for evaluation instead of accuracy. For this metric, the only article for comparison (baseline) is the one presented by Wu *et al.* [7] on

Table 7. Best AUC when validating in-domain. Whenever two results are compared, the best one is in **bold**.

Experiment	Result	Features	Classifier	Baseline	Features
A(W)	0.7891	LIWC + POS1	RF	-	-
AB(W)	0.8031	C4G	RF	-	-
ABD(W)	0.7697	C4G	RF	-	-
AD(W)	0.7612	LIWC	RF	-	-
B(W)	0.8544	C4G	RF	-	-
BD(W)	0.7715	C4G	RF	-	-
C(V)	**0.7153**	LIWC + POS3	RF	0.6625 [7]	Glove
D(W)	0.6573	POS3	RF	-	-

Table 8. Best AUC by doing cross-topic validation.

Experiment	Result	Features	Classifier
AB(W)→D(W)	0.7533	LIWC + POS1	RF
AD(W)→B(W)	0.7166	POS3	RF
BD(W)→A(W)	0.7509	C4G	RF

Table 9. Best AUC by doing cross-modality validation. In-domain results were trained and validated with the target domain. When compared, the best in-domain result is underlined. When comparing the result of transfer with the baseline, the best result is in **bold**.

Experiment	Result	Features	Classifier	Baseline in-domain	Our best in-domain
ABD(W)→C(V)	0.6225	POS1	RF	**0.6625**[7]	0.7200
AB(W)→C(V)	0.6351	LIWC + POS1	RF	**0.6625**[7]	0.7200
C(V)→AB(W)	0.6267	LIWC + POS1	NB	-	-
C(V)→ABD(W)	0.5959	LIWC + POS1	NB	-	-

the court dataset. From Table 7 we can observe that, validating in-domain, our experiment surpass the best result reported by them.

From Table 9 we can see that we get a slightly better result by training with 2 topics of written text instead of 3; this result is 4.1% below the best result reported by Wu *et al.* validating in-domain. This is particularly relevant because of three reasons: (1) We are training in an artificial environment and validating in a real one, (2) we are getting evidence of the multimodal nature of the selected features, and (3) our representation is simple compared to theirs (they encode the texts using Glove with the pre-trained Wikipedia 2014+ Gigaword corpus, while we use a LIWC vector concatenated with a bag of POS tags unigrams).

By observing our result tables, it is easy to detect that RF performs the best in most of the experiments, followed by SVM to some extent. Therefore,

Times the feature achieved the best result

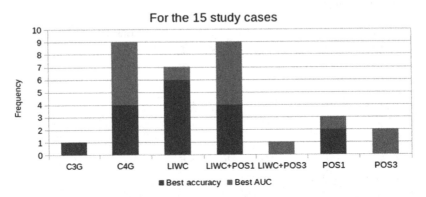

Fig. 2. The frequency represents, out of the 15 study cases, how many times the given feature (x-axis) reached the best result for accuracy and AUC separately.

Times the feature achieved the best result

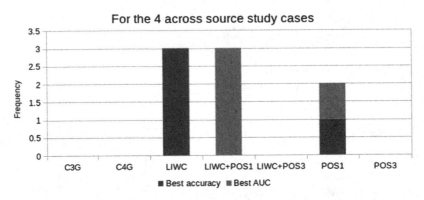

Fig. 3. The frequency represents, out of the 4 study cases where cross-modality validation was done, how many times the given feature (x-axis) reached the best result for accuracy and AUC separately.

Random Forest seems like a good candidate for deception detection, at least given the proposed representations of text in this study. Figures 2 and 3 show those representations given how many times they achieved the best result for the different study cases.

Among the 15 study cases (Fig. 2), we can observe that the most dominant representations are the character 4-grams, the LIWC vectors and their concatenation with POS tags unigrams. From these three, LIWC was more consistent for accuracy rather than AUC, while the other two are more balanced, in favor of AUC.

By analyzing just the 4 cases where cross-modality transfer is done (Fig. 3), we can observe that LIWC vectors, POS tags unigrams and their concatenation get the best results, while character 4-grams don't appear any longer. Again, LIWC works better when measuring accuracy, while LIWC+POS1 works better when evaluating with AUC. Although character 4-grams perform well validating in-domain (specially for single topics), their performance is highly degraded when testing the model on external domains (specially for cross-modality experiments); although that representation is able to capture some style, it relies heavily on vocabulary, explaining why it is not useful for transfer.

6   Conclusions and Future Work

In this paper, we studied the use of many representations and classifiers for deception detection through text, motivated by the idea of transferring knowledge from one modality -source of information- to another one (particularly from written text to transcripts extracted from video). Also, we expected to deal with topic-free learning. For this work, the, a domain is composed both by a given set of topics and a modality.

With those two objectives in mind, we found that character 4-grams have a good performance when validating in-domain, therefore being useful when constructing systems for specific domains. However, their ability to transfer knowledge into unknown topics or a new modality is poor compared to other representations used here.

We found that, either for transferring learning or learning in-domain, LIWC vectors and/or POS 1-grams give good results, reaching numbers around the state of the art when testing over a real-life dataset for deception detection. By training in-domain (accuracy 69.42%, AUC 0.7153), we actually surpass previous results. When transferring from written text on unrelated topics (accuracy 63.64%, AUC 0.6351), we achieve numbers around the state of the art for works that learn directly from the target domain.

Talking about the classifiers we tested (NB, SVM, DT, RF), at least for the given text representations RF shows a tendency as the best classifier for deception detection, either at validating in-domain or for cross-domain transfer (both for cross-topic and cross-modality). Less frequently, SVM tends to give good results too.

This work was motivated by the idea of constructing a multimodal system for deception detection in videos, similar to the one presented by Wu et al. [7]. In this sense, the present paper works on multimodal deception detection from text analysis by transferring learning. Future work implies analyzing body language and voice to add additional modalities to the present work. Talking about text only, we would like to study the effect of selecting particular features from the current used vectors based on their relevance for classification in the current datasets and new datasets if available, including ones in other languages as Spanish.

Appendix A   Results achieved by each classifier for all the proposed representations in the 15 study cases

See (Tables 10, 11, and 12)

Table 10. Results gotten by NB for the 15 case studies with all the proposed representations.

Naive Bayes

Experiment	C3G		C4G		LIWC		LIWC+POS1		LIWC + POS3		POS1		POS3	
	Acc	AUC	Acc	AUC	Acc	AUC	Acc	AUC	Acc	AUC	Acc	AUC	Acc	AUC
A(W)	62.50	0.6518	65.00	0.6501	66.50	0.7310	66.00	0.6882	65.00	0.6499	62.00	0.6569	63.50	0.6430
AB(W)	67.25	0.7023	68.00	0.6897	62.75	0.6860	65.50	0.7055	61.75	0.6607	61.00	0.6893	61.25	0.6505
ABD(W)	62.50	0.6451	62.83	0.6353	61.33	0.6427	62.67	0.6715	60.67	0.6262	57.50	0.6728	60.67	0.6322
ABD(W)→C(V)	53.72	0.5456	54.55	0.5596	52.89	0.5786	55.37	0.5298	50.41	0.5351	51.24	0.5175	49.59	0.5152
AB(W)→C(V)	51.24	0.5011	52.89	0.5346	57.02	0.6307	56.20	0.5760	52.89	0.5348	57.02	0.5355	50.41	0.5380
AB(W)→D(W)	56.50	0.5659	54.50	0.5454	52.00	0.5773	54.00	0.5679	59.00	0.5992	54.00	0.5648	57.00	0.5910
AD(W)	55.75	0.5812	60.50	0.6307	60.00	0.6553	62.75	0.6575	61.25	0.6381	58.75	0.6364	61.00	0.6428
AD(W)→B(W)	54.50	0.5740	57.50	0.5923	43.00	0.3654	46.00	0.4062	53.50	0.5609	54.50	0.6364	59.00	0.6012
B(W)	70.00	0.7177	70.00	0.7019	64.50	0.7312	69.00	0.7434	72.50	0.7511	67.50	0.7263	71.50	0.7413
BD(W)	63.00	0.6452	63.25	0.6373	59.50	0.6412	63.75	0.6745	60.75	0.6288	59.50	0.6624	60.50	0.6301
BD(W)→A(W)	56.00	0.5873	54.50	0.5515	56.50	0.6599	57.50	0.6737	57.00	0.6217	55.00	0.6571	55.50	0.6139
C(V)	59.50	0.6081	65.29	0.6663	54.55	0.5617	49.59	0.5100	53.72	0.5638	49.59	0.4989	53.72	0.5683
C(V)→AB(W)	55.00	0.5742	54.75	0.5544	58.25	0.6135	58.75	0.6267	56.75	0.5622	54.75	0.5819	55.75	0.5488
C(V)→ABD(W)	52.83	0.5340	52.83	0.5305	57.67	0.5942	57.33	0.5959	53.50	0.5300	53.33	0.5612	52.67	0.5169
D(W)	47.00	0.4567	52.50	0.5215	56.00	0.6011	58.00	0.5826	55.50	0.5877	60.00	0.6057	56.50	0.5900

Table 11. Results gotten by SVM for the 15 case studies with all the proposed representations.

SVM

Experiment	C3G		C4G		LIWC		LIWC + POS1		LIWC + POS3		POS1		POS3	
	Acc	AUC	Acc	AUC	Acc	AUC	Acc	AUC	Acc	AUC	Acc	AUC	Acc	AUC
A(W)	63.50	0.6350	67.00	0.6700	72.50	0.7250	71.50	0.7150	64.50	0.6450	69.50	0.6950	57.00	0.5700
AB(W)	65.50	0.6550	71.50	0.7150	72.00	0.7200	70.00	0.7000	68.75	0.6875	68.00	0.6800	64.00	0.6400
ABD(W)	64.50	0.6450	66.33	0.6633	67.83	0.6783	68.83	0.6883	65.83	0.6583	67.33	0.6733	62.83	0.6283
ABD(W)→C(V)	44.63	0.4460	50.41	0.5037	52.07	0.5242	52.07	0.5225	57.02	0.5725	53.72	0.5400	57.02	0.5719
AB(W)→C(V)	48.76	0.4872	47.93	0.4783	55.37	0.5559	55.37	0.5568	51.24	0.5150	51.24	0.5161	46.28	0.4648
AB(W)→D(W)	61.00	0.6100	57.50	0.5750	60.50	0.6050	62.00	0.6200	59.50	0.5950	61.50	0.6150	58.00	0.5800
AD(W)	63.25	0.6325	63.75	0.6375	68.25	0.6825	68.00	0.6800	63.25	0.6325	67.00	0.6700	59.75	0.5975
AD(W)→B(W)	58.50	0.5850	58.50	0.5850	58.50	0.5850	61.00	0.6100	59.50	0.5950	65.00	0.6500	52.50	0.5250
B(W)	73.50	0.7350	77.50	0.7750	76.00	0.7600	74.50	0.7450	74.50	0.7450	69.50	0.6950	70.00	0.7000
BD(W)	64.75	0.6475	68.75	0.6875	68.00	0.6800	66.75	0.6675	64.50	0.6450	67.50	0.6750	62.75	0.6275
BD(W)→A(W)	58.50	0.5850	63.00	0.6300	63.50	0.6350	66.50	0.6650	64.50	0.6450	67.50	0.6750	63.50	0.6350
C(V)	61.98	0.6201	69.42	0.6941	52.07	0.5204	52.89	0.5287	67.77	0.6773	52.07	0.5204	57.85	0.5776
C(V)→AB(W)	55.25	0.5525	51.75	0.5175	60.00	0.6000	54.75	0.5475	52.25	0.5225	53.00	0.5300	55.00	0.5500
C(V)→ABD(W)	54.50	0.5450	50.67	0.5067	55.83	0.5583	53.33	0.5333	51.00	0.5100	51.00	0.5100	53.17	0.5317
D(W)	56.00	0.5600	56.00	0.5600	59.50	0.5950	63.00	0.6300	57.00	0.5700	61.50	0.6150	56.00	0.5600

Table 12. Results gotten by RF for the 15 case studies with all the proposed representations.

Random forest

Experiment	C3G		C4G		LIWC		LIWC + POS1		LIWC + POS3		POS1		POS3	
	Acc	AUC	Acc	AUC	Acc	AUC	Acc	AUC	Acc	AUC	Acc	AUC	Acc	AUC
A(W)	69.50	0.7710	67.50	0.7735	71.00	0.7621	70.50	0.7891	69.00	0.7657	71.00	0.7663	65.50	0.7245
AB(W)	71.75	0.7885	72.00	0.8031	71.00	0.7834	72.50	0.7948	69.00	0.7787	69.50	0.7620	65.25	0.7579
ABD(W)	68.33	0.7551	67.83	0.7697	67.50	0.7563	70.50	0.7671	66.17	0.7378	68.17	0.7377	64.17	0.7088
ABD(W)→C(V)	46.28	0.4713	56.20	0.5932	60.33	0.5633	62.81	0.6182	57.02	0.5398	63.64	0.6225	51.24	0.5428
AB(W)→C(V)	55.37	0.5699	48.76	0.5593	57.85	0.5638	60.33	0.6351	57.02	0.5981	58.68	0.6189	54.55	0.5787
AB(W)→D(W)	56.50	0.6243	59.50	0.6476	59.00	0.7131	64.50	0.7533	59.50	0.6699	63.00	0.6702	61.00	0.6568
AD(W)	65.25	0.7096	67.00	0.7168	71.25	0.7612	68.25	0.7435	68.00	0.7333	66.50	0.7090	63.00	0.6751
AD(W)→B(W)	56.50	0.5985	63.50	0.7116	58.00	0.5999	61.00	0.6820	57.00	0.6107	65.50	0.7166	57.00	0.6576
B(W)	75.00	0.8413	76.50	0.8544	72.50	0.8147	74.50	0.8388	75.00	0.8309	72.00	0.8153	75.50	0.8113
BD(W)	67.00	0.7321	67.75	0.7715	68.75	0.7623	67.25	0.7546	67.00	0.7495	64.00	0.7072	66.00	0.7112
BD(W)→A(W)	68.00	0.7505	66.50	0.7509	68.00	0.7262	66.50	0.7457	59.50	0.7070	64.50	0.6980	62.00	0.6619
C(V)	54.55	0.6231	59.50	0.6679	63.64	0.6697	63.64	0.6806	65.29	0.7153	58.68	0.6417	54.55	0.5956
C(V)→AB(W)	58.25	0.5981	55.50	0.5844	54.25	0.5547	59.00	0.6211	57.00	0.6143	57.25	0.6163	50.25	0.5603
C(V)→ABD(W)	53.83	0.5631	53.67	0.5582	52.83	0.5316	55.33	0.5781	56.33	0.5847	55.00	0.5815	50.50	0.5614
D(W)	60.00	0.6347	64.00	0.6565	57.00	0.6367	60.50	0.6539	60.50	0.6463	57.00	0.5888	63.50	0.6573

References

1. Pérez-Rosas, V., Mihalcea, R.: Cross-cultural deception detection. In: Proceedings of the 52nd Annual Meeting of the Association for Computational Linguistics (Volume 2: Short Papers), pp. 440–445. Association for Computational Linguistics (2014)
2. Ekman, P.: Telling Lies: Clues to Deceit in the Marketplace, Politics, and Marriage, Revised edn. WW Norton & Company, New York City (2009)
3. Newman, M.L., Pennebaker, J.W., Berry, D.S., Richards, J.M.: Lying words: predicting deception from linguistic styles. Pers. Soc. Psychol. Bull. **29**(5), 665–675 (2003)
4. Pérez-Rosas, V., Abouelenien, M., Mihalcea, R., Burzo, M.: Deception detection using real-life trial data. In: Proceedings of the 2015 ACM on International Conference on Multimodal Interaction, pp. 59-66. ACM (2015)
5. Abouelenien, M., Pérez-Rosas, V., Zhao, B., Mihalcea, R., Burzo, M.: Detecting deceptive behavior via integration of discriminative features from multiple modalities. IEEE Trans. Inf. Forensics Secur. **12**(5), 1042–1055 (2017)
6. Abouelenien, M., Pérez-Rosas, V., Zhao, B., Mihalcea, R., Burzo, M.: Gender-based multimodal deception detection. In: Proceedings of the Symposium on Applied Computing (2017). https://dl.acm.org/citation.cfm?doid=3019612.3019644
7. Wu, Z., Singh, B., Davis, L.S., Subrahmanian, V.: Deception detection in videos. arXiv preprint arXiv:1712.04415 (2017)
8. Sapkota, U., Bethard, S., Montes, M., Solorio, T.: Not all character N-grams are created equal: a study in authorship attribution. In: Proceedings of the 2015 Conference of the North American Chapter of the Association for Computational Linguistics: Human Language Technologies, pp. 93-102 (2015)
9. Toutanova, K., Klein, D., Manning, C., Singer, Y.: Feature-rich part-of-speech tagging with a cyclic dependency network. In: Proceedings of HLT-NAACL 2003, pp. 252–259 (2003)

Author Index

Printed in the United States
By Bookmasters